BLACKS IN THE NEW WORLD
August Meier, Series Editor

The Democratic Party and the Negro

Lawrence Grossman

The Democratic Party and the Negro

Northern and National Politics
1868-92

UNIVERSITY OF ILLINOIS PRESS
Urbana Chicago London

LIBRARY OF CONGRESS CATALOGING IN PUBLICATION DATA

Grossman, Lawrence, 1945–
  The Democratic Party and the Negro.

  (Blacks in the new world)
  A revision of the author's thesis, City University
of New York, 1973.
  Bibliography: p.
  Includes index.
    1. Democratic Party—History. 2. Afro-Americans
—Politics and suffrage. 3. United States—Politics
and government—1865–1898. I. Title. II. Series.
JK2317.1868.G752   329.3'009'034   75-30546
ISBN 0–252–00575–9

For Mom and Dad,
Mimi and Fran

Preface

This book is a history of Democratic racial policy in the late nineteenth century. It examines the party's evolving political attitude toward the Negro in the quarter-century between the presidential elections of 1868 and 1892, the reasons why a metamorphosis took place, and its limits. Much has already been written about the Southern Democratic approach to this issue in the post-Reconstruction years. Therefore I have concentrated on parts of the picture not yet examined: the national scene, and Northern state and local politics. Southern developments receive attention only as they influenced or reflected Northern and national trends.

The six chapters divide naturally into four parts. The first two chapters follow the national Democracy from its white supremacist national campaign of 1868, through the gradual capture of the party by new departure racial moderates in the early 1870's, to the ending of Reconstruction and the establishment of a solid Democratic South. Unbending in their opposition to federal intervention in Southern race relations, the new departure Democrats of the 1870's made that opposition seem reasonable and responsible by coupling it with pledges to abide by the Reconstruction amendments to the Constitution which gave blacks civil equality and the ballot. In the third chapter the scene shifts northward. Beginning in 1873 and continuing on into the 1890's, there emerged a second, or newer departure. State and local Democrats in the North muted old appeals to white prejudice and competed with Republicans for black favor through pro-Negro legislation and grants of patronage. Simultaneously, some Negroes, dissatisfied with Republican behavior, espoused political independence or became Democrats. The extent of Democratic-Negro rapprochement varied from state to state and from city to city in the North, but it was, as a whole, of major significance. The fourth chapter analyzes what happened when Grover Cleveland, a Northern Democrat with a good record on race, became in 1885 the first Democratic president since before the Civil War. Cleveland's race policy, a combination of both new departures, raised Negro hopes that the national Democracy might finally have outgrown its ancient hostility toward blacks. But then follows the denouement in the subsequent two chapters. Once the Republicans, back in control of the federal government, tried to pass legislation protecting the Negro ballot in the South, the entire Democratic party backed the Southern wing's desire to maintain white supremacy by preventing national interference with political affairs in Dixie. Yet, even while fellow-traveling with Southern racists, the Northern Democracy kept up its search for Negro support, with some success. Indeed, I suggest that Northern Democratic racial liberalism helped to blunt and defeat Republican desires to safeguard Negro suffrage.

This study has some potentially significant aspects. For too long historians writing about either Reconstruction or the Gilded Age have minimized the Democratic role, leading the reader to believe that the course of Reconstruction was determined almost exclusively by Republican factions, and that an accurate picture of American politics in the 1870's and 1880's can exclude detailed attention to the Democrats. A full analysis of Democratic policy on the key issue of race should begin to redress the historiographical imbalance. Also, when historians do mention the late nineteenth century Democracy, they usually ask whether there were any differences of principle between the two major parties before 1896. This book, when compared to earlier studies of Republican policy, shows that, on the race question, at least, the answer is a qualified yes. The partisan gap on this issue narrowed during and after Reconstruction, especially in Northern state and local politics—but a gap nevertheless remained on the point of federal intervention in the South, which became a chasm in the Lodge bill struggle of 1890–91. Only after 1892 can one speak of a solid political consensus on the place of the Negro in American life—precisely at the time that new cleavages of a social and economic nature appeared on the national scene. Finally, the research for this study has convinced me that despite recent interest in the history of American race relations, much of the story, at least for the late nineteenth century, has not been told. To cite just one example, the importance of the black role in Northern party politics which brought about an otherwise inexplicable series of state civil rights laws in the 1880's has up to now been uncharted historical territory.

In the long process of preparing this book, I have come to owe much to many people. The guiding spirit of the entire project has been Professor LaWanda Cox. She first awakened my serious interest in the subtle interaction of race and politics in the post–Civil War period, then supervised this study as a dissertation, and has always contributed incisive criticism, kind encouragement, and sage advice regarding this work and many other matters. Professor Stanley P. Hirshson provided much help. His knowledge of American political history, especially in connection with the race question, his eye for style, and his warm friendship are appreciated. I am also thankful to Professors Ari Hoogenboom, Elsie Lewis, and Hans Trefousse, who read the manuscript in dissertation form and made useful suggestions. The insights of Professor August Meier, editor of this series, were invaluable. A Danforth Foundation fellowship enabled me, to begin work on this book; a congenial association with the administration, faculty, and students of Stern College for Women, Yeshiva University, facilitated its completion. My parents and sisters have sustained me spiritually and materially always.

—L. G.

Contents

List of Tables

1

The Racist Democracy
1868

A disunited Democratic party faced the presidential election of 1868. The Civil War had splintered its ranks into War Democrats, who cooperated with Republicans on a "Unionist" ticket in 1864; regular Democrats, who backed the war effort but criticized President Abraham Lincoln's handling of it; and Copperheads, openly sympathetic to the South. With Republicans exploiting their opponents' dubious allegiance to the Union, these differences left a legacy of Democratic disharmony even after Appomattox. Aside from the loyalty issue, Democrats, like Republicans, divided on the currency issue between hard-money men and inflationists.[1]

One of the few bonds uniting Democrats through the war years and Reconstruction was opposition to Republican racial policy. The Democracy had come to institutionalize anti-Negro feeling during the 1850's, as Democrats opposed to slavery or its spread into the territories joined the new Republican party. By 1860 the Democratic organization consisted of Southerners committed to the peculiar institution who were about to secede from the Union, and Northerners with no strong convictions about the immorality of slavery. In wartime the Northern Democracy not only opposed freeing the slaves and other Republican efforts to aid blacks, but also sought votes by appealing to white prejudice. After the end of hostilities Democrats opposed the Civil Rights

1. Though there is no full-scale study of the wartime Democratic organization, the factional cleavages are delineated in Harold M. Hyman, "Election of 1864," in *History of American Presidential Elections, 1789–1968,* ed. Arthur M. Schlesinger, Jr., and Fred L. Israel (New York: Chelsea House, 1971), II, 1155–1244. On the currency see Irwin Unger, *The Greenback Era: A Social and Political History of American Finance, 1865–1879* (Princeton: Princeton University Press, 1964), pp. 79–85.

Act of 1866 and the Fourteenth Amendment, formulated in 1866 and ratified in 1868, that established in law an equal civil status for the Southern freedmen. Democrats were even more outraged at Republican passage of the 1867 Reconstruction Acts which granted Negroes unrestricted suffrage in the secession states. Exploiting white racism, the Northern Democracy won victories in the fall elections of 1867, and new Democratic legislatures in New Jersey and Ohio revoked their states' earlier ratifications of the Fourteenth Amendment. The party's 1868 state conventions all condemned Republican Reconstruction, especially black suffrage.[2] There was, then, much truth to the Republican taunt that "the only test of Democratic soundness is hatred of the Negro."[3]

Despite this united opposition to Negro rights, Democrats differed over political strategy in handling the issue. The split, at this stage expressed more in nuances of rhetoric than in differences over policy, reflected divergent assessments of what was expedient and varying degrees of commitment to white supremacy. Everyone realized that to attain victory in 1868—when little success could yet be expected in the South, with its thousands of new black Republican voters—Democrats would have to win over some of the Northern opposition vote. However, moderate Democrats knew that conservative Republicans disturbed by the extreme measures against the South and political equality for Negroes shunned affiliation with a political organization suspected of disloyalty.[4] Secession in 1861 had been linked with support for slavery; during the war Northern Democrats had fought emancipation of the slaves; Democratic backing

2. Many samples of Democratic anti-Negro rhetoric during the war are provided in V. Jacque Voegeli, *Free but Not Equal: The Midwest and the Negro during the Civil War* (Chicago: University of Chicago Press, 1967). A detailed analysis of Democratic policy in the early Reconstruction years is Edward L. Gambill, "Northern Democrats and Reconstruction, 1865–1868" (Ph.D. dissertation, University of Iowa, 1969). State party platforms for 1868 are reprinted in *American Annual Cyclopaedia*, 1868, in the articles about individual states. A South Carolina Democratic platform in April did accept qualified Negro suffrage, but a revised platform two months later repudiated this concession.

3. New York *Independent*, March 12, 1868, p. 1.

4. Such Republican fears are expressed in James L. Bates to Thomas Ewing, January 8, 1868, Box 3, Thomas Ewing Papers, Ohio Historical Society, and David Davis to his brother, April 22, 1868, Folder 98, Davis Papers, Chicago Historical Society.

for President Andrew Johnson against Congress had revolved around the question of equal citizenship for both races. Thus, in many Republican minds, Democratic hostility to the Negro was bound up with Confederate sympathies. Moderate Democrats therefore wanted to supplement their opposition to Negro rights with assurances that the party did not desire to give up the fruits of Union victory by an abrupt overthrow of Reconstruction. But they were not sure how to reconcile these contradictory political impulses.[5] In contrast, Democratic extremists, many of whom had been wartime Copperheads, favored a pure racist stance. They expected to capture the White House by making the election of 1868 a simple referendum on white supremacy.[6] This strategy, successful in the 1867 state elections, assumed that there were many Republicans anxious to repudiate the principle of Negro suffrage as embodied in the Reconstruction Acts, even at the risk of bringing former rebels back to power in the South.

Whether framed in conservative or reactionary terms, the status of the Negro in the South was sure to be "the absorbing question" of the 1868 election.[7] Samuel J. Tilden, an influential New York Democrat, believed that white Americans would not accept "a partnership in self-government with a mass of voters . . . incompetent at the present time to exercise the suffrage wisely or safely and without any of the training, habits, or aspirations of freemen." A racist campaign by the Democrats, Tilden felt, would appeal "to the adopted citizens—whether Irish or German; to all the working men," as well as to conservative Re-

5. John Quincy Adams to Horatio Seymour, March 19, 1868, Seymour Papers, Fairchild Collection, New York Historical Society; Adams to Charles Francis Adams, May 13, 1868, Reel 586, Adams Family Papers, Massachusetts Historical Society; James R. Doolittle to Manton Marble, January 27, 1868, Vol. 17, Marble Papers, Library of Congress; Doolittle to George H. Paul, February 19, 1868, Box 5, Paul Papers, State Historical Society of Wisconsin; Indiana Congressman Michael Kerr, in *Congressional Globe*, 40 Cong., 2 sess., pp. 578, 1973 (January 18, March 18, 1868).

6. La Crosse (Wisconsin) *Democrat*, February 10, 1868, clipping in Vol. 17, Marble Papers; *Democratic Almanac*, 1868, pp. 17–18; Senators Garrett Davis of Kentucky and Willard Saulsbury of Delaware, in *Congressional Globe*, 40 Cong., 2 sess., pp. 1122, 1437 (February 12, 26, 1868).

7. William Bigler to Samuel J. Tilden, February 3, 1868, Box 8, Tilden Papers, New York Public Library; also in John Bigelow, ed., *Letters and Literary Memorials of Samuel J. Tilden* (New York: Harper and Brothers, 1908), I, 217.

publicans. "The pride of a superior race and self esteem, well founded in this case, are a universal power." Formulating this strategy in an address to the New York Democratic state convention in March, Tilden explained the necessity to bar Southern Negroes from the polls while welcoming all whites, whatever their character or intelligence. The body politic, he theorized, should admit "whatever element could be absorbed into the homogenous mass . . . whatever element could be admitted into the family, which is the basis of society." Chinese, Indians, and Negroes, who would never be allowed to intermarry with whites, must not share political power with them. However, European immigrants, who "spring from the same parent stock with ourselves," and amalgamate naturally with native families, should enjoy total equality. Tilden further lured the immigrant vote with a warning that, once the federal authority dictated suffrage laws, it might disfranchise foreign-born Americans.[8] The praise that Tilden's speech evoked from the powerful New York organization foreshadowed the major role that race would play in the upcoming campaign.[9]

Meanwhile, Democratic factions struggled over whom to nominate for president, rekindling internal differences. George Pendleton of Ohio was the leading candidate. Despite great popularity in the West, his coolness toward the Union effort during the war and his inflationary stand on currency alienated moderates and hard-money men. Desperate for a nominee who could draw Republicans and War Democrats, moderates considered the candidacy of Republican Chief Justice Salmon P. Chase. While politics often creates strange alliances, the Chase movement seemed totally illogical: the Democracy stood for white supremacy, and Chase had been one of the earliest political advocates of Negro equality and a major architect of the Re-

8. Tilden to Bigler, February 28, 1868, Box 14, Bigler Papers, Historical Society of Pennsylvania; also in Bigelow, ed., *Letters*, I, 219–20; John Bigelow, ed., *The Writings and Speeches of Samuel J. Tilden* (New York: Harper and Brothers, 1885), I, 401–19. For the prewar roots of this racial theory, see George Fredrickson, *The Black Image in the White Mind: The Debate on Afro-American Character and Destiny, 1817–1914* (New York: Harper and Row, 1971), p. 99.

9. New York *World*, March 18, 1868, p. 4; Horatio Seymour to Tilden, March 24, 1868, Box 8, Tilden Papers, also in Bigelow, ed., *Letters*, I, 224–25.

publican party. Yet it was possible that his intense presidential ambitions might dilute his racial egalitarianism. The serious and protracted attempt to reconcile Chase's long-standing commitment to equal rights with the Democrats' anti-Negro program was an important stage in the complicated evolution of Democratic policy on race.[10]

Paradoxically, "the more pronounced Republicans" favored Chase for president early in 1868. But he alienated the Radicals by his conduct as presiding officer at President Johnson's impeachment trial which began in March, adjourned for the Republican convention, and reconvened in May. Former supporters complained that Chase had abandoned the Republicans by not favoring the impeachers in his rulings from the chair, and General Ulysses S. Grant received a unanimous nomination.[11]

Democrats began to negotiate with Chase during the impeachment trial. Though he disclaimed interest in the presidency, the chief justice spelled out his political views to all who asked: universal suffrage, amnesty for Confederates, and opposition to the Republican policy of stationing federal troops in the South as mandated by the Reconstruction Acts. Chase advised his Democratic friends that the only way they could regain political respectability was to concede voting rights to blacks and recognize Southern governments set up under congressional reconstruction. If they did so, the grateful freedmen would vote for their old masters, restoring Democratic ascendancy in the South and the nation. Clearly, despite his surface denials, Chase wanted to run for president on such a platform, and he hoped to convince Democrats that they could only erase the memory of past errors "when the negro question is definitively settled."[12]

10. This episode in Chase's career has been treated by historians, but not in the context of the Democrats' developing racial policy. See Charles H. Coleman, *The Election of 1868: The Democratic Effort to Regain Control* (New York: Columbia University Press, 1933), pp. 102–40; Donnal V. Smith, "Salmon P. Chase and the Nomination of 1868," in *Essays in Honor of William E. Dodd,* ed. Avery Craven (Chicago: University of Chicago Press, 1935), pp. 291–319; Edward S. Perzel, "Alexander Long, Salmon P. Chase, and the Election of 1868," *Bulletin of the Cincinnati Historical Society,* XXIII (January, 1965), 3–18.

11. New York *Independent,* February 27, 1868, p. 1, May 21, 1868, p. 4.

12. The quotation is from a letter written by Chase's private secretary Jacob Schuckers to Alexander Long, May 9, 1868, Box B, Long Papers, Cincinnati

Chase Democrats sought a compromise Reconstruction plank for their national platform which would satisfy both the chief justice and the white-supremacist Democratic masses. Suggestions ranged from holding new constitutional conventions in the South, to ignoring the suffrage issue entirely.[13] August Belmont of New York, chairman of the Democratic National Committee and a leading moderate, offered a formula that avoided the substantive question of Negro suffrage, but insisted that it was a state matter, not one to be decided by the federal government. Belmont asked Chase in late May whether he would run on this platform. In his immediate written response to Belmont the chief justice reiterated his belief in universal suffrage but evaded answering the question put to him.[14] However, by mid-June, learning of his growing popularity among Democrats who viewed his candidacy as the only alternative to defeat, Chase offered a choice of "one of two forms of expression" for the Democratic platform: "Either restoration on the basis of universal suffrage, without any declaration one way or the other, about suffrage in the States; or, recognition of the fact that universal suffrage is a democratic principle, the application of which is to be left in the States, under the Constitution, to the States themselves. . . ."[15]

Historical Society. Also see Chase to Murat Halstead, March 26, 1868, MS in New York Historical Society; Chase to John D. Van Buren, April 6, 1868, Letterbook 117, pp. 346–48, Chase Papers, Library of Congress; Chase to Alexander Long, April 19, 1868, Box B, Long Papers, reprinted in Jacob W. Schuckers, *The Life and Public Services of Salmon Portland Chase* (New York: D. Appleton, 1874), pp. 578–79, and Robert B. Warden, *An Account of the Private Life and Public Services of Salmon Portland Chase* (Cincinnati: Wilstach, Baldwin, 1874), pp. 686–87; Chase to Henry W. Hilliard, April 27, 1868, Vol. 111, Chase Papers, LC, also in Schuckers, *Life of Chase*, pp. 528–29.

13. John D. Van Buren to Horatio Seymour, May 1, 20, 1868, Seymour Papers, Fairchild Collection, NYHS; New York *World*, June 3, 1868, p. 4.

14. Chase to Belmont, May 30, 1868, Vol. 18, Marble Papers; also in August Belmont, *Letters, Speeches and Addresses* (n.p.: By the author, 1890), pp. 114–17.

15. Evidence of pro-Chase feeling can be found in S. L. M. Barlow to George B. McClellan, June 2, 1868, Series 2, Vol. 26, McClellan Papers, Library of Congress; Chase to Murat Halstead, June 1, 1868, Vol. 111, John J. Cisco to Chase, June 1, 1868, Jacob Schuckers to Chase, June 6, 1868, J. L. Whitaker to Chase, June 9, 1868, Vol. 100, Chase Papers, LC; August Belmont to Manton Marble [June, 1868], Vol. 17, Marble Papers. Chase's proposed platform was first articulated in Chase to William Cullen Bryant, June 19, 1868, Bryant-Godwin Papers, New York Public Library; also in Schuckers, *Life of Chase*,

The first alternative was a puzzling self-contradiction; the second, ignoring the clause of the Fourteenth Amendment that reduced the representation of states disfranchising blacks, was a major concession to the Democrats. It upheld the states' rights position by making universal suffrage anywhere in the country a mere "principle" subject to state implementation. Democrats anxious to capture Chase were satisfied, even though the acceptance of universal suffrage as a party tenet was difficult to swallow.[16]

Principled white supremacists, generally committed to Pendleton's cause, rejected both Chase and his ambiguous platform. Reflecting their views, Senator-elect Allen Thurman of Ohio, who owed his seat to the successful Democratic tide of 1867, wrote:

> To go outside the party for a candidate or to take a dubious man, would lose us more than we could possibly gain by it. The strength of our party consists in its hostility to the unconstitutional acts, extravagance, corruption, negro worship and excessive taxation of the Radicals, and to abandon this hostility, or modify it until it should amount to nothing, would . . . take all the fire and zeal out of our people and enable the radicals to obtain a very easy victory.[17]

The Democratic national convention opened at Tammany Hall in New York City on July 4. In the two preceding weeks Congress had readmitted Arkansas, the Carolinas, Louisiana,

---

pp. 558–59, and Warden, *Account of Chase*, pp. 701–2. His suggestions were then printed up under the title of "Mr. Chase's Views," available in Jacob Schuckers Papers, Library of Congress, and in Schuckers, *Life of Chase*, pp. 567–68.

16. Horatio Seymour, quoted in Chicago *Tribune*, June 22, 1868, p. 2; James C. Kennedy to William Cassidy, June 18, 1868, Box 8, Horatio Seymour Papers, New York State Library; John D. Van Buren to Chase, June 25, 1868, Box 13, Frederick Aiken to Chase, July 3, 1868, Box 1, Chase Papers, Historical Society of Pennsylvania; Aiken to Chase, June 25, 1868, Container 100, Chase Papers, LC; J. Glancy Jones to Alexander H. Stephens, June 22, 1868, Vol. 44, Stephens Papers, Library of Congress.

17. Thurman to William Bigler, June 24, 1868, Box 14, Bigler Papers. Other adverse opinions are Charles P. Brown to William Allen, June 20, 1868, Vol. 17, Allen Papers, Library of Congress; A. E. Burr to Gideon Welles, June 29, 1868, Welles Papers, New York Public Library; S. L. M. Barlow to George B. McClellan, June 30, 1868, Series 2, Vol. 26, McClellan Papers.

Georgia, Alabama, and Florida to statehood on the condition that their constitutions pledge never to disfranchise Negroes. All but Georgia complied. Senators and congressmen from Arkansas had already taken their seats, and those from the other newly regenerated states would soon join them.[18] Chairman Belmont, welcoming the Democratic delegates to the convention, denounced the new Southern regimes and charged Republicans with a plot to force black rule on the old Confederacy.[19]

The Democratic platform, far from embodying Chase's views, reflected the extremist position. It accepted the death of slavery and secession but upheld the right of "citizens" of a state to set voting requirements, and announced that all steps previously taken to reconstruct the South were "unconstitutional, revolutionary, and void."[20] This would surely play into Republican hands, confirming popular suspicions that Democratic opposition to Negro rights was part of a design to overthrow the results of the war.

The convention deadlocked for twenty-one ballots over the presidential nomination as Pendleton, the front-runner, could not get the two-thirds vote necessary under party regulations. Instead of turning to Chase (who was willing, in the end, to run even on the extremist platform), the delegates compromised on Horatio Seymour, the wartime governor of New York, an advocate of hard money and, as events would show, a man little interested in the race issue. Chase did poorly, receiving only one-half vote from California on the twelfth, thirteenth, and seventeenth through nineteenth ballots, and four Massachusetts votes on the twenty-first ballot.[21]

18. James G. Randall and David Donald, *The Civil War and Reconstruction,* 2nd ed., rev. (Boston: D. C. Heath, 1969), pp. 618–19.

19. *Official Proceedings of the National Democratic Convention at Tammany Hall, New York City, July 4–9, 1868* (Boston: Rockwell and Rollins, 1868), p. 4.

20. Kirk H. Porter and Donald B. Johnson, eds., *National Party Platforms, 1840–1964* (Urbana: University of Illinois Press, 1966), pp. 37–38.

21. *Proceedings of Democratic Convention, 1868,* pp. 121, 124, 134, 137, 146, 151. The final ballot nominating Seymour is tabulated *ibid.*, p. 161. For Chase's acceptance of the platform in the hope of being nominated, see Chase to John D. Van Buren, July 8, 1868, copy, Series 2, Chase Papers, Cincinnati Historical Society, also in Schuckers, *Life of Chase,* p. 590, and Warden, *Account of Chase,* p. 707.

The unsuccessful Chase boom further fragmented the party. By advocating the chief justice and a conciliatory Reconstruction plank, moderates antagonized extremists. But more significant in the long run, the fact that some Democrats, for reasons of expediency, were ready to nominate a believer in racial equality and eager to compromise with him on Reconstruction opened the first important crack in the Democracy's solid anti-Negro front. Nevertheless, Chase's dismal failure at the convention showed that the great majority of Democrats opposed any retreat from the party's old commitment to white supremacy.

After adopting an extreme Reconstruction plank and rejecting Chase, the Democracy confirmed its negrophobia by choosing, with negligible opposition, General Frank Blair of Missouri to run for vice-president. A crude racist who advocated the colonization of American Negroes outside the country, Blair had prepared a letter prior to the convention which expressed his views on Reconstruction. This "Broadhead letter" noted that even a Democratic victory in the fall could not bring legislative repeal of Reconstruction because the Senate would remain Republican under all circumstances. Therefore, a Democratic president would simply have "to declare these acts null and void, compel the army to undo its usurpations at the South, disperse the carpet-bag State governments, allow the white people to reorganize their own governments and elect Senators and Representatives."[22] The convention chose Blair as Seymour's running mate by acclamation largely on the strength of this uncompromising opposition to Republican Reconstruction and Negro rights, which was consistent with the Democratic platform.[23]

22. For Blair's personality and attitudes, see F. P. Blair, Jr. to James Rollins, March 23, 1868, Montgomery Blair to F. P. Blair, Jr., May 17, 1868, Container 3, Montgomery Blair to ———, May 16, 1868, James Rollins to ———, June 25, 1868, F. P. Blair, Jr., to Montgomery Blair, July 1, 1868, Container 8, Blair Papers, Library of Congress; James B. Beck to John W. Stevenson, undated, 1868, Vol. 29, Stevenson Papers, Library of Congress. The Broadhead letter is in New York *World*, July 3, 1868, p. 1, and reprinted in William E. Smith, *The Francis Preston Blair Family in Politics* (New York: Macmillan, 1933), II, 405–7.

23. *Proceedings of Democratic Convention, 1868*, pp. 165–70; Thomas Ewing, Jr., to Hugh Ewing, July 23, 1868, Box 4, Hugh Ewing Papers, Ohio Historical Society.

Moderate Democrats grumbled and extremists exulted about their platform and Blair,[24] while Republicans concluded that the Democracy, by couching its opposition to Negro rights in terms which threatened more bloodshed, had handed Grant victory. Republican Senator Oliver P. Morton of Indiana quoted the Democratic Reconstruction plank on the Senate floor and had the clerk read the Broadhead letter aloud. Morton then announced: "General Blair has relieved the Republican party of a good deal of labor."[25] Democratic senators tried to answer back but were themselves divided. Moderate Charles Buckalew of Pennsylvania said that, while his whole party agreed on Reconstruction's illegality, the organization was not of one mind over what to do about it. Blair's view was not universally held by Democrats, and Buckalew personally felt that Reconstruction "may become valid" if Southerners accepted it. In contrast, Democratic Senator Garrett Davis of Kentucky saw the coming election as a struggle between whites and blacks for race supremacy. If Grant won by the margin of Negro votes, whites would not submit.[26]

The same cleavage that divided Buckalew and Davis also separated the two Democratic nominees. While Blair stressed race as the overriding issue, Seymour shied away from it, preferring to attract Northern businessmen with attacks on Republican economic policy and pleas for sectional reconciliation.[27] Indeed, Seymour stated in his letter accepting the nomination that, if elected, he would not "make sudden or violent changes"

24. Moderate opinion is expressed in New York *World,* July 10, 1868, p. 4; Sam Ryan to Horatio Seymour, July 14, 1868, Seymour Papers, Fairchild Collection, NYHS; James R. Doolittle to Manton Marble, July 20, 1868, Vol. 18, Marble Papers. For extremist comment see *Old Guard,* VI (August, 1868), 628; A. E. Burr to Gideon Welles, July 14, 1868, Welles Papers, Library of Congress; Montgomery Blair to Mrs. Blair, July 14, 1868, Container 41, Blair Papers.

25. *Congressional Globe,* 40 Cong., 2 sess., pp. 3871–72 (July 9, 1868).

26. *Ibid.,* pp. 3875–79, 3907 (July 9, 10, 1868). Also see Davis to Horatio Seymour, August 12, 1868, Box 9, Seymour Papers, NYSL.

27. The contrast is clear in speeches that the two men delivered from the same platform immediately following the convention, reported in New York *World,* July 11, 1868, p. 1. Also consult Seymour to Tilden, July 20, 1868, Box 8, Tilden Papers.

in Reconstruction policy, and privately expressed alarm at the shrillness of extremists like Blair. "We must," he counseled, "teach moderation."[28]

Unfortunately for the cause of moderation, custom dictated that a candidate for president not campaign actively. There was no such limitation on the vice-presidential hopeful, and Frank Blair set the tone of the Democratic canvass, traveling across the country urging whites to foil the Republican plot to defile their racial purity. He went so far as to charge Republicans with promising white women to Negroes, and assured his audiences that Grant's victory would mean the introduction in America of such African practices as polygamy and concubinage. This was no mere vote-getting device as it might be for other politicians; Blair's race prejudice was totally sincere.[29]

As the campaign progressed, the whole Democratic party moved in Blair's direction. The moderates increasingly stressed race in an effort to shift attention away from the Democrats' muddled stand on the currency.[30] Even the New York organization, previously a bastion of moderation, secured a picture of the heavily Negro Louisiana legislature, produced thousands of copies, and sent them out as campaign literature in an open racist appeal.[31] But Dixie Democrats were most enthusiastic about the platform and Blair's speeches—and, unfortunately for the Democratic cause, whenever Southerners echoed them, it was an easy matter for Republicans to demonstrate the ongoing "revolutionary" intentions of ex-Confederates and the party

28. *Proceedings of Democratic Convention, 1868*, pp. 176–81; Seymour to James R. Doolittle, August 4, 1868, in Duane Mowry, ed., "Post-Bellum Days: Selections from the Correspondence of the Late Senator James R. Doolittle," *Magazine of History*, XVII (August–September, 1913), 57.

29. New York *World*, July 23, 1868, p. 8, August 7, 1868, pp. 1, 8, September 26, 1868, p. 1; F. P. Blair, Jr., to Mrs. Francis Minor, October 13, 1869, Container 53, Blair Papers.

30. Coleman, *Election of 1868*, pp. 287–88; editorials in New York *World*, July 24–October 14, 1868; S. S. Cox, *Speeches of S. S. Cox in Maine, Pennsylvania, and New York during the Campaign of 1868* (New York: Douglas Taylor's Democratic Printing Establishment, 1868).

31. S. L. M. Barlow to Tilden, September 2, 28, October 7, 1868, William Henry Hurlbut to Tilden, September 22, 1868, Box 8, Tilden Papers.

they supposedly controlled.[32] Although some Northern Democrats saw the danger posed by their ideological ties with unrepentant rebels, efforts to encourage moderate voices in the South had little success.[33]

When the Democrats suffered crushing losses in the September and October state elections, many realized that the national ticket was in trouble, and that "the *moderate* men must take hold of the party reins, or we are gone."[34] The moderates tried: Belmont, in the name of the national Democracy, and Tilden, representing the New York organization, issued statements denying that Democrats stood for violent change. The New York *World*, the most powerful moderate newspaper in the country, urged Blair to resign from the ticket and asked Seymour to "bring back the canvass to the moderate and proselytizing ground on which it was his original wish to place it."[35] Extremists exerted enough influence to keep Blair's name on the ballot, but Seymour did take to the stump. Concentrating on the financial question, Seymour made an eleventh-hour attempt to woo

32. A good example of Southern extremism (delivered before a Northern audience, no less) is Benjamin H. Hill, *Great Speech of the Hon. Benjamin H. Hill, of Georgia, delivered before the "Young Men's Democratic Union," October 6, 1868* (New York: n.p., 1868). Republican campaigners simply read such inflammatory Southern utterances to Northern audiences as proof of continued disloyalty. See the clippings in Box 35 of the Henry L. Dawes Papers, Library of Congress. The influence on Northern opinion is apparent in Peter Cooper to Nahum Capen, September 10, 1868, copy, Cooper-Hewitt Papers, Cooper Union, New York City.

33. August Belmont to Manton Marble, July, 1868, Vol. 18, Marble Papers; William S. Rosecrans to Horatio Seymour, August 5, September 15, 1868, Seymour Papers, Fairchild Collection, NYHS; Rosecrans to Tilden, September 12, 1868, Vol. 18, Seymour to Rosecrans, September 24, 1868, Vol. 19, Marble Papers; Robert E. Lee, in New York *World*, September 9, 1868, p. 4.

34. C. M. Gould to Samuel S. Cox, October 15, 1868, Reel 1, Cox Papers, Brown University; microfilm copies at Rutherford B. Hayes Memorial Library.

35. Belmont and Tilden in New York *World*, October 29, 1868, p. 3. The anti-Blair movement was sparked *ibid.*, October 19, 20, both p. 4. See also George T. McJimsey, *Genteel Partisan: Manton Marble, 1834–1917* (Ames: Iowa State University Press, 1971), pp. 129–30. For information on a simultaneous but independent attempt to substitute Chase for Seymour, see Clement Vallandigham to Samuel J. Tilden, October 17, 1868, telegram, Box 8, Tilden Papers; Thomas Hendricks to Salmon P. Chase, October 20, 1868, MS in New York Historical Society; Horatio Seymour to Cyrus H. McCormick, October 20, 1868, Series 1A, Box 30, McCormick Papers, State Historical Society of Wisconsin.

Republicans by disclaiming any intention of overthrowing Reconstruction.[36]

It was too late for sudden moderation: in November, Seymour won only 80 electoral votes to Grant's 214, though the Democrats polled 47 percent of the popular vote and carried the closely contested state of New York.[37] Each Democratic faction blamed the other for the result. Extremists insisted that many Democrats had stayed home on election day because the party was not sufficiently devoted to white supremacy. Some old-liners considered Seymour's defeat fortunate, since his lukewarm opposition to Reconstruction made him a rather dubious Democrat. "The present organization," announced the Copperhead *Old Guard* magazine, "may be properly called a *mulatto* Democracy. . . . Now let us have a *white* Democracy."[38] However, moderates felt that Grant could have been defeated if the whole party had followed Seymour's conciliatory course, if Blair had not scared off potential Republican recruits, and if the Reconstruction plank had been milder. Seymour himself attributed the result to the desire of businessmen to have old conflicts settled, and "our platform in 1868 looked to unsettling them." Chairman Belmont was so disgusted with the extremists that in a moment of despair he privately proposed to "build up a new party, take hold of new issues, so as to get the people with us and not to remain in the leading-strings of old political hacks."[39] But the moderates, now so self-righteous, had been mouthing Frank Blair's rhetoric until the early state election results showed that such crude extremism was counterproductice.

These contrasting explanations for defeat showed that the 1868 campaign had widened the cleavage within the Democracy. Extremists were more convinced than ever that only white

36. Adverse responses to the *World*'s course appear in letters dated October 17–21, 1868, Marble Papers. Seymour's last-ditch campaigning was reported in New York *World*, October 24, 1868, p. 4.

37. *Tribune Almanac*, 1869, pp. 88, 48.

38. *Old Guard*, VI (December, 1868), 883–84.

39. New York *World*, November 5, 1868, p. 4; Seymour to George L. Miller, December 20, 1869, Seymour Papers, Fairchild Collection, NYHS; Belmont to Manton Marble, November 6, 1868, Vol. 20, Marble Papers.

supremacist propaganda could build a new Democratic majority in the nation. In contrast, the moderates expected to achieve the same end by muting inflammatory appeals to racism and finding new issues. The fate of the party would hinge on which assessment was accurate, and the future course of the nation's racial policy might depend on which faction won control of the party.

2

A New Departure
1869-84

In the years immediately following Seymour's defeat, Democratic moderates took over the party reins and, building on the strategy suggested in the Chase movement of 1868, devised a clever long-range plan to regain power. Official acquiescence in Reconstruction would renew Democratic respectability among Northern voters, while a hands-off Southern policy justified by states' rights theory might allow Dixie Democrats to recapture control of the South, legally or otherwise. This theoretical capitulation to Republican Reconstruction, combined with opposition to its practical enforcement, became known as the "new departure." Though denounced by Republicans as hypocritical, the new departure contributed to the collapse of Reconstruction in the 1870's and the partial eclipse of the race issue in national politics of the 1880's.

Formulation

After the 1868 election Democratic moderates gave up opposition to the Reconstruction Acts as futile, while old-liners kept up the fight. Moderate New York Congressman Samuel S. ("Sunset") Cox urged Democrats to "accept the situation as to the Status of the States South and endeavor to regulate the relations of the federal government to the States on the principle of State Autonomy . . . let that be bygones. . . ."[1] The reference to state autonomy indicates that even those party leaders accepting Reconstruction would fight federal efforts to enforce it. Never-

1. S. S. Cox to Manton Marble, February 13, 1869, Vol. 21, Marble Papers. Similar sentiments are in New York *World*, November 9, 1868, p. 4.

theless, principled white supremacists considered even this position tantamount to complete surrender, and called for continued resistance to all Republican innovations in race relations.[2]

The two wings of the Democratic party found a common cause and temporary unity when the Republicans sponsored a new constitutional amendment. While the Reconstruction Acts had brought black suffrage to the South, few Negroes enjoyed the franchise elsewhere. Five New England states had long allowed black voting; New York granted the privilege to Negroes owning $250 in property; and the blacks of Wisconsin, Iowa, Minnesota, Nebraska, and Tennessee had gained voting rights since the war's end. But members of the race in every other state outside the old Confederacy were politically powerless.[3] In 1869 Republicans proposed a Fifteenth Amendment, nationalizing Negro suffrage and placing it under federal protection.

Whatever their attitude toward the Reconstruction Acts, Democrats in Congress fought the new amendment. The party was most vocally represented in debate by border state racists who warned of the Negro's biological incapacity for responsible political behavior.[4] Democratic moderates joined the attack but used a different rhetoric. Not explicitly disagreeing with the extremists on black inferiority, moderates preferred to emphasize the opposition's alleged bad faith in going back on the Republican platform in 1868, which had promised to leave voting rights in the Northern and border regions under state control. Present state legislatures elected before the federal amendment had even been proposed did not reflect popular opinion on the issue, argued Democratic moderates.[5] Despite the intensity of their opposition, Democrats were unable to prevent congres-

2. Dayton *Ledger*, March 4, 1869, p. 2; New York *Day Book*, April 17, May 22, 1869, both p. 4; *Democratic Almanac*, 1869, p. 39.

3. William Gillette, *The Right to Vote: Politics and the Passage of the Fifteenth Amendment* (Baltimore: Johns Hopkins University Press, 1969), pp. 26–27, 80.

4. Remarks of Senators Garrett Davis of Kentucky, George Vickers of Maryland, Thomas Bayard and Willard Saulsbury of Delaware, in *Congressional Globe*, 40 Cong., 3 sess., pp. 716, 905, 169 (Appendix), 1310 (January 29, February 5, 17, 1869).

5. Remarks of Senators Charles Buckalew of Pennsylvania and James Dixon of Connecticut, *ibid.*, pp. 543, 912 (January 23, February 5, 1869).

sional passage of the amendment in February, 1869. The measure then went to the state legislatures for ratification.[6]

Democrats in almost every Northern and border state fought ratification.[7] The tenacity of Democratic opposition was most clearly illustrated in Indiana; Hoosier Democrats at first professed not to "believe the Radical majority in the present Legislature will even consider an amendment that their National platform repudiated." When Republicans pressed for ratification, the state Democracy, announcing that "the prejudice of caste is a fiat of the Almighty," refused to allow passage by a legislature elected before the issue had been raised. Democratic legislators walked out, preventing a quorum in either House, and then resigned to force special elections "for the purpose," as one of them put it, "of securing to the People of Indiana, and particularly to my own constituency, the right to express their voice in the adoption of the Constitutional amendment."[8] Campaigning for reelection on a platform asserting that "the Government was formed *for* white men, in the *interest* of white men . . . *by* white men," all the Democrats regained their seats, determined to tie up ratification with similar tactics until the next general election.[9] Reflecting party sentiment, a resident of Fulton County urged his senator: "In God's name Charley come home a thousand times rather than allow this to be done."[10] But Democratic plans to prevent ratification failed. Republicans pushed the amendment through the state senate by locking its doors with

6. Thomas F. Bayard to James A. Bayard, February 23, 1869, Container 178, Bayard Papers, Library of Congress; New York *World*, February 27, 1869, p. 4. Gillette's *Right to Vote*, pp. 46–78, gives an excellent account of the proposed amendment in Congress.

7. Roll calls in the state legislatures on ratification are available in Edward McPherson, ed., *The Political History of the United States of America during the Period of Reconstruction* (Washington: Solomons and Chapman, 1875), pp. 484–562. The only Northern states where Democrats conceded the issue in 1869 were Maine and New Hampshire, both solidly Republican states where blacks already voted.

8. Indianapolis *Sentinel*, February 22, 1869, p. 2, March 5, 1869, p. 1; Charles B. Laselle to Conrad Baker, March 3, 1869, copy, Laselle Papers, Indiana Division, Indiana State Library.

9. Indianapolis *Sentinel*, March 5, 1869, p. 2; William S. Holman to Samuel S. Cox, March 23, 1869, Reel 1, Cox Papers; J. J. Bingham to ————, March 29, 1869, Laselle Papers.

10. Milo R. Smith to C. B. Laselle, March 27, 1869, Laselle Papers.

the Democrats inside. When minority members of the House of Representatives resigned again, the Republican speaker ruled that two-thirds of those holding seats sufficed for a quorum, and ratification followed.[11]

While such Democratic zeal typified the prevalent attitude in the party's Northern and border wing, it was not generally shared by Southerners. Blacks were already voting in the states of the old Confederacy, and there was no chance of defeating ratification. Indeed, Alabama, Arkansas, Florida, Louisiana, the Carolinas, and Virginia ratified in 1869, and Congress would soon make ratification a condition for the readmission of Georgia, Mississippi, and Texas to the Union. Many pragmatic Southern Democrats accepted the situation in the hope of winning over some of the black vote, and therefore remained silent about or actively favored the Fifteenth Amendment.[12] In Virginia, for example, occurred the first official political acceptance of Negro suffrage by Southern Democrats. A convention composed of Democrats and some renegade Republicans formed a new Virginia Conservative party in January, 1869; explicitly recognizing and soliciting black votes, the delegates nominated candidates for state office. The Conservatives won their election in July; the voters simultaneously approved a state constitution enfranchising Virginia Negroes, but rejected a separately submitted clause placing political disabilities on ex-Confederates. By exploiting Republican factionalism and embracing black suffrage in return for the political rehabilitation of former rebels, the Conservatives prevented a real Reconstruction regime in Virginia. Even more important, they showed the national Democracy that a tactical retreat from racist rhetoric might yield political benefits.[13]

11. The episode is treated in William C. Gerichs, "The Ratification of the Fifteenth Amendment in Indiana," *Indiana Magazine of History*, IX (September, 1913), 131–66, and more recently in Emma Lou Thornbrough, *The Negro in Indiana before 1900* (Indianapolis: Indiana Historical Bureau, 1957), pp. 245–48.

12. Gillette, *Right to Vote*, pp. 92–104, highlights Southern passivity and acquiescence. Also see W. Grayson Mann to John C. Breckinridge, February 18, 1869, Vol. 265, Breckinridge Papers, Library of Congress, and John Edwards to Andrew Johnson, July 12, 1869, Reel 39, Johnson Papers, Library of Congress.

13. Jack P. Maddex, Jr., *The Virginia Conservatives, 1867–1879: A Study in Reconstruction Politics* (Chapel Hill: University of North Carolina Press, 1970), pp. 35–85.

In the summer of 1869, with eventual ratification of the Fifteenth Amendment by the requisite number of states a certainty, Northern Democratic unity evaporated. Moderates, buoyed by the Virginia election results, knew that Negro suffrage in the South was beyond recall; while keeping up opposition to the amendment, they tried to prepare their party for inevitable defeat on this issue.[14] Extremists maintained their old stance of no compromise,[15] but the erosion of their strength was presaged in two key state elections in the fall of 1869: the politically flexible New York Democracy won, while its doctrinaire Ohio counterpart lost.

Democratic leaders in New York, remembering the lessons of 1868, planned a conservative campaign for 1869 that would appeal to wavering Republicans. Through a policy of silence on the Reconstruction Acts the Democrats implicitly accepted the Negro franchise where it was already in effect, but fought hard against its extension. Specifically, this meant a pledge to revoke New York's earlier ratification of the Fifteenth Amendment, and opposition to a Republican-sponsored state referendum abolishing New York's property qualification for black voters. The opportunistic slogan of "acquiesce to negro suffrage when we must, and defeat it when we can"[16] brought success. On election day New Yorkers defeated the Negro voting referendum by over 3,000 votes and elected a Democratic legislature which, in January, 1870, annulled the state's ratification of the Fifteenth Amendment.[17] The New York election of 1869 was the first sign that, by assuaging suspicions that they meant to overthrow what

14. New York *World*, July 8, 19, 1869, both p. 4; I [vory] C[hamberlain] to Manton Marble, undated, 1869, Vol. 21, John P. Stockton to Marble, July 9, 1869, F. J. Porter to Marble, July 20, 1869, Vol. 22, Marble Papers.

15. Cincinnati *Enquirer*, July 1, 1869, p. 4; *Old Guard*, VII (June, 1869), 402, 404.

16. New York *World*, September 8, 1869, p. 4. The New York campaign can be followed *ibid.*, September 23, 1869, p. 3, September 25, 1869, p. 6, October 28, 1869, p. 3, October 29, 1869, p. 1; *American Annual Cyclopaedia*, 1869, p. 488; Manton Marble to S. L. M. Barlow, August 9, 1869, Barlow Papers, Henry E. Huntington Library.

17. New York *World*, November 4, 1869, p. 4; McPherson, ed., *Political History of Reconstruction*, p. 562. This nullification of New York's ratification was never recognized by the secretary of state.

had already been accomplished in the South, moderate Democrats could win control of a pivotal Northern state.

Extremists ran the Ohio campaign of 1869. Disdaining the moderate path of silence on the Reconstruction Acts, Ohio Democrats repeated the tactics of 1868: they exploited white racial prejudice with fierce attacks on Negro suffrage as a whole, North and South. Since Ohio voters had defeated a state referendum on black suffrage two years earlier, Democrats believed that enough Republican white supremacists could be won over to insure a Democratic victory. Gubernatorial candidate George Pendleton sounded the keynote. Predicting that the Supreme Court was "only waiting an opportunity to declare the reconstruction acts unconsitutional," he pleaded: "Let us people our country with the best races of men." The Democratic strategy failed, and Republicans captured the governorship.[18]

These 1869 elections threw Democrats into political confusion. The inertia built up by past policies insured that the party's public stance would remain at least temporarily anti-Negro, but many Democratic leaders privately recognized that the sooner the race question were buried, the better. Democratic platforms and legislators in Northern and border states, except for some New England defections, kept up massive opposition to the Fifteenth Amendment in the early part of 1870.[19] Yet, even while the party press in Ohio insisted that most Buckeyes were white supremacists despite Pendleton's defeat, the personal correspondence of Democratic politicos in the state indicated a recognition that Negro suffrage was an obsolete issue.[20] The

18. Pendleton is quoted in New York *World*, September 13, 1869, p. 1. On the campaign in Ohio see Cincinnati *Enquirer* and Dayton *Ledger*, September-October, 1869; Llewellyn Baber to Thomas Ewing, February 17, 1869, John Thompson to Thomas Ewing, Jr., July 27, 1869, Container 75, Ewing Papers, LC; Llewellyn Baber to Allen G. Thurman, May 20, 1876, Thurman Papers, Ohio Historical Society; William Lawrence, *Negro Suffrage: Ohio Holds the Casting Vote on the XVth Amendment* (n.p.: n.p., 1869); Durbin Ward, *Life, Speeches and Orations of Durbin Ward of Ohio* (Columbus: A. H. Smythe, 1888), p. 166.

19. *American Annual Cyclopaedia*, 1870, pp. 210, 403, 536, 606; McPherson, ed., *Political History of Reconstruction*, pp. 556–62.

20. Dayton *Ledger*, October 18, November 19, 1869, both p. 2; Cincinnati *Enquirer*, December 9, 1869, p. 4; Thomas Ewing, Jr., to Hugh Ewing, September 30, 1869, Box 5, Hugh Ewing Papers; John H. James to R. N. Osbell, De-

course of the astute New Yorker "Sunset" Cox betrays a wide divergence between lingering outward recalcitrance even among moderates, and secret capitulation. On the floor of Congress in January, 1870, Cox described Negro legislators in the South as "mulatto barbers and black field hands, who had sharpened their brains with their ox-goads," but in February he privately recognized the inevitability of nationwide black suffrage, suggested a complete Democratic abandonment of racist appeals, and asked: "What would be the effect of a policy of acceptance of the inevitable Colored Cuss: He is here! in Senate and as a voter, and he will soon be everywhere whether we like it or not . . . I think it's foolish—we are,—not to look into the *Whites* of his eye, 'Squar!' He's an element of the future!"[21]

Democratic response to the Fifteenth Amendment's official promulgation in March, 1870, provided further evidence that moderates were quietly taking over the party. Many Southern Democrats, who already had been living with Negro suffrage for two years, were prepared to make the best of the situation "by dividing and controlling the colored vote."[22] Though eleven Northern states would now see blacks at the polls for the first time, and the new voters would hold a potential balance of power in seven, most Northern Democrats too were ready to make "some sacrifice of prejudice" and accept Negro suffrage.[23] Thus Ohio Democrats, so antagonistic the previous fall, offered no resistance to the new voters in the spring elections of 1870; a few Democratic legislators even helped the Republicans abrogate obsolete Ohio laws imposing heavy penalties on Negroes who attempted to vote.[24] The Democratic majority in the New

---

cember 31, 1869, Letterbook 163, p. 320, James Papers, Ohio Historical Society; James R. Hubbell to Salmon P. Chase, October 19, 1869, Vol. 101, Chase Papers, LC; Joseph H. Geiger to Chase, October 23, 1869, MS in New York Historical Society.

21. *Congressional Globe*, 41 Cong., 2 sess., p. 499 (January 4, 1870); Cox to Manton Marble, February 27, 1870, Vol. 24, Marble Papers.

22. William Durwell to Alexander H. Stephens, May 9, 1870, Vol. 53, Stephens Papers. Also see Southern Democratic platforms in *American Annual Cyclopaedia*, 1870, pp. 15, 31, 302, 457, 681.

23. Gillette, *Right to Vote*, p. 82; New York *World*, April 1, 1870, p. 4.

24. Dayton *Herald*, March 30, 31, 1870, both p. 2; Cincinnati *Enquirer*, April 5, 1870, p. 1; Charles R. Williams, ed., *Diary and Letters of Rutherford B.*

York legislature, unashamedly opportunistic, tried to gain credit for enfranchising the state's blacks by sponsoring and passing a bill that ended New York's property restriction on Negro suffrage. The Democrats declared that their bill had nothing to do with the recently promulgated Fifteenth Amendment, which had made the property qualification a dead letter anyway.[25]

There was formidable resistance to the amendment only in the border states, the West Coast, and Indiana. The Maryland and West Virginia Democratic organizations split over whether to continue Negro-baiting tactics, and Kentucky Democrats explicitly barred blacks from participation in party affairs. The Delaware Democracy carried out a skillful anti-Negro propaganda campaign which evoked a white backlash against the race, establishing Democratic control and Negro degradation in the state for years to come.[26] In the Far West Democratic leaders urged nullification of the Fifteenth Amendment, through force if necessary.[27] Still angry at the way their state's ratification had occurred, the Indiana party ran an old-fashioned racist campaign in 1870—and won. Democratic moderates barely managed to sidetrack a joint resolution of Indiana's new Democratic legislature denouncing the Fifteenth Amendment as a fraud and demanding its revocation.[28]

Hayes (Columbus: Ohio State Archeological and Historical Society, 1925), III, 96, 102; Ohio, *Journal of the House of Representatives*, 1870, pp. 739–50; *Journal of the Senate*, 1870, pp. 41, 338.

25. Albany *Argus*, April 1, 8, 1870, both p. 2; New York *World*, April 24, 1870, p. 5, May 3, 1870, p. 4; New York, *Journal of the Senate*, 1870, p. 848; *Journal of the Assembly*, 1870, p. 1567; John D. Van Buren to Salmon P. Chase, April 1, 1870, MS in New York State Library. Gillette, *Right to Vote*, pp. 160–61, provides a concise analysis of Northern moderate Democratic attitudes within the context of national party trends.

26. Excellent essays on the border state situation are collected in Richard O. Curry, ed., *Radicalism, Racism, and Party Realignment: The Border States during Reconstruction* (Baltimore: Johns Hopkins University Press, 1969), pp. 1–219.

27. *American Annual Cyclopaedia*, 1870, p. 79; *Congressional Globe*, 41 Cong., 2 sess., pp. 3568, 3658–59, 3758 (May 18, 20, 24, 1870).

28. Daniel W. Voorhees, *The Political Issues in Indiana: Speech of Hon. D. W. Voorhees delivered in the Academy of Music, Indianapolis, March 31, 1870* (n.p.: n.p., 1870), p. 19; Indianapolis *Sentinel*, April 2, 8, 1870, January 31, 1871, all p. 2; John B. Stoll, *History of the Indiana Democracy, 1816–1916* (Indianapolis: Indiana Democratic Publishing Company, 1917), p. 243; Francis M. Trissal, *Public Men of Indiana: A Political History from 1860 to 1890* (Hammond: W. B. Conkey, 1922), I, 69.

With the presidential election of 1872 on the horizon, Democrats had a choice of three possible positions on Reconstruction. The diehards insisted on a repetition of the 1868 strategy of total, explicit resistance.[29] At the other end of the Democratic spectrum, the New York *World* and others in the moderate vanguard called for outright acceptance of the new order as the only way to blunt Republican charges that the Democracy still intended to subordinate blacks.[30] The party's national leadership chose a middle path of vagueness in order to keep the organization from splintering. It was plainly anachronistic to continue with talk of expunging the amendments and unraveling the Reconstruction Acts, but outright acquiescence would alienate much of the Democratic rank and file who viewed such a capitulation as humiliating rather than realistic.[31]

The party's official pronouncements through 1870 and early 1871 were therefore enigmatic. In June, 1870, Democratic members of Congress issued an address to voters which pleaded, "Let there be no dissension about minor matters, no time lost in the discussion of dead issues"—but what was "minor" or "dead" was left to the imagination of the reader.[32] Congressman Samuel J. Randall of Pennsylvania, head of the National Democratic Executive Resident Committee in Washington, announced that

29. Former Confederate Vice-President Alexander H. Stephens and his brother Linton led this group. See James D. Waddell, *Biographical Sketch of Linton Stephens Containing a Selection of his Letters, Speeches, State Papers, etc.* (Atlanta: Dodson and Scott, 1877), pp. 318–19, 322, 331–46; Alexander H. Stephens to Linton Stephens, October 8, 1870, Linton Stephens to Alexander H. Stephens, October 10, 1870, Reel 5, Stephens Correspondence, Manhattanville College; Alexander H. Stephens to Montgomery Blair, January 31, 1871, Container 9, Blair Papers; T. Byrdsall to Alexander H. Stephens, March 15, 1871, Vol. 61, Stephens Papers; New York *Day Book*, January 14, February 18, 1871, both p. 4; *Pomeroy's Democrat* (New York), January 18, February 22, March 22, 1871, all p. 4.

30. Editorials in New York *World*, August, 1870–May, 1871; Samuel J. Randall, quoted in George W. Booker to Alexander H. Stephens, March 12, 1871, Vol. 61, Stephens Papers; Benjamin H. Hill, Jr., *Senator Benjamin H. Hill of Georgia: His Life, Speeches and Writings* (Atlanta: H. C. Hudgins, 1891), pp. 55–59.

31. A cynical observer claimed that most Democrats did "not know where or how they stand." William H. Hidell to Alexander H. Stephens, October 22, 1870, Vol. 58, Stephens Papers.

32. New York *World*, June 25, 1870, p. 1.

his party was appealing for votes in the 1870 elections on the bland issue of "economy and honesty in the management of the public treasury," and he excluded any material on the Fifteenth Amendment from the list of Democratic campaign literature. State party platforms in 1870 also shied away from the sensitive Reconstruction issue.[33] In April, 1871, congressional Democrats had difficulty preparing another annual address to the people. When the extremists drew up a statement, it had to be "toned down to suit the squeamish stomachs" of the moderates, and "it was finally signed each side giving its own construction to the paper." This address was a bit more explicit than that of 1870, asking Democrats "to discontinue and discourage any violations of the rights of any portion of the people secured under the Constitution or any of its amendments."[34] The policy of the straddle gained momentum when the old-line Kentucky Democracy framed a platform in May, 1871, which ignored the amendments and simply endorsed the congressional address.[35] By this time even the most extreme party leaders were ready to go along, consoling themselves with the thought that, as long as there was no explicit acceptance of the amendments, Democrats could dismantle Reconstruction once they gained national power.[36]

But the noncommittal policy was shattered on May 18, 1871, when the Democrats of Montgomery County, Ohio, adopted a resolution on Reconstruction, meant as a model for the state

33. Randall quoted *ibid.*, October 22, 1870, p. 5; Randall to ———, undated, 1870, Box 4, Randall Papers, University of Pennsylvania; *American Annual Cyclopaedia*, 1870, *passim*.

34. The resolution is in New York *World*, April 21, 1871, p. 1, and the circumstances of its preparation are described in F. P. Blair to Alexander H. Stephens, May 3, 1871, Vol. 62, Stephens Papers. Blair was now a senator from Missouri.

35. *American Annual Cyclopaedia*, 1871, pp. 435–36; Henry Watterson to Parke Godwin, February 22, 1871, Bryant-Godwin Papers; B. W. Duke to John W. Stevenson, May 17, 1871, Vol. 29, Stevenson Papers.

36. Remarks of Frank Blair in *Congressional Globe*, 41 Cong., 3 sess., Appendix, pp. 114–17 (February 15, 1871); Blair to Alexander H. Stephens, March 10, 1871, Vol. 61, Stephens Papers; Stephens to Blair, May 8, 1871, Vol. 12, Carl Schurz Papers, Library of Congress; also in Ulrich B. Phillips, ed., *Correspondence of Robert Toombs, Alexander H. Stephens, and Howell Cobb* (Washington: U.S. Government Printing Office, 1913), pp. 713–16; New York *Democrat*, May 5, 1871, p. 2.

platform, which specifically accepted the new amendments. This plank, written by former Copperhead leader Clement Vallandigham, who was planning a political comeback, acquiesced in "the natural and legitimate results of the war . . . including the three several [sic] amendments *de facto* to the Constitution, recently declared adopted, as a settlement in fact of all the issues of the war. . . ." This was the first official Democratic pronouncement openly admitting the amendments' validity, but it simultaneously attacked the federal government's right to implement them. Vallandigham's platform, called the new departure, reaffirmed "the original theory and character of the Federal Government," the old idea of states' rights. Explaining his position to the state convention at Columbus on June 1, Vallandigham invited his party to enjoy the best of both worlds: the "sound doctrine of strict construction" would remove federal interference from the South, while symbolic acceptance of Negro civil and political equality would remove the taint of disloyalty from the Democracy in the North.[37] Despite charges of betrayal from those who preferred a policy of silence on the amendments, new departurism spread rapidly among moderates, some of whom had been thinking along similar lines as early as the Chase movement of 1868.[38] Ohio Democrats endorsed the

37. James L. Vallandigham, *A Life of Clement L. Vallandigham* (Baltimore: Turnbull Brothers, 1872), pp. 438–39; Dayton *Herald*, June 7, 1871, p. 2. On the background of Vallandigham's move, see Clifford H. Moore, "Ohio in National Politics, 1865–1896," *Ohio Archeological and Historical Quarterly*, XXXVII (April–June, 1928), 268–72; Indianapolis *Sentinel*, February 27, 1871, p. 2; James H. Lambert to Alexander H. Stephens, March 1, 1871, Vol. 61, Stephens Papers; Vallandigham to Lewis D. Campbell, May 4, 1871, Campbell Papers, Ohio Historical Society; Cincinnati *Enquirer*, May 18, 1871, p. 4.

38. For negative sentiment, see *Pomeroy's Democrat*, May 31, 1871, pp. 1, 4, June 4, 1871, pp. 1, 4; C. Chauncey Burr to Alexander H. Stephens, June 25, 1871, Vol. 63, Stephens Papers; W. D. Northend to F. P. Blair, June 18, 1871, Barton Able to Blair, June 23, 1871, Container 3, Blair Papers; James Ferguson to William Allen, June 19, 1871, Vol. 17, Allen Papers. Qualified acceptance is expressed in John James to Vallandigham, May 16, 1871, James to Lewis D. Campbell, May 27, 1871, Letterbook 164, pp. 71–73, 75, James Papers; Llewellyn Baber to Thomas Ewing, Jr., O. T. Moore to Ewing, Jr., May 24, 1871, Container 78, Ewing Papers, LC; Cincinnati *Enquirer*, May 20, 25, 1871, both p. 4. Enthusiastic responses are Salmon P. Chase to Vallandigham, May 20, 1871, Letterbook 119, p. 141, Chase Papers, LC; William S. Groesbeck to S. S. Cox, June 3, 1871, MS in Ohio Historical Society; Thomas Hendricks quoted in Cincinnati *Enquirer*, July 28, 1871, p. 4; New York *World*, June 2, 3, 12, 1871, all p. 4.

platform, followed by nine more Northern state organizations and that of Arkansas. Nevertheless, Democrats suffered losses at the polls in the fall elections of 1871. It is difficult to tell whether the result was due primarily to rank and file anger at the new departure, as extremists claimed, or to the Tweed Ring scandals in New York, which tainted the national Democracy with the stigma of corruption.[39]

The new departure's significance was not its immediate effect on party fortunes. Indeed, Congressman Randall recognized this as he told Pennsylvania Democrats that acceptance of the amendments would not carry their state in 1871, but that since "we would have to take the 'new departure' in . . . 1872 . . . we might as well take it now."[40] In the long run, by officially removing race and the related issue of "'the results of the war'" from partisan debate, the Vallandigham policy would revive the trust of Northern voters in the Democracy. As August Belmont exclaimed somewhat prematurely on hearing of the new departure, "the game of charging us with disloyalty and Copperheadism is played out."[41] At the same time new departurists would insist on strict construction of federal powers under the amendments, thereby crippling Republican efforts to enforce

---

39. The nine other Northern Democratic organizations were those of California, Illinois, Iowa, Maine, Massachusetts, Minnesota, New Jersey, Pennsylvania, and Wisconsin. Platforms are in *American Annual Cyclopaedia,* 1871. The new departure proved most difficult to sustain during the fall campaigns in Ohio and Pennsylvania. On Ohio, see John R. Nickel to Alexander H. Stephens, August 5, 1871, Vol. 63, Stephens Papers; H. Cameron to Thomas Ewing, Jr., June 2, 1871, Hugh Ewing to Thomas Ewing, Jr., July 11, 1871, Container 78, Ewing Papers, LC; Llewellyn Baber to Montgomery Blair, July 10, 1871, Container 3, Blair Papers. The Pennsylvania situation is described in W. Watson to Samuel J. Randall, June 29, 1871, W. McClelland to Randall, July 6, 21, 1871, Box 4, Randall Papers; R. E. Monaghan to William Bigler, August 1, 1871, and enclosed circular, Box 15, Bigler Papers. The election returns are printed in *Tribune Almanac,* 1872, pp. 57–60, 67, 70, 73, 76, and various assessments of these results emerge from C. S. Barret to Samuel J. Randall, October 15, 1871, Benjamin Green to Randall, November 1, 1871, Box 5, Randall Papers; Richard Vaux to William Bigler, February 2, 1872, Box 15, Bigler Papers; Salmon P. Chase to Alexander Long, November 29, 1871, Box B, Long Papers.
40. Quoted in Joseph Hemphill to Alexander H. Stephens, August 16, 1871, Vol. 64, Stephens Papers.
41. Belmont to George McCook, June 5, 1871, Vol. 28, Marble Papers.

Negro rights and allowing Southern Democrats the freedom to seize and hold political control of their region.

But even before Vallandigham enunciated this overall strategy, Democrats in Congress, intent on preventing further Republican measures on behalf of the Negroes, were working out the specific tactics. Republicans recognized that promulgation of the Fourteenth and Fifteenth Amendments would not of itself insulate the freedman from ongoing white violence and intimidation in the South, and the party pushed through Congress a series of three enforcement acts in 1870 and 1871 which provided further protection for blacks. Whatever internal differences Democrats might have over the status of the Fifteenth Amendment, they all stood to lose from its effective implementation. The party needed white control of the South as a stepping stone to national power, and the Negro vote would have to be neutralized somehow. Effective enforcement of Negro rights meant indefinite Republican rule in the South, and Democrats in Congress unanimously opposed the legislation.[42]

Party spokesmen developed two lines of attack on enforcement which the Democracy would repeat for the next twenty years. First, when confronted with evidence of Southern violence, Democratic lawmakers countered with outright denial, or denunciation of Republicans for precipitating the outbreaks. Senator John P. Stockton of New Jersey said that "the fifteenth amendment will enforce itself" in the South without further legislation, irrelevantly citing the lack of violence when blacks voted in his own home ward. As for charges that a violent Ku Klux Klan terrorized the freedman, Senator Thurman blamed the Reconstruction Acts, though adding, "I am not justifying the Ku Klux." The minority report of a joint congressional committee assigned to investigate the Klan was released in February, 1872; it echoed Thurman. This Democratic report asked that Southern whites guilty of violence be punished, but it blamed

42. Congressional roll calls on the three enforcement acts are available in Edward McPherson, ed., *Handbook of Politics for 1870* (Washington: Philp & Solomons, 1870), p. 44; *Handbook of Politics for 1872*, pp. 8, 87. All Democrats voted nay each time.

Republican Reconstruction policies, since "the worst governments produce the most disorders." A general amnesty for Confederates would remedy the situation without formal revocation of Negro suffrage.[43] More important was the Democratic tactic of drawing a sharp distinction on constitutional grounds between the possible validity of the recent amendments and the definite illegality of the enforcement legislation, an approach that Vallandigham was to use in his new departure. California Senator Eugene Casserly was the first congressional Democrat who declared that the Fifteenth Amendment, even if legitimate, merely nullified state voting laws which discriminated against blacks. Since federal enforcement power touched states only, it was powerless against individuals or organized bands suspected of interference with Negro voting. Therefore the federal enforcement acts covering such crimes were unconstitutional.[44] Democrats interpreted the Fourteenth Amendment's guarantee of "equal protection under the laws" in the same limited way. In late 1871 Senator Charles Sumner, Republican of Massachusetts, proposed a civil rights bill outlawing racial discrimination in public accommodations, places of amusement, public schools, cemeteries, and jury selection. Senator Thurman, speaking for the Democracy, attacked the measure's constitutionality on the grounds that the Fourteenth Amendment gave federal authority no power over the discriminatory acts of individuals, and his party colleagues chimed in with appeals to white fear of Negro "social equality."[45] Senator Casserly privately predicted in 1871 that strict Democratic interpretation of the amendments would "wreck" all federal legislation under them, and in later years the

43. *Congressional Globe*, 41 Cong., 2 sess, pp. 3567–68, 2397 (May 18, April 4, 1870); U.S. House, *Report of the Joint Select Committee to Inquire into the Condition of Affairs in the Late Insurrectionary States*, House Report 22, 42 Cong., 2 sess., 1872, I, 292–96, 448, 463, 509. One Democratic member, in a separate report, demanded an end to black voting. *Ibid.*, pp. 515–17.

44. Remarks of Casserly, *Congressional Globe*, 41 Cong., 2 sess., Appendix, p. 472 (May 20, 1870).

45. Remarks of Thurman, *Congressional Globe*, 42 Cong., 2 sess., p. 280, Appendix, p. 26 (December 2, 1871, February 6, 1872). Also see other Democratic comment *ibid.*, pp. 791, 3252, Appendix, pp. 9–11, 599 (February 2, May 9, January 30, May 29, 1872).

Supreme Court, following Democratic reasoning, would do the wrecking.[46]

Three roll calls in the House of Representatives early in 1872 showed that, despite the disappointing outcome of the 1871 elections, new departure moderates had consolidated their control of the Democracy. Republicans moved a resolution affirming the validity of the recent amendments "and such reasonable legislation of Congress as may be necessary to make them in their letter and spirit most effectual." Only eight Democrats, all from the North, supported the motion, while fifty-seven Democrats voted to deny congressional authority to enforce the amendments, and several more abstained. Democrat James Brooks of New York then offered an alternative new departure formula, simply recognizing the amendments with no mention of congressional power to legislate. This time fifty-five Democrats voted yea, while just twenty-two extremists opposed the measure. A sectional analysis of this roll call is revealing:

TABLE 1. *Democratic Votes on Brooks Resolution, February 5, 1872*

	Yes	*No*
New England	4	0
Mid-Atlantic	17	1
Midwest	13	2
Border	11	13
South	10	6
Total	55	22

If the congressmen were correctly representing their constituents in this vote, only in the border states did a majority of Democrats still refuse to acknowledge the amendments. Old-liners were furious that so many Northern Democrats backed the Brooks proposal. But party solidarity returned a week later, when the Democratic contingent unanimously opposed a Re-

46. Casserly to Manton Marble, March 12, 1871, Vol. 27, Marble Papers; Rayford W. Logan, *The Betrayal of the Negro: From Rutherford B. Hayes to Woodrow Wilson* (New York: Collier, 1968), pp. 105–24.

publican resolution stating the legality of the three enforcement acts previously passed.[47] Thus on the eve of the 1872 presidential campaign most Democrats were in the new departure camp, ready to pledge verbal obedience to the Reconstruction amendments while opposing federal implementation of political and civil equality for Negroes.

1872: The Point of No Return

The Democrats confirmed their new departure by endorsing a "Liberal" anti-Grant Republican for president in 1872. This strategy of joining forces with dissident Republicans failed to stop Grant's reelection bid, but it did go a long way toward restoring Democratic political respectability. As new departurists realized, such respectability was essential for carrying out the policy of non-enforcement of the amendments.

Creation of a Liberal-Democratic bloc to defeat Grant presented more difficulties than similar movements in the Virginia and Missouri state elections in 1869 and 1870 which had required agreement only on state issues.[48] A national coalition, besides agreeing on a joint presidential nominee, would have to work out a common policy on Reconstruction. The Liberals planned an early national convention, hoping to nominate a ticket palatable to the Democracy. As for a platform plank on Reconstruction, despite the contrast in their original positions on the civil equality of the races, new departure Democrats by

47. The first two roll calls are in *Congressional Globe*, 42 Cong., 2 sess., pp. 832–33 (February 5, 1872). In this and all subsequent sectional breakdowns of Democratic votes, Delaware, Maryland, West Virginia, Tennessee, Kentucky, and Missouri are treated as border states, and the other former slave states are considered "South." Extremist hostility to the Brooks resolution is seen in *Pomeroy's Democrat*, February 10, 1872, p. 1, and D. M. Dubose to Alexander H. Stephens, March 7, 1872, Vol. 68, Stephens Papers. The final roll call is in *Congressional Globe*, 42 Cong., 2 sess., p. 974 (February 12, 1872).

48. On Virginia see above, pp. 18–19. The Missouri coalition, like Virginia's, was formed primarily to remove political disabilities from ex-Confederates. For detailed accounts, consult Thomas S. Barclay, *The Liberal Republican Movement in Missouri, 1865–1871* (Columbia: State Historical Society of Missouri, 1926); William E. Parrish, *Missouri under Radical Rule, 1865–1870* (Columbia: University of Missouri Press, 1965); Parrish, "Reconstruction Politics in Missouri, 1865–1870," in Curry, ed., *Radicalism, Racism, and Party Realignment*, pp. 1–36.

now accepted the amendments which Liberals had espoused, while both elements opposed federal enforcement laws and the proposed civil rights bill.[49] But the remnants of old-line Democracy still held out against even a symbolic surrender of white supremacy and might refuse to rally behind the new anti-Grant crusade unless it were made clear that this was a coalition of convenience only, not a shift in party doctrine.[50]

Liberal Republicans began their convention on May 1. As expected, their platform affirmed the permanence of the Reconstruction amendments, including "impartial suffrage," and recognized "the equality of all men before the law" while demanding the restoration of local self-government in the South— exactly the formula that Vallandigham had put forward in 1871. The Liberal platform ignored Sumner's civil rights bill.[51] If the nature of their resolutions had been expected, their choice for the presidential nomination was not. Instead of naming a Conservative Republican known to oppose Radical Reconstruction, like the former envoy to Great Britain Charles Francis Adams or Supreme Court Justice David Davis, the convention turned to Horace Greeley, editor of the New York *Tribune*. Nothing could have antagonized the Democrats more. Greeley had been first a partisan Whig, then a Radical Republican, and throughout a long career had consistently gone out of his way to stigmatize Democrats and all things Democratic. Asked how he expected the Democracy to respond to the nomination, Greeley replied: "Well, the democrats . . . are queer and do a good many queer

49. Two perceptive articles by Patrick A. Riddleberger on the Liberal attitude toward Reconstruction are "The Break in the Radical Ranks: Liberals vs. Stalwarts in the Election of 1872," *Journal of Negro History*, XLIV (April, 1959), 136–57, and "The Radicals' Abandonment of the Negro during Reconstruction," *ibid.*, XLV (April, 1960), 88–102. The compatibility of Liberal Republicanism and new departure Democracy is evident in the similarities between editorials on Reconstruction in the New York *World* and the Chicago *Tribune*, a representative Liberal paper, through the early part of 1872. Of course, no generalization about the Liberals holds for a man like Charles Sumner, who would eventually join the movement.

50. J. Glancy Jones to Carl Schurz, January 26, 1872, Vol. 14, Schurz Papers; Jones to Alexander H. Stephens, March 7, 1872, Herbert Fielder to Stephens, March 12, 1872, Vol. 68, D. M. DuBose to Stephens, April 17, 1872, Vol. 69, Stephens Papers.

51. Porter and Johnson, eds., *Party Platforms*, p. 41.

things. You don't know just what they are up to till they do it."
Democratic Congressman Michael Kerr of Indiana was more
succinct: "What the Democrats will do towards Greeley, God
only knows."[52]

While many Democrats, especially in the South, were ready
to swallow Greeley as the only way to beat Grant and restore
"local self-government" to the secession states, extremists could
not forget the Liberal's enthusiasm for Negro rights, and they
demanded an independent Democratic nominee to challenge
both Grant and Greeley.[53] Congressman Daniel Voorhees of
Indiana launched a crusade to head off a Democratic endorsement of Greeley. On the floor of Congress Voorhees noted that
Greeley had applauded Republican Reconstruction, including
Sumner's civil rights bill, until very recently. Was it not con-
ceivable that, once elected, Greeley might repudiate the Liberal
platform and pour more suffering and humiliation on the white
South? Returning home, Voorhees told his Terre Haute constituents that he had hoped to attack Indiana Republicans in the

52. The standard biography of Greeley is Glyndon G. Van Deusen, *Horace Greeley: Nineteenth Century Crusader* (Philadelphia: University of Pennsylvania Press, 1953), and a recent account of his nomination is Matthew T. Downey, "Horace Greeley and the Politicians: The Liberal Republican Convention in 1872," *Journal of American History*, LIII (March, 1967), 727–50. The statements of Greeley and Kerr are from Albany *Argus*, May 6, 1872, p. 2, and M. C. Kerr to Edward A. Atkinson, May 13, 1872, Box 3, Atkinson Papers, Massachusetts Historical Society.

53. For Southern satisfaction, consult William L. R. Brockenbrough to John W. Stevenson, May 24, 1872, Vol. 30, Stevenson Papers; Linton Stephens to Alexander H. Stephens, May 5, 1872, Reel 5, Stephens Correspondence; Wade Hampton to John Mullaly, May 19, 1872, in Charles E. Cauthen, ed., *Family Letters of the Three Wade Hamptons, 1782–1901* (Columbia: University of South Carolina Press, 1953), p. 144; Southern state platforms in *American Annual Cyclopaedia*, 1872. Evidence of similar Northern feeling is provided in James R. Doolittle to George B. Smith, May 7, 1872, Box 4, Smith Papers, State Historical Society of Wisconsin; John Tapley to Doolittle, May 4, 1872, H. A. Tenney to Doolittle, May 8, 1872, Box 4, Doolittle Papers, State Historical Society of Wisconsin; S. Churchill to Lyman Trumbull, May 17, 1872, Gustave Koerner to Trumbull, May 24, 1872, Vol. 76, Trumbull Papers, Library of Congress. A few examples of the intense hostility among extremists are *Pomeroy's Democrat*, May 5, 1872, p. 4; George B. Smith to James R. Doolittle, May 13, 1872, Box 4, Doolittle Papers; James B. Wall to Samuel J. Randall, May 19, 1872, Box 5, Randall Papers; Wall to Thomas F. Bayard, May 30, 1872, Container 179, Bayard Papers; Jeremiah S. Black to Editor of York (Pennsylvania) *Gazette*, May 20, 1872, copy, Vol. 55, Black Papers, Library of Congress; George McDowell to Alexander H. Stephens, May 31, 1872, Vol. 69, Stephens Papers.

upcoming campaign for their support of the civil rights bill, but with a negrophile at the head of his own ticket this would be ludicrous. "What harmony will there be," he asked, "between the entire Democratic side of the House in Congress, and their candidate . . . on the point of [racial] equality in schools?" There was also some opposition to Greeley from moderate Democrats motivated by personal animosity.[54] National Democratic leaders were unsure about the direction of public opinion, and therefore refused to commit themselves for or against Greeley. Surveying the confused Democratic scene, former Senator Casserly predicted a choice "between defeat with Greeley, and defeat without him, with a split in the party into the bargain as in 1860."[55]

Since firm national guidance was lacking, state Democratic organizations would chart the party's course; with Greeley assured of substantial Southern support, Northern and border state conventions held the key to Democratic policy. Through May and early June the Democrats of Tennessee, New York, Iowa, and Kansas officially favored coalition with the Liberals, while opponents prevailed in Pennsylvania and Delaware.[56] The turning point came on June 12 at the Indiana convention. If a Greeley endorsement were to be prevented, it would have to be done by the Hoosier Democracy, an old-line bastion in which Daniel Voorhees was a major power. Despite predictions of a hard fight, Greeley sentiment swept the convention, and Voorhees was persuaded to keep silent. Thomas Hendricks, previously noncommittal, received the nomination for governor and declared: "We have turned our backs on the past—we stand in the present and

54. Voorhees, in *Congressional Globe*, 42 Cong., 2 sess., pp. 3379–81 (May 13, 1872), and Chicago *Tribune*, May 26, 1872, p. 10. Moderate antagonism toward Greeley was centered around the New York *World*. See M[anton] M[arble] to I[vory] C[hamberlain], May 3, 1872, telegram, Vol. 31, Marble Papers; Marble to S. L. M. Barlow, May 6, [1872], Barlow Papers; editorials in New York *World*, May–July, 1872.

55. Eugene Casserly to Samuel J. Tilden, June 13, 1872, Box 9, Tilden Papers. The perplexities plaguing the party leadership are evident in remarks of Thomas Hendricks in Dayton *Herald*, May 9, 1872, p. 2; Hendricks to David Davis, May 4, 1872, Folder 108, Davis Papers; August Belmont, in Washington *Patriot*, May 6, 1872, p. 1; Belmont to Samuel Bowles, May 7, 1872, Vol. 5, Wells Papers, Library of Congress.

56. *American Annual Cyclopaedia*, 1872, pp. 235, 405, 423, 585, 664–65, 753–54.

look to the future."[57] Democrats in several more states followed Indiana into the coalitionist camp. With approbation of Greeley at the national convention now a certainty, embittered Democratic extremists made secret plans to bolt and organize a "purer" Democracy of their own.[58]

The Democratic national convention opened on July 9 with a speech by James R. Doolittle, a former Republican senator from Wisconsin, stressing the compatibility of new departure Democracy with the Liberal Republican platform of local self-government and equal rights for all. Speaking for the old-liners, Senator Thomas Bayard of Delaware asked for a brief and vague Reconstruction plank that would not commit the party to anything, but Southern new departurists responded that Democrats could recapture control of the secession states even while openly upholding the recent amendments. The delegates proceeded to endorse the Liberal platform by a margin of 670 to 62. In the presidential balloting Greeley received 732 of the 770 votes cast, a result that he interpreted as "conclusive proof that not merely is slavery abolished, but that its spirit is extinct" even among Democrats.[59] Ostensibly, race was no longer a partisan issue, and the new departure dream of a respectable Democracy immune from charges of disloyalty had come true.

But despite Greeley's euphoria, there was evidence that Democratic racial attitudes had not really changed. Many Democrats refused to stand behind the decisions of their national convention. Although Democratic leaders who had been lukewarm or hostile to Greeley wheeled into line after the convention, much

57. M. C. Kerr to Edward A. Atkinson, May 26, 1872, Box 3, Atkinson Papers; David Davis to James E. Harvey, June 4, 1872, Folder 109, Davis Papers; M. C. Kerr to Manton Marble, June 13, 1872, Vol. 31, Marble Papers; George W. Julian Journals, pp. 130–31 (June 15, 1872), Julian Papers, Indiana Division, Indiana State Library; Stoll, *History of the Indiana Democracy*, p. 250. Hendricks is quoted in Dayton *Herald*, July 1, 1872, p. 2.

58. *American Annual Cyclopaedia*, 1872. Significant resistance did surface in Kentucky, Maryland, and New Jersey. Plans for a bolt are formulated in an anonymous circular entitled "Confidential," dated June 26, 1872, in Box 4, Smith Papers.

59. *Official Proceedings of the National Democratic Convention held at Baltimore, July 9, 1872* (Boston: Rockwell and Churchill, 1872), pp. 16–19, 47–53, 65–66, 80.

of the rank and file refused to follow. A few anti-Greeley Democrats, disgusted at their party's capitulation, organized a new white supremacist "straight-out" Democracy; their presidential nominee was Charles O'Conor, a New York lawyer who still believed in the scriptural authority of slavery. O'Conor vacillated, finally declining the nomination, but his name remained on the ballot in several states.[60] More ominously, many Democrats who would have nothing to do with this splinter group sat on their hands during the campaign. In Illinois, for example, a leader complained that Democrats "don't attend meetings or enthuse worth a cent," and a careful canvass of De Witt County in the central part of the state found 140 Democrats refusing to vote for Greeley.[61] Reports from other states told a similar tale of widespread apathy.[62] Clearly, the lopsided majorities which had endorsed Greeley and the new departure platform at the national convention did not reflect grass-roots party feeling.

Not only was Greeley's implication that the Democracy had capitulated to his views misleading; indeed, the exact opposite was the case. It was ironic that, while many Democrats could not stomach their party's espousal of racial equality before the law and at the ballot box, the Greeley Liberals themselves were committed only symbolically to this principle, since almost all of them had gone over to the Democratic new departure stand on the substantive question of enforcement. Thus, despite his Radical Republican background, Greeley himself opposed federal in-

60. On the "straight-outs" see C. Chauncey Burr to Alexander H. Stephens, July 16, 1872, Vol. 70, Stephens Papers; Blanton Duncan to Jeremiah S. Black, July 19, 1872, Vol. 56, Black Papers; Cincinnati *Enquirer*, August 8, 1872, p. 5; *Pomeroy's Democrat*, August–October, 1872; Samuel J. Bayard to J. B. Guthrie, September 8, 1872, S. J. Bayard Papers, Princeton University. On O'Conor consult S. S. Cox to Parke Godwin, October 16, 1872, Reel 1, William Cullen Bryant Papers in Goddard-Roslyn Collection, Microfilm, New York Public Library.

61. A. M. Herrington to John M. Palmer, August 7, 1872, Box 43, Lyman Trumbull to Cyrus H. McCormick, September 16, 1872, Box 47, Series 1A, McCormick Papers.

62. J. P. Towne to George B. Smith, September 7, 1872, Box 4, Smith Papers; William H. Hidell to Alexander H. Stephens, July 30, 1872, Vol. 70, Stephens Papers; John D. Van Buren to Salmon P. Chase, June 16, 1872, Box 13, Chase Papers, HSP; Henry Watterson to Whitelaw Reid, August 19, 1872, Container 176, Eugene Casserly to Reid, September 26, 1872, Container 79, Reid Papers, Library of Congress.

tervention in the South now that blacks had the franchise. He counseled the race to practice self-help rather than agitate for government aid, adding that the Negro would be better off if he kept away from "intoxicating drink."[63] Greeley made no public statement on the civil rights bill during the campaign for fear of antagonizing Sumner, but his private opposition was known.[64] Was this not Democratic policy? Virtually all prominent Democrats, from "Sunset" Cox to Frank Blair, publicly echoed their platform pledge not to reopen the question of black civil and political equality; however, they also advocated the return of white rule in the South, a goal attainable once the federal presence was withdrawn.[65] Few Democrats were as explicit as Jeremiah S. Black, a cabinet member in the Buchanan administration and now a Democratic elder statesman, who predicted that, while Greeley's election would not bring immediate revocation of the last two amendments, "it will begin the process of their gradual extinction."[66] Nevertheless, the party's goal of white supremacy did entail such "gradual extinction" in practice if not in law. Divided over whether to work for Greeley, O'Conor, or to sit out the campaign, the Democracy as a whole shared the ultimate hope of wresting political power away from Southern Negroes.

Though determined to restore white rule in the South, Democrats appealed for Negro votes in 1872. There had been sporadic and unsuccessful attempts, since 1867 in the South and 1870 in the North, to enlist black Democrats.[67] But in 1872 the Recon-

63. Fredrickson, *Black Image*, pp. 182–83; New York *World*, May 17, 1872, p. 1; Cincinnati *Enquirer*, July 27, 1872, p. 1.

64. Gideon T. Norman to Horace Greeley, November 12, 1872, Box 3, Greeley Papers, New York Public Library; Edward A. Pollard, *A Southern Historian's Appeal for Horace Greeley* (Lynchburg, Va.: Daily Republican Book and Job Printing Establishment, 1872), pp. 27–29.

65. Samuel S. Cox, *Grant or Greeley* (New York: S. W. Green, 1872); Blair, in *Congressional Globe*, 42 Cong., 2 sess., Appendix, p. 381 (May 20, 1872). Also see items cited below in footnotes 83 and 84.

66. Black to William H. Welsh, August 3, 1872, copy, Vol. 56, Black Papers.

67. Southern attempts to carry the black vote in 1868 can be traced in the following: R. Abbey to Samuel J. Tilden, July 3, 1868, Box 8, Tilden Papers; Jonathan Leftwich to Andrew Johnson, July 27, September 9, 1868, William T. Dortch to Johnson, August 3, 1868, Reel 34, Johnson Papers; Price Williams to Horatio Seymour, August 30, 1868, Box 9, Seymour Papers, NYSL; Ben H.

struction amendments were no longer a bone of contention between the parties, and the Greeley campaign was therefore the
first real Democratic opportunity to seek Negro support. Nevertheless, winning blacks over to the Democracy remained difficult. Negro population in the United States was distributed
unevenly among the sections: 75 percent in the secession states,
almost 20 percent in Union border states, and the remainder in
the North.[68] Virtually all of these blacks were Republicans, and
for good reason. The Democracy had justified and protected the
slave system for decades; after emancipation, it had fought all
Republican measures designed to aid the freedman. Aside from
issues relating to slavery, free-state blacks, proscribed as an inferior caste, had long found their worst enemies in the Democratic camp.[69] Forthright demands by leaders of the race for
equal rights and the ballot before and after Appomattox could
only sharpen Democratic antagonism.[70]

Despite firm Republican affiliation, some Negroes did not like
the way their party treated them. As a Canadian Negro wrote to
an American friend in 1871: "You are in the hands of a terrible
Despotism with the Democratic party on the one hand against

Irwin to Alexander H. Stephens, August, 1868, Vol. 44, Stephens Papers; John D.
Van Buren to Seymour, September 5, 1868, Seymour Papers, NYHS; William M.
Browne to William B. Reed, September 7, 1868, Box 111, James Buchanan Pa-
pers, Historical Society of Pennsylvania. Northern Democratic efforts to gain
Negro favor after passage of the Fifteenth Amendment are noted in *New Era*
(Washington, D.C.), April 21, May 5, 1870, both p. 2, May 12, 1870, p. 3; *New
National Era*, September 29, 1870, p. 3, March 9, April 26, 1871, both p. 1; New
York *Day Book*, February 18, 1871, p. 4; Roi Ottley, *"New World A-Coming":
Inside Black America* (Boston: Houghton Mifflin, 1943), p. 209; Vallandigham,
Vallandigham, pp. 433–35.

68. U.S. Department of Commerce, Bureau of the Census, *Negro Population,
1790–1915* (Washington: U.S. Government Printing Office, 1918), p. 44.

69. Some evidences of fervent black Republicanism are L. Lane to Jacob
White, November 8, 1869, Pennsylvania State Equal Rights League Papers, Box
2G, Leon Gardiner Collection, Historical Society of Pennsylvania; *New Era*,
February 24, September 15, 1870, both p. 2; *American Annual Cyclopaedia*,
1869, p. 700. On prewar Northern Democratic hostility to blacks see Leon F.
Litwack, *North of Slavery: The Negro in the Free States, 1790–1860* (Chicago:
University of Chicago Press, 1961).

70. Elsie M. Lewis, "The Political Mind of the Negro, 1865–1900," *Journal of
Southern History*, XXI (May, 1955), reprinted in *The Negro in the South since
1865: Selected Essays in American Negro History*, ed. Charles E. Wynes (New
York: Harper and Row, 1968), pp. 22–28; August Meier, *Negro Thought in
America, 1880–1915* (Ann Arbor: University of Michigan Press, 1963), pp. 3–16.

you, and half-hearted Republicans on the other. . . ."[71] Members
of the race were upset that certain Republicans opposed the
Fifteenth Amendment. Also, the party was reluctant to appoint
blacks to office, excluded them from juries, and seemed to be
misusing idealistic slogans as a cover for corruption and lawless-
ness in the South.[72] Disturbed that Republicans were taking
Negro support for granted, some black leaders made overtures
to the Democracy before the 1872 election in the hope that a
stance of political independence would force both parties to bid
for the black vote.

Peter Clark of Ohio and George T. Downing of Rhode Island
were the most prominent advocates of this strategy in the early
1870's, and would remain so until the 1890's. A leading Negro
educator in Cincinnati, Peter Clark had long criticized the Republican organization for its conservatism on racial matters; in
1869 he berated it for insufficient zeal in pushing the Fifteenth
Amendment. By 1871 Clark had joined the Liberal Republicans,
denouncing Grant's policy of military intervention in the South
as calculated only to embitter race relations there. Angry about
Republican foot-dragging on Sumner's civil rights bill and the
party's failure to award patronage to blacks, he publicly urged
Cincinnati Negroes in the spring of 1872 to ignore party labels
in the local election and vote for those candidates, Republican
or Democrat, pledging to give blacks municipal jobs.[73] Downing

71. P. Lester to William Still, April 30, 1871, Still Papers, Box 9G, Leon
Gardiner Collection.

72. Mary Grew to Pennsylvania Abolition Society, undated, 1869, Pennsylvania Abolition Society Minutes, 1847–1916, p. 247, Historical Society of Pennsylvania; *New Era*, January 20, March 3, 1870, both p. 2; *New National Era*,
August 31, 1871, p. 3; September 14, 28, 1871, both p. 1; Dayton *Herald*,
January 24, 1872, p. 2.

73. Biographical data on Clark can be culled from Dovie King Clark, "Peter
Humphries Clark," *Negro History Bulletin*, V (May, 1942), 176; Charles T.
Greve, *Centennial History of Cincinnati and Representative Citizens* (Chicago:
Biographical Publishing, 1904), I, 887; L. D. Easton, "Colored Schools," in
*History of the Schools of Cincinnati and Other Educational Institutions, Public
and Private*, ed. Isaac Martin (Cincinnati: n.p., 1900), p. 187; George Wash-
ington Williams to Frederick Douglass, May 3, 1876, Reel 10, Douglass Papers,
Library of Congress. Clark's militancy before and during the Civil War is ex-
pressed in *Proceedings of a Convention of the Colored Men of Ohio Held in the
City of Cincinnati on the 23rd, 24th, 25th and 26th days of November, 1858*
(Cincinnati: Moore, Wilstach, Keys, 1858), p. 9; Peter H. Clark, *The Black*

was a wealthy Newport caterer who also functioned as a one-man lobbyist for Negro rights in Washington, aided by the friendship of Charles Sumner. Disillusioned with the Republicans as early as 1869, he threatened Republican senators two years later that Negroes might desert the party if the civil rights bill were not passed, and he asked in a public letter: "Would any party treat a corresponding strength as the Republican party treats its black strength?" Since Democrats were no longer exploiting crude racism, Downing predicted a division of the Negro vote unless the Republicans paid more than lip service to party ideals.[74]

But Clark and Downing expressed a minority view; in 1872 most blacks still distrusted the Democracy too much to consider it a reasonable alternative to solid Republicanism. Frederick Douglass expressed mainstream Negro opinion in his denunciation of Downing's stand as "repulsive, scandalous, and shocking." "Comparisons between the two parties," he wrote, "are simply revolting." When invited to join the anti-Grant Liberal movement in 1871, Douglass replied: "I had better put a pistol to my head and blow my brains out, than to lend myself in any wise to the destruction or the defeat of the Republican party." He called Vallandigham's new departure a hoax because, while not repealing the amendments, a Democratic national administration "might ignore odious local laws that Southerners

Brigade of Cincinnati (Cincinnati: Joseph Boyd, 1864), pp. 5–7. For his postwar political course, see Dayton *Ledger*, September 24, 1869, p. 2; *New Era*, May 5, 1870, p. 1; Cincinnati *Enquirer*, April 6, 1871, p. 4, January 2, March 14, 1872, both p. 8.

74. Background information on Downing is available in S. A. M. Washington, *George Thomas Downing: Sketch of His Life and Times* (Newport: Milne Printery, 1910); Downing to Alexander Crummell, April 19, 1860, Reel 1, Crummell Papers, Schomburg Collection, New York Public Library; Downing to Blanche K. Bruce, July 10, 1876, Box 1, Bruce Papers, Moorland-Spingarn Collection, Howard University; Downing to John Jay, March 5, 1877, Jay Family Papers, Columbia University; Downing to Charles Sumner, May 28, 1855, February 19, 1863, May 5, 1866, January 1, 1867, Sumner Papers, Houghton Library, Harvard University. His steady movement away from the Republicans is obvious in *Proceedings of the Colored National Labor Convention held in Washington, D.C. on December 6–10, 1869* (Washington: Office of the New Era, 1870), p. 3; Downing to Charles Sumner, February 7, 1871, Sumner Papers; *New National Era*, February 23, 1871, p. 3; New York *Herald*, April 29, 1871, p. 4.

would be ready to enact; they would certainly be deaf and blind concerning Ku-Kluxism and kindred outrages."[75] A national Negro convention held at New Orleans in April, 1872, followed Douglass's lead and endorsed the regular Republican ticket.[76]

Nevertheless, Democrats and Liberals hoped to win over many Negroes by capturing Charles Sumner. Revered by blacks as a champion of racial equality, Sumner despised Grant. However, he hesitated to join the Greeley coalition for fear that a national administration under Democratic influence might impair the status of the freedman. Sumner maintained his silence through the spring of 1872 while privately advising Negroes to assume an independent political stance which would impel "all parties" to recognize the principle of "Equal Rights."[77] On July 29, in a public letter to Negroes, Sumner finally committed himself to the anti-Grant movement. He echoed Greeley's assertion that, through official endorsement of racial equality and the nomination of a veteran anti-slavery man for president, Democrats "have set their corporate seal to the sacred covenant. They may continue Democrats in name, but they are in reality Republicans."[78] Sumner failed to see or refused to acknowledge that, on the contrary, Liberal Republicans had become Democrats on the vital issue of federal enforcement of Negro rights.

Relying on Greeley's old pro-Negro record and encouraged by Sumner's course, Democrats, especially in Southern and border states, tried to split the black vote. In former slave states Democrats tried cajolery and flattery as well as the usual forceful means. The Texas party paid Negroes to stump the state for Greeley, and the Florida Democracy sent black delegates to the

75. *New National Era*, June 8, 1871, p. 2; Douglass to Cassius M. Clay, July 26, 1871, Reel 1, Douglass Papers; also in Philip S. Foner, ed., *The Life and Writings of Frederick Douglass* (New York: International Publishers, 1955), IV, 252–53; *New National Era*, January 11, 1872, p. 2.

76. *New National Era*, May 2, 1872, pp. 1–2.

77. David Donald describes the evolution of Sumner's position in 1872 in *Charles Sumner and the Rights of Man* (New York: Alfred A. Knopf, 1970), pp. 539–55. Sumner's advice to Negroes is in Sumner to George T. Downing, April 8, 1872, Downing Papers, owned by Reverend Howard DeGrasse Asbury.

78. Charles Sumner, *The Works of Charles Sumner* (Boston: Lee and Shepard, 1883), XV, 184–85.

state party convention.[79] Northern Democratic appeals to the race were half-hearted. Even though the Negro electorate held a theoretical balance of power in the key states of Connecticut, Indiana, New Jersey, New York, Ohio, and Pennsylvania, leading Greeleyites assumed from the outset that "niggers go Grant."[80] Even so, Northern Democratic newspapers printed the names of all blacks they could find who favored Greeley.[81] Also the anti-Grant coalition had Southern black Greeleyites and white Liberal Republicans with good records on race address Northern Negro audiences. Such tactics aroused much animosity in the black community and led to some violent confrontations.[82]

There was little that Democrats and Liberals, North or South, could offer the Negro in exchange for his vote, since Greeleyite affirmation of the Reconstruction amendments was fraught with new departure ambiguity. When Democrats discussed the Southern issue in the 1872 campaign, they preached a natural identity of interests between the freedmen and their former masters. Grant's defeat would remove the evil influence of Republican "outsiders" who interfered with the South's racial harmony.[83] This was a sugar-coated way of saying that a Greeley administration would leave the South in the hands of white Democrats. In-

79. W. C. Nunn, *Texas under the Carpetbaggers* (Austin: University of Texas Press, 1962), pp. 69–70; Joe M. Richardson, *The Negro in the Reconstruction of Florida, 1865–1877* (Tallahassee: Florida State University, 1965), p. 233. Also see Cassius M. Clay to Henry Watterson, May 15, 1872, Vol. 1, Watterson Papers, Library of Congress; Clay to Whitelaw Reid, May 10, 1872, Container 81, Edward A. Pollard to Reid, May 26, 1872, Container 132, Reid Papers; J. W. Chrisfield to A. W. Bradford, July 17, 1872, Box 9, Bradford Papers, Maryland Historical Society.

80. M[anton] M[arble] to I[vory] C[hamberlain], May 3, 1872, telegram, Vol. 31, Marble Papers. Also note Jacob D. Cox to David A. Wells, May 23, 1872, Vol. 5, Wells Papers, LC. The importance of the Northern black vote is calculated in Gillette, *Right to Vote*, p. 82.

81. Albany *Argus*, July 8, 1872, p. 1, July 12, 22, 26, 1872, all p. 2; Washington *Patriot*, July 22, 1872, p. 1; Dayton *Herald*, July 30, 1872, p. 2.

82. Cincinnati *Enquirer*, August, 1872; Grace Julian Clarke, *George W. Julian* (Indianapolis: Indiana Historical Commission, 1923), p. 354.

83. *Speech of Allen G. Thurman at Tiffin, Ohio, September 6, 1872* (Columbus: Columbus Daily Sentinel Office, 1872), p. 7; *Speeches of Hon. Francis Kernan of New York and Hon. R. M. T. Hunter of Virginia at the Mass Meeting in New York on Thursday Evening, September 12, 1872* (New York: John Polhemus, 1872), pp. 7,11; Dayton *Herald*, October 26, 1872, p. 2.

deed, Democratic rhetoric often slipped into outright threats against blacks. Leading Democratic newspapers warned the race that if it voted as a bloc for Grant, a violent white Democratic backlash against Negroes might follow.[84]

Political arguments based upon threats could only alienate black voters. Negro meetings throughout the nation passed pro-Grant and anti-Greeley resolutions.[85] To insure a solid black vote, the regular Republicans published special campaign literature aimed at Negroes and circulated a rumor charging that Greeley's New York *Tribune* employed a lily-white staff.[86] There were black Greeleyites, and they did hold a national convention —but no prominent member of the race would have anything to do with the movement, not even Peter Clark or George T. Downing.[87] The coalition's last prominent Negro hope, P. B. S. Pinchback, lieutenant governor of Louisiana, decided in late August not to oppose the regular Republican ticket.[88] It was obvious by midsummer that not even Sumner could influence the Negroes. As a disappointed Georgia Democrat reported, "The freedmen know no political names but Grant and Lincoln."[89]

84. Cincinnati *Enquirer*, August 27, 1872, p. 4; Washington *Patriot*, July 30, 1872, p. 2; James B. Beck to Carl Schurz, July 24, 1872, Vol. 18, Schurz Papers; Mary Doline O'Connor, *Life and Letters of M. P. O'Connor* (New York: Dempsey and Carroll, 1893), pp. 335–36.

85. *American Annual Cyclopaedia*, 1872, p. 585; Chicago *Tribune*, May 17, 1872, p. 1; Cincinnati *Enquirer*, August 16, 1872, p. 5; Lucretia H. Newman Coleman, *Poor Ben: A Story of Real Life* (Nashville: Publishing House of the A. M. E. Sunday School Union, 1890), pp. 117–18.

86. Frederick Douglass, *U.S. Grant and the Colored People* (Washington: n.p., 1872); William Lloyd Garrison and others, *Grant or Greeley—Which? Facts and Arguments for the Consideration of the Colored Citizens of the United States Being Extracts from Letters, Speeches and Editorials by Colored Men and Their Best Friends* (n.p.: Republican National Congressional Committee, 1872); Samuel Wright to ———, June 3, 1872, Box 7, Greeley Papers, Library of Congress.

87. On the convention, see Cincinnati *Enquirer*, September 18, 1872, p. 2. Evidence of other Negro support for Greeley is in L. G. Dynes to George W. Julian, June 15, 1872, Julian Papers; R. R. Finley to E. L. Gross, July 25, 1872, Finley to J. K. Dubois, August 29, 1872, Series 1A, Box 43, McCormick Papers; Herbert Aptheker, ed., *A Documentary History of the Negro People in the United States* (New York: Citadel Press, 1951), pp. 567–68.

88. James Lewis to P. B. S. Pinchback, Pinchback to Lewis, August 27, 1872, Box 1, Pinchback Papers, Moorland-Spingarn Collection, Howard University.

89. James Callaway to Horatio Seymour, August 8, 1872, Box 11, Seymour Papers, NYSL.

Greeley suffered overwhelming defeat in November, carrying just Georgia, Kentucky, Maryland, Missouri, Tennessee, and Texas. While Seymour had received 47 percent of the popular vote in 1868, Greeley won just 44 percent. Hardly anyone but Sumner and Greeley was surprised that blacks had voted almost as a unit for Grant.[90] Of more interest was the failure of the Liberals to win over many regular Republicans, and of greatest importance were widespread defections among Democrats. Though only about 20,000 Democrats voted for O'Conor on the straight-out ticket, thousands more refused to vote at all.[91] Despite Greeley's promise to remove the federal presence from the South, some rank and file Democrats were not yet ready for the humiliation of accepting the Reconstruction amendments which they had fought, and many of those who were ready could not take the extra step of voting for a presidential candidate who had been a Radical Republican. Even some Democrats who cast Greeley ballots held their noses while doing so, like the man from southern Illinois who later recalled that it

> was enough to make the master of ceremonies in the bottomless, laugh in his own face to see men who believe in their inmost hearts in the exclusive rule of *White Men*, voting for the man who had proudly carried Cuffee in his pocket for 30 years. . . . When the returns came, we thanked God, that the Negroes voted *enmasse* chiefly for Grant. We do not desire Democrats to be under a shade of political obligation to Sambo; it is degrading to them. They are wasting time that could be better spent on the White Race, than on licking "black and tan" feet for office.[92]

In the immediate aftermath of the election it seemed possible that the Democracy might repudiate the new departure as Greeley Democrats, seeking a scapegoat for defeat, blamed Negro suffrage. James R. Doolittle charged that Grant's title to the presidency was tainted because he was "chosen in an elec-

90. W. Dean Burnham, *Presidential Ballots, 1836–1892* (Baltimore: Johns Hopkins University Press, 1955), pp. 246–49; George W. Julian, *Political Recollections, 1840–72* (Chicago: Jansen, McClurg, 1884), pp. 348, 350; Sumner to George T. Downing, December 6, 1872, Downing Papers.

91. Burnham, *Presidential Ballots*, pp. 110–18.

92. P. R. Sawyer to William Allen, July 27, 1875, Vol. 18, Allen Papers.

tion when 700,000 negroes held the balance of power." According to the Cincinnati *Enquirer*, "negrodom decides the issue." The Washington *Patriot* warned that American policy "is to be shaped by a herd of semi-barbarians." A Georgia Democrat, citing as evidence the solid Negro Grant vote in his town, concluded that the freedmen "have no more business with the ballot, than the mule they follow at the plow."[93]

However, once the bitterness of defeat wore off, Democrats recognized that with the Greeley campaign the new departure had passed the point of no return. Democratic state platforms in 1873 and 1874 reiterated the national platform of 1872.[94] The ranks of those who still held out against official acceptance of the amendments dwindled until even *Pomeroy's Democrat*, the leading straight-out newspaper, capitulated.[95] The Democracy as a whole agreed with the New York *World* that "the new amendments to the Constitution are no longer an issue; they are all accomplished facts."[96] Over the next few years Democratic acquiescence in Negro civil and political equality became more credible as many Liberal Republicans, several having abolitionist and Radical backgrounds, drifted into the Democracy with the disintegration of the Liberal organization.[97] Since Democrats no longer questioned the Reconstruction amendments and talked instead about other more "relevant" issues like the economy and corruption in government, it became difficult for regular Republicans to argue convincingly that a disloyal Democracy still sought to reverse the "results of the war."

This very return to political respectability would make the ongoing Democratic commitment to local self-government in the

93. Doolittle to Augustus Schell, December 4, 1872, draft, Box 5, Doolittle Papers; Cincinnati *Enquirer*, November 3, 1872, p. 4; Washington *Patriot*, November 9, 1872, p. 2; Gideon T. Norman to Horace Greeley, November 12, 1872, Box 3, Greeley Papers, NYPL.

94. *American Annual Cyclopaedia*, 1873, 1874.

95. *Pomeroy's Democrat*, March 28, 1874, p. 2.

96. New York *World*, September 13, 1873, p. 4.

97. On the fate of the Liberals after 1872, see Earl D. Ross, *The Liberal Republican Movement* (New York: Henry Holt, 1919), pp. 192–237. Democrats were eager to absorb as many as they could, as evidenced in Samuel P. Randall to Richard Vaux, May 5, 1875, Box 10, Vaux Papers, Historical Society of Pennsylvania.

South appear more reasonable and moderate than ever before. If everyone accepted the amendments after 1872, why should national authorities interfere in Southern affairs? Democrats reiterated their constitutional argument that the amendments were just prohibitions on states giving the central government no new powers; surely, they claimed, the amendments would enforce themselves. But beyond this insistence on states' rights and opposition to "centralization," Democrats openly spoke of the need to reduce Southern Negroes to "a subordinate place in the body politic."[98] Was this aim consistent with the amendments? Most Democrats glossed over the contradiction, but the influential Albany *Argus* suggested a solution in 1874 that the party would echo well into the twentieth century: the freedmen, recognizing their own incapacity, would voluntarily leave politics to their paternalistic white neighbors. Once federal troops were gone, blacks would recognize "the natural law" of white superiority, no matter what the Constitution said.[99] As Republican interest in the seemingly intractable Southern problem declined through the 1870's, the new departure strategy of allowing the subversion of Negro rights in the South while pledging verbal fealty to those rights was on the road to success. The public Democratic position after 1872, then, was "resolute warfare for the supremacy of the whites" without "illegal or unjust interference with the blacks."[100]

Consolidation

Although the Greeley campaign sealed Democratic commitment to the new departure, 1873 was a bleak year for the party faithful. Grant was back in office with an overwhelming

98. Cincinnati *Enquirer*, April 17, 1873, p. 4. Also see *ibid.*, January 6, 1874, p. 4; Albany *Argus*, March 21, 1873, p. 2; New Work *World*, September 5, 1873, p. 4.

99. Albany *Argus*, August 10, 1874, p. 2. Another common view was that the race question would disappear as blacks drifted South into Mexico and Central America, leaving the United States almost lily-white. See Theodore Randolph to Thomas F. Bayard, April 28, 1874, Container 179, Bayard Papers; New York *World*, May 12, August 7, 1873, September 6, 1874, all p. 4.

100. Albany *Argus*, July 11, 1873, p. 2.

mandate, both Houses of Congress had substantial Republican majorities, and seven Southern states were still unredeemed from Republican rule. Little could anyone foresee the reversal soon to come. The 1874 elections would give the Democrats control of the House of Representatives and end Reconstruction in three more secession states. Two years later the national election would put the entire South in Democratic hands. New departure strategy initiated in 1871 and 1872, then, did not immediately improve party fortunes, but its delayed dividends proved worth waiting for.

Renewal of debate in the House of Representatives on Sumner's civil rights bill in January, 1874, placed Northern Democrats in an awkward position. In contrast to Southern and border state Democrats who had no inhibitions about mounting a racist attack on the measure, Northerners faced a dilemma: they recognized the unpopularity of civil rights, especially mixed schools, among their white constituents, but also feared that appeals to white supremacy might destroy their own new image of respectability. Republicans seeking a moderate political alternative to Grantism would shun a Democracy that still used rhetoric associated with disloyalists. As Northern Democrats maintained an embarrassed silence, the halls of Congress echoed with speeches by their colleagues from former slave states asserting Caucasian superiority, and warning of miscegenation.[101]

A Republican taunt that "there has yet . . . been no man from the North who calls himself a Democrat who has risen to oppose this bill or make a speech against its provisions"[102] finally goaded the Northerners into debate. "Sunset" Cox first took up the challenge. Avoiding inflammatory language, he denied that his party was prejudiced against Negroes, and hurled back at Republicans the charge of inciting blacks to hate whites. According to Cox, the civil rights bill could help no one because only "self-help, not State help" brought progress to any people. He ended his speech with a subtle appeal to white racial fears, predicting that

101. *Congressional Record*, 43 Cong., 1 sess., pp. 376–77, 406, 454–55, 556 (January 5, 6, 7, 10, 1874).

102. Ben Butler, Representative from Massachusetts, *ibid.*, p. 457 (January 7, 1874).

Negroes would prevent the Republicans from deleting the mixed-school clause of the bill. When the measure reached the Senate floor, Thurman of Ohio spoke for Northern Democrats; his transformation from a race-baiter to a "friend" of blacks was remarkable. Having only "the kindliest feelings" for Negroes, recognizing that "they are human beings as I am," and "willing to see them enjoy every civil right that I enjoy," Thurman nevertheless believed that Sumner's bill would only injure them.[103] Northern opponents of the legislation avoided the Southerners' use of racial slurs and emphasized the constitutional issue instead: since the bill operated upon individuals who discriminated against blacks, it was not sanctioned by the Fourteenth Amendment, which only touched states. Democrats embellished this argument with references to the Supreme Court's ruling in the Slaughterhouse Cases of 1873, a decision limiting the amendment's scope.[104] Though pruned of its school clause, the civil rights bill was still not law as Congress recessed for the midterm election campaign.

The 1874 elections were tailor-made for a successful application of the new departure. All Democrats now accepted the authority of the amendments while calling for the withdrawal of federal troops from the South as a step toward restoration of "local self-government." With Reconstruction a settled matter and fears of a resurgent Confederacy muted, Democrats seized on two spectacular new issues: widespread scandals in the Grant administration, and a severe economic depression.

Yet Democrats continued to disagree over certain matters related to race and the South. First, how did the civil rights question fit into the new departure framework? A minority wing of Northerners, in control only of the New England, New York, Michigan, and Minnesota organizations, hoped to attract undecided Republican voters by minimizing war-related matters, and therefore ignored civil rights. The New York *World* stressed the color-blind nature of this type of campaign when it pre-

103. Cox and Thurman, *ibid.*, pp. 614, 4088 (January 13, May 20, 1874).
104. *Ibid.*, pp. 342, 4086 (December 19, 1873, May 20, 1874); Eugene Casserly to Thomas F. Bayard, June 26, 1874, Container 179, Bayard Papers; New York *World*, May 1, 25, 1874, both p. 4.

dicted that on election day "every honest citizen, white or black, will be encouraged; every public robber . . . white or black, will be discomfited."[105] But all Southern Democrats and most Northerners, sure that "the anti-negro is the certain card,"[106] could not forego the temptation of fanning a white backlash by exploiting the threat of Negro "social equality" should the Republicans win. For example, Delaware Democrats called Sumner's bill blasphemy against God, Daniel Voorhees called white prejudice "wisdom," and the Cincinnati *Enquirer* blamed all racial conflict in the South on "the infamous 'Civil Rights Bill.' "[107] These Democrats perceived that while white opinion accepted black suffrage on the grounds of elementary fairness, racial integration was far less popular; race prejudice in the form of opposition to civil rights was still a potential Democratic vote-getter. A more serious rift of a sectional nature threatened the Democrats as reports from the South indicated widespread white atrocities against blacks. Republicans told the voters that such violence proved the hollowness of the new departure: Southern Democrats, backed by the national party, still intended to subordinate their former slaves by keeping them from the polls. Faced with this Republican effort to stress the old issues, Northern Democrats responded in a self-contradictory way. On the one hand they blamed Republicans for fomenting racial strife in order to divert public attention from the "real" issues, and pointed out that peace reigned in those Southern states already redeemed by Democrats.[108] But on the other hand, Northern Democrats

105. New York *World*, November 3, 1874, p. 6. The New York strategy can be followed in the pages of the *World* and the Albany *Argus*, September–November, 1874; August Belmont to Manton Marble, September 17, 1874, Vol. 37, Marble Papers; *American Annual Cyclopaedia*, 1874, p. 611. For other state platforms downplaying race, see the *Cyclopaedia*, pp. 240, 514, 521, 558–59, 564, 596.

106. Richard Vaux to John W. Stevenson, August 11, 1874, Vol. 31, Stevenson Papers.

107. *American Annual Cyclopaedia*, 1874, p. 258; Voorhees in Indianapolis *Sentinel*, August 8, 1874, p. 3; Cincinnati *Enquirer*, September 9, 1874, p. 4. Also see F. J. Porter to Manton Marble, July 23, 1874, Vol. 37, Marble Papers; Theodore Randolph to Whitelaw Reid, August 4, 1874, Container 134, Reid Papers; *American Annual Cyclopaedia*, 1874, pp. 15, 415, 477, 577, 601, 787.

108. Albany *Argus*, September 1, 5, 1874, both p. 2; New York *World*, August

privately and publicly denounced their Southern allies for hand-
ing the Republicans a campaign weapon that might smash the
new departure image, for while many Northern Republicans
were tired of federal intervention and willing to give the South
a chance to work out its own solution to the race problem, they
were not ready to abandon the freedman to outright terrorism.
Former Senator Casserly complained to a friend: "Every 'out-
rage' reported from the South, gives me a chill to the very
marrow,—for it gives new life to Radicalism. . . ." The Cincinnati *Enquirer* openly denounced "some of the people down
South" who "will find out after a while that every time a 'nigger'
is killed in their section new blood is infused into the veins of
the attenuated Republican party of the North." By September
the paper read all lawless Southerners out of the party.[109]

Democrats nevertheless swept the 1874 elections, carrying
the closely contested states of Indiana, New Jersey, New York,
and Ohio, as well as normally Republican Massachusetts, Ne-
vada, New Hampshire, and Pennsylvania. The Democracy also
"redeemed" Alabama, Arkansas, and Texas. While the previous
House of Representatives had a 103-vote Republican majority,
the new one would be Democratic by almost the same margin.
The victory was national, having to do with economic discontent
and revulsion against corruption in government. Though Democratic use of the civil rights issue probably won over many of
the Southern whites who had previously cooperated with the
Republicans, it was of minor significance in the North: Democratic successes in states where race was not stressed were as
great as their triumphs elsewhere. The election results, above
all, marked a decline of Northern suspicions that Democrats
intended to destroy the "results of the war." The new departure

---

28, 30, September 2, 1874, all p. 4. Cf. Albert V. House, Jr., "Northern Congressional Democrats as Defenders of the South during Reconstruction," *Journal of
Southern History*, VI (February, 1940), 58.

109. Casserly to Thomas F. Bayard, September 10, 1874, Container 179,
Bayard Papers; Cincinnati *Enquirer*, September 4, 9, 1874, both p. 4. Similar
sentiments are in Albany *Argus*, September 17, 1874, p. 2, and New York *World*,
October 14, 1874, p. 4.

of 1871 and Greeley's campaign of 1872, so futile in the short run, had now, by muting the old issues, allowed the Democrats to succeed on new issues.[110]

A jubilant Democracy announced its continued opposition to the civil rights bill and all proposals enforcing the Reconstruction amendments. There was, Democrats insisted, "a palpable distinction" between the amendments themselves, which were sacrosanct, and legislation based on them, which only produced "mischief." White Democrats would regain control of the last four Southern states under Republican rule once the federal government was "restricted to its proper sphere."[111] In the lame-duck session of Congress, before the new Democratic House took over, Republicans pushed through their civil rights bill against solid Democratic opposition, but a Democratic filibuster headed off a proposed new enforcement bill safeguarding black suffrage in the South.[112]

After March, 1875, a Democratic House was able to prevent new federal legislation protecting Negroes, and the party turned its attention to the 1876 presidential contest. Democrats hoped to repeat the successful new departure tactics of 1874: emphasis on corruption and hard times, insistence that no one disputed the amendments, and agitation for an end to federal interference with "local self-government." The major threat to the Democrats would come from Republican attempts to destroy the new departure's moderate facade by charging that "if the Democrats

110. The results are collected in *Tribune Almanac*, 1875, pp. 44–90 *passim*, and the factors behind the Democratic victories are discussed in Unger, *Greenback Era*, pp. 249–50, and Thurlow Weed to John A. Dix, November 7, 1874, Dix Papers, Columbia University. For the impact of the new departure, see Cincinnati *Enquirer*, May 5, 1875, p. 4, and Thomas J. McCormack, ed., *Memoirs of Gustave Koerner, 1809–1896: Life Sketches Written at the Suggestion of his Children* (Cedar Rapids, Ia.: Torch Press, 1909), II, 591.

111. New York *World*, November 11, 1874, p. 4; Albany *Argus*, November 7, 1874, p. 2.

112. Democratic response to passage of the civil rights bill was mild. The Cincinnati *Enquirer* called on all states under Democratic control to nullify the law, but only Delaware did so, authorizing owners of establishments affected by the Act to provide separate accommodations for "obnoxious" customers. See Cincinnati *Enquirer*, March 26, 1875, p. 4, and Gilbert T. Stephenson, *Race Distinctions in American Law* (New York: D. Appleton, 1910), p. 112. On the Democratic filibuster against the enforcement bill, consult Thomas F. Bayard to Manton Marble, February 12, 1875, Vol. 39, Marble Papers.

elect their President—more blood—fresh graves—the country must prepare for the repeal of all three of the amendments."[113] In order to win the White House and put a final end to Reconstruction, the Democracy would have to give the lie to such assertions by muzzling hot-headed Southerners.

The 1876 Democratic campaign started well, as the national convention adopted a new departure platform and nominated Governor Samuel J. Tilden of New York for president, but a bloody racial confrontation at Hamburg, South Carolina, in mid-July spoiled Democratic strategy. As predicted, Republicans resurrected the race issue, tying violence against Southern Negroes to the spirit of unrepentant Confederacy. The Republican presidential candidate, Rutherford B. Hayes, told his own supporters to stress that *"a Democratic victory will bring the Rebellion to power."* Equally dangerous to Democratic hopes was the charge that Tilden, if elected, would allow payment to Confederates for property destroyed by Union troops. One of Tilden's closest confidants noted that "the cry of the bloody shirt . . . has been after all the pièce de résistance of the Republicans in this canvass, the shirt and the rebel claims."[114]

Democrats saw that, despite their own efforts to spotlight other issues, Republicans had succeeded in focusing popular attention "yet on race, civil war, etc."[115] Tilden's backers worked to counter this Republican offensive. Southerners campaigning in the North received explicit instructions to cool their rhetoric.[116] The New York Democracy, controlled by Tilden, was careful to nominate a gubernatorial candidate with "no con-

113. John W. Stevenson to Thomas F. Bayard, July 8, 1875, Container 179, Bayard Papers. Also note Eugene Casserly to Manton Marble, March 12, 1875, Vol. 40, Marble Papers; James L. Kemper to Montgomery Blair, April 28, May 2, 1876, Container 10, Blair Papers; Cincinnati *Enquirer*, January 14, 1876, p. 4; Charles Mason Remey, ed., *Life and Letters of Charles Mason, Chief Justice of Iowa, 1804–1882* (Washington: By the editor, 1939), XI, 1844.

114. The Democratic platform is in Porter and Johnson, eds., *Party Platforms*, pp. 49–51. Hayes's encouragement of the bloody shirt is seen in Hayes to Carl Schurz, August 9, 1876, in Williams, ed., *Diary and Letters of Hayes*, III, 340. The last quotation is from the John Bigelow Diaries, November 11, 1876, New York Public Library.

115. S. S. Cox to Samuel J. Tilden, July 15, 1876, Box 11, Tilden Papers.

116. William Bigler to Tilden, September 30, 1876, A. J. Smith to Tilden, October 11, 1876, Box 12, *ibid.*

gressional or war records," and called in its platform for "public rebuke and punishment" of Southern lawbreakers.[117] A friend of Tilden, Scott Lord of New York, introduced a resolution in the House noting reports that the Fifteenth Amendment was being violated in certain states and declaring that such activity "should meet with certain, condign, and effectual punishment" in "any court having jurisdiction." Passage of the measure by the Democratic House put the party on record against intimidation of black voters, but the high number of Southern and border state Democrats who abstained or voted nay showed the unpopularity of any hint, however veiled, that federal courts might have a role to play in enforcement.[118] Tilden's letter accepting the nomination reaffirmed the amendments, called for "cordial fraternity and good will among citizens, whatever their race or color," and promised to use all legal means "to protect . . . all citizens, whatever their former condition, in every political and personal right." He wrote a separate letter pledging to veto any legislation paying Confederate war claims.[119] The long-range change in Democratic strategy was underlined when a New Jersey man sent Tilden a group picture of South Carolina's heavily Negro legislature and offered to produce thousands of copies for campaign purposes, a racist tactic that the party had used in 1868. Tilden, though, would have none of it, and did not even acknowledge receipt of the suggestion.[120]

As further evidence of its new spirit, the Democracy made unprecedented efforts to win the friendship of blacks, whose enthusiasm for Republicanism had waned since 1872 because of the party's foot-dragging on civil rights and patronage, and reports of Republican corruption in the South.[121] The official

117. Roswell P. Flower to Tilden, September 4, 1876, *ibid.*; *Appleton's Annual Cyclopaedia*, 1876, p. 603.

118. *Congressional Record*, 44 Cong., 1 sess., pp. 5419–22 (August 10, 1876); Albany *Argus*, August 14, 1876, p. 2; *Nation*, XXIII (August 17, 1876), 97. Also see Scott Lord to Tilden, July 31, 1876, Box 11, Tilden Papers.

119. *Official Proceedings of the National Democratic Convention Held in St. Louis, Missouri, June 1876* (St. Louis: Woodward, Tiernan and Hale, 1876), p. 183; Tilden to Abram S. Hewitt, October 23, 1876, Box 12, Tilden Papers.

120. Romeo F. Chabert to Tilden, October 18, November 1, 1876, Box 12, Tilden Papers.

121. Negro disillusionment with Republicans can be traced in the following:

Democratic attitude on Negro voting as expressed in their campaign textbook of 1876 showed how far the organization had come since 1868: black suffrage "of itself was not wrong, but was made an instrument by designing politicians."[122] To prove that Republicans did not really care about the welfare of the race, Democrats cited the recent collapse of the Freedman's Savings Bank, a private institution set up after the war under government sponsorship to train former slaves to save their money. The Cincinnati *Enquirer*, a white supremacist newspaper in pre–new departure days, now lectured Republicans that "it is bad enough to steal from a white man, but to rob a poor negro is the quintessence of meanness."[123] There were active black Democrats in the former slave states, especially South Carolina, and Northern cities also had small contingents of Negro Tildenites.[124] While this was more than the Greeley coalition

Congressman Alonzo Ransier of South Carolina in *Congressional Record*, 42 Cong., 1 sess., p. 4786 (June 9, 1874); Foner, ed., *Life and Writings of Douglass*, IV, 95; George T. Downing in New York *Tribune*, July 4, 1874, p. 4; Hiram Revels to U. S. Grant, November 6, 1875, reprinted in *Congressional Record*, 45 Cong., 3 sess., Appendix, p. 224 (February 27, 1879); P. B. S. Pinchback in *Convention of Colored Newspaper Men* (Cincinnati: n.p., 1875), p. 1; John Smyth to Blanche K. Bruce, February 13, 1876, Maurice Bauman to Bruce, February 14, 1876, C. H. Thomas to Bruce, April 20, 1876, Box 1, Bruce Papers.

122. *The Campaign Text Book* (New York: Democratic National Committee, 1876), p. 246.

123. Cincinnati *Enquirer*, November 4, 1876, p. 4. The issue was also used in *Campaign Text Book*, pp. 544–52, and Albany *Argus*, October 12, 1876, p. 2. The Bank's history is told by Walter L. Fleming in *The Freedmen's Savings Bank: A Chapter in the Economic History of the Negro Race* (Chapel Hill: University of North Carolina Press, 1927). See also Carl R. Osthaus, *Freedmen, Philanthropy, and Fraud: A History of the Freedman's Savings Bank* (Urbana: University of Illinois Press, 1976).

124. Florida: Richardson, *The Negro in the Reconstruction of Florida*, pp. 235–37; Louisiana: E. G. W. Butler to M. Blair, October 12, 1876, Box 10, Blair Papers; William Ivy Hair, *Bourbonism and Agrarian Protest: Louisiana Politics, 1877–1900* (Baton Rouge: Louisiana State University Press, 1969), p. 4; Maryland: Robert McLane to Samuel J. Tilden, September 21, 1876, Box 12, Tilden Papers; Mississippi: T. Marion Shields to Tilden, October 22, 1876, *ibid.*; Vernon Lane Wharton, *The Negro in Mississippi, 1865–1890* (Chapel Hill: University of North Carolina Press, 1947), p. 200; North Carolina: Frenise A. Logan, *The Negro in North Carolina, 1876–1894* (Chapel Hill: University of North Carolina Press, 1964), p. 21; South Carolina: Manly Wade Wellman, *Giant in Gray: A Biography of Wade Hampton of South Carolina* (New York: Charles Scribner's Sons, 1949), pp. 257–72; Martin R. Delany to T. Bourne, May 19, 1876, Box 11, T. Bourne to Samuel J. Tilden, October 7, 1876, Box 12, Tilden Papers; Tennessee: Andrew J. Chambers to Samuel J. Randall, July 3,

had done in 1872, the great majority of Negroes could not overlook the ongoing violence, intimidation, and white arrogance in
the South, and they knew that a new departure Democrat in the
White House would do nothing to stop the injustices of "local
self-government." Blacks therefore generally stayed Republican; their spokesmen explained that the race could only afford
to divide politically when both parties would practice, not merely preach, the equal rights of all men.[125]

Democrats were disappointed when a special commission
decided the disputed election of 1876 in favor of the Republicans, but they rejoiced at President Hayes's Southern policy.
Relying on promises from white leaders to protect suffrage
rights, Hayes removed the federal presence from the last three
secession states under Republican control, thus ending Reconstruction. As Democrats constantly reminded him, Hayes had
implemented Democratic states' rights doctrine.[126] Republican
abandonment of Reconstruction was a complex phenomenon
stemming from several causes, but the Democratic role was
vital. As long as Democrats held out against the amendments,
Republicans could justify federal intervention on the grounds

---

20, 1876, Boxes 25, 26, Randall Papers; Texas: Lawrence D. Rice, *The Negro in
Texas, 1874–1900* (Baton Rouge: Louisiana State University Press, 1971), p. 41;
Virginia: Maddex, *Virginia Conservatives*, p. 196; Colored Democratic Associa-
tion to Tilden, November 8, 1876, Box 12, Tilden Papers. Evidence for the
existence of Negro Tilden clubs in Indianapolis, Harrisburg, New York City, and
Detroit are in Cincinnati *Commercial*, reprinted in New York *World*, September
1, 1876, p. 2; William Battis Alderman to Tilden, November 9, 1876, Box 12,
Tilden Papers; New York *World*, October 27, 1876, p. 1; David M. Katzman,
Before the Ghetto: Black Detroit in the Nineteenth Century (Urbana: University
of Illinois Press, 1973), p. 183.

125. P. B. S. Pinchback, "On the Effects of the Hayes-Tilden Campaign," p.
15, in Box 1, Pinchback Papers; Speeches of Senator Blanche K. Bruce and
Representative John R. Lynch of Mississippi, in *Congressional Record*, 44 Cong.,
1 sess., pp. 2103, 3783, 3825 (March 31, June 13, 15, 1876).

126. The complicated negotiations which led to Hayes's inauguration are
discussed by C. Vann Woodward in *Reunion and Reaction: The Compromise of
1877 and the End of Reconstruction* (Boston: Little, Brown, 1966). For Democratic approval of the new Southern policy, see Cincinnati *Enquirer*, April 23,
1877, January 4, 7, 1878, all p. 4; Albany *Argus*, March 16, April 30, December
4, 1877, all p. 2; *Congressional Record*, 45 Cong. 2 sess., p. 1347 (February 26,
1878); Democratic state platforms in *Appleton's Annual Cyclopaedia*, 1877,
1878; George S. Converse to Samuel S. Cox, October 18, 1877, Reel 1, Cox
Papers.

that disloyalists, North and South, wanted to subordinate the Negro in true Confederate style. But the new departure, with its symbolic surrender to Reconstruction, was paradoxically the death knell of Reconstruction. Moderate Democratic rhetoric allowed the North to believe that there was a national consensus accepting civil and political equality for blacks. This heightened the pressure on Republicans to stop their interference in Southern affairs (which was becoming increasingly futile anyway) and made Hayes's policy inevitable.

After 1876 the Democracy no longer had to fight Republican regimes in the secession states; it could assume instead a defensive posture, warding off Republican efforts to break the solid Democratic South. In 1878, when Hayes and his party saw that Southern Democrats had no intention of protecting the black ballot, there was little the Republicans could do. For the next decade Democrats would be strong enough in either or both congressional houses to block federal enforcement of Negro rights. The new departure was a success. As Northern interest in the matter declined, everyone pledged verbal allegiance to the Reconstruction amendments, but the Democrats used every excuse to prevent Congress from carrying them out. Republican Senator George Edmunds of Vermont described the Democrats' hypocritical position:

> It is all very nice for a few dozen gentlemen on the other side to get up and say that they are in favor of the Constitution of the United States with all its trimmings and refuse to do anything about it. . . . when it comes . . . to proposing to do anything about it, then the gentlemen say, Oh no; oh no; it is too late, or it is too early; it is too vague, it is too mysterious, it is too something; never let us do anything about it at all.[127]

The Democrats soon became so cocky that they overreached themselves, substituting aggression for defense. Despite Demo-

127. Edmunds, in *Congressional Record*, 45 Cong., 3 sess., p. 1007 (February 5, 1879). On the shift in Republican attitudes after the 1878 elections, see Stanley P. Hirshson, *Farewell to the Bloody Shirt: Northern Republicans and the Southern Negro, 1877–1893* (Bloomington: Indiana University Press, 1962), pp. 45–56.

cratic majorities in House and Senate created by the 1878 elections, President Hayes still had power under the federal election laws to station soldiers at the polls. In 1879, invoking the principle of states' rights, congressional Democrats attached riders to vital appropriation bills barring the execution of the election laws. Though Hayes was not using his power to station troops at Southern elections, he refused to give up the prerogative and vetoed a series of appropriation bills because of the riders.[128] Republicans turned the issue against the Democrats in the 1879 state elections; Republican victories that year showed that, while the Northern electorate wanted to leave the South alone, it would not back an aggressive Democracy, with its large ex-Confederate component, in a crusade to dismantle the federal election laws. Democratic insistence on the riders was perceived as a threat to the "results of the war." Learning prudence, the Democrats backed down on the appropriation bills.[129] Then, in 1880, knowing that some Northern voters still rejected the Democracy "because of Southern ascendancy in it,"[130] the party nominated for President General Winfield S. Hancock, a Union war hero, on a new departure platform. Surely "a soldier who poured out his life blood and dared death daily . . . will see to it that none of the proper fruits of the war are lost." For Negro consumption the Democrats resurrected the ghost of the Freedman's Bank, "the wickedest and meanest swindle which the Republican party is responsible for."[131] Republicans repeated their sectional tactics of 1879, calling the Democratic nominee a mere puppet of violent Confederates, and Republican candidate James A. Garfield barely defeated Hancock. But the Southern

128. Cincinnati *Enquirer*, March 28, May 19, July 30, August 4, September 8, October 4, 1879, all p. 4; Hirshson, *Bloody Shirt*, pp. 56–57.

129. Hirshson, *Bloody Shirt*, pp. 57–59; Cincinnati *Enquirer*, November 17, 28, 1879, both p. 4; Albany *Argus*, November 11, 29, December 1, 1879, all p. 4; George T. B. Carr to W. H. English, November 7, 1879, William H. English Papers, Indiana Historical Society.

130. Montgomery Blair to Samuel J. Tilden, June 13, 1880, Box 15, Tilden Papers.

131. Porter and Johnson, eds., *Party Platforms*, p. 56; Albany *Argus*, July 16, 1880, p. 4. The Freedman's Bank is emphasized in *The Campaign Text Book* (New York: Democratic National Committee, 1880), p. 377.

question was a secondary issue by now. Garfield and his Republican successor Chester A. Arthur did even less than Hayes to afford Negroes federal protection.[132]

Besides public boredom with matters of race and Democratic propaganda against federal involvement, another major reason for Northern acceptance of "local self-government" in the South was that it did seem to pacify the region. The violence accompanying Democratic seizure of power in the South in the 1870's had embarrassed the party's Northern wing, which was trying to ride new departure politics to victory. But in the period between redemption and the 1890's a group of upper-class Southern white leaders known variously as Bourbons, Redeemers, or Conservatives followed a racial strategy that dovetailed with national Democratic policy. Allied with northeastern business interests, this post-Reconstruction Southern ruling class had to fight off sporadic challenges from discontented poorer whites. To retain control, therefore, the Redeemers strove to win the Negro's confidence and vote in those areas where blacks were not yet disfranchised through fraud or subterfuge. The paternalistic stance that a number of white leaders took toward the race, while calculated to achieve political results, was also, to an extent, a true reflection of the noblesse oblige spirit that the wealthiest slaveowners had shown before emancipation, and it contrasted favorably with the crude racism characteristic of lower-class whites.[133] For example, Lucius Lamar of Mississippi, as congressman and senator, traded patronage favors with leading Negroes of his state and always retained their high regard.[134]

132. Herbert J. Clancy, *The Presidential Election of 1880* (Chicago: Loyola University Press, 1958), pp. 175–81; Hirshson, *Bloody Shirt*, pp. 78–122.

133. C. Vann Woodward, *Origins of the New South, 1877–1913* (Baton Rouge: Louisiana State University Press, 1951), pp. 79–81, 209–12; Woodward, *The Strange Career of Jim Crow*, 2nd rev. ed. (New York: Oxford University Press, 1966), pp. 47–59; Paul M. Gaston, *The New South Creed: A Study in Southern Mythmaking* (New York: Alfred A. Knopf, 1970), pp. 119–50.

134. Lamar to Blanche K. Bruce, October 27, 1875, Box 1, Robert E. Leachman to Bruce, December 20, 1877, Box 2, Lamar to Bruce, October 18, 1879, Box 4, W. B. Inge to Bruce, January 26, 1880, Box 5, Bruce Papers; *Congressional Record*, 44 Cong., 1 sess., pp. 4878–79, 5541 (July 25, August 12, 1876); Woodward, *Strange Career of Jim Crow*, p. 58.

Wade Hampton was elected governor of South Carolina in 1876 after pledging to "know no party, nor race, in the administration of the law." During his tenure in the statehouse Hampton encouraged liberal appropriations for black schools and vetoed a bill instituting the chain gang on the grounds that a disproportionate number of its victims would be Negro.[135] Such Conservatives certainly did not speak for all Southern whites; their paternalism was in no sense a commitment to racial equality, and indeed they were not themselves consistent in their policies, at times betraying a willingness to head off political revolt by catering to white prejudice. Nevertheless, Redeemer ideology was perfectly suited to new departure doctrine. Northern Democrats by the late 1870's could argue that the benevolent rule of local whites made federal intervention in the South an anachronism. As the Albany *Argus* editorialized, with the Negro in good hands, Northerners could, in clear conscience, "let the Southern people influence and impress the negroes in their own way. . . ."[136]

By the early 1880's the new departure dream was solid reality. Not yet in control of the presidency, Democrats had enjoyed a revival in North and South by pledging fealty to the Reconstruction amendments, keeping Congress from enforcing them, and exploiting Northern weariness with old issues. Northern Democrats, hand in hand with Southern Redeemers, had convinced

135. Hampton's pre-election pledge is in Cincinnati *Enquirer*, October 2, 1876, p. 4. His racial policies while governor are noted in Wellman, *Giant in Gray*, p. 299. Also see *Congressional Record*, 47 Cong., special sess., p. 372 (April 21, 1881); George Brown Tindall, *South Carolina Negroes, 1877–1890* (Columbia: University of South Carolina Press, 1952), pp. 19–40; William J. Cooper, Jr., *The Conservative Regime: South Carolina, 1877–90* (Baltimore: Johns Hopkins University Press, 1968), pp. 86–88, 215. A more skeptical assessment is Joel Williamson, *After Slavery: The Negro in South Carolina during Reconstruction, 1861–1877* (Chapel Hill: University of North Carolina Press, 1965), pp. 406–7. Both Lamar and Hampton wrote on Negro suffrage in "Ought the Negro to Be Disfranchised? Ought He to Have Been Enfranchised?" *North American Review*, CXXVIII (March, 1879), 231–44.

136. Albany *Argus*, March 11, 1879, p. 2. For similar Northern Democratic views, consult Thomas Hendricks, "Ought the Negro to Be Disfranchised?" and "Retribution in Politics," *North American Review*, CXXVIII (March, April, 1879), 267–70, 337–51; Senator George Pendleton of Ohio in *Congressional Record*, 47 Cong., special sess., pp. 277–78 (April 13, 1881).

many Republicans that there was no longer a race question in national politics.[137] Meanwhile, the new departure was bringing unforeseen changes on the Northern racial front.

137. Springfield (Mass.) *Republican*, April 11, 1883, p. 9; Carl Schurz, "Party Schisms and Future Problems," *North American Review*, CXXXIV (May, 1882), 433; Benjamin F. Butler to J. D. Foster, October 16, 1882, Letterbook 10, Butler Papers, Library of Congress.

3

A Newer Departure:
Closing the Gap between
Northern Democrats and Negroes
1873-92

The Problem

While the national Democracy was keeping federal authority from protecting Southern Negroes in the two decades following 1872, a new, more positive relationship between Democrats and Negroes emerged in the North. In contrast to the pre–new departure mood of hostility between the two groups, blacks and Democrats began to explore the possibilities of political rapprochement above the Mason-Dixon Line. On some occasions and in some places Negroes took the initiative by adopting an independent political stance in state and local elections. In other situations the Democracy made the first move with patronage or favorable state legislation. Although most Northern blacks stayed Republican, the greater openness of some to novel political options and the increased Northern Democratic desire to please the race deserve careful analysis, especially in light of the unbending Democratic support for and connivance at white supremacy in Dixie. Indeed, by the late 1880's the issue of Negro rights in the South seemed divorced from state and local racial politics in the North.

The argument for Negro abandonment of unanimous Republicanism was simple. As Peter Clark and George T. Downing warned even before 1872, so long as Republicans took the black vote for granted, they would not grant benefits to Negroes. Descriptions of corruption in Southern Republican state governments alienated some Negroes, and the gradual dismantling of

Reconstruction combined with erosion of Republican concern for the freedmen to provide further grounds for pessimism about the party's direction. Cries of betrayal from blacks greeted President Hayes's withdrawal of the federal presence from Dixie in 1877 and President Arthur's 1882 decision to channel Southern patronage to white factions instead of to Negroes. Black men North and South who felt frustrated in their efforts to attain political preferment through the Republican organization added their voices to the chorus of the discontented. The next blow was the 1883 decision by a Republican Supreme Court striking down the Civil Rights Act of 1875—clear proof, to angry blacks, that the party had deserted them. What difference was there now between Republican and Democratic race policy, they asked.[1] Negroes pressed successfully for Northern state civil rights laws to replace the federal statute, and they scrutinized the attitudes of both parties to these proposals.[2] Charles Sumner's advice of 1872 seemed most relevant in the 1880's: make the two parties bid for black favor by adopting, or at least threatening to adopt, an uncommitted political stand.

The middle and late 1880's marked the high tide of Negro rebellion against Republican neglect. While ongoing Democratic interference with the full exercise of their rights in the South made deviation from the Republican fold in national elections tantamount to betrayal of the race, arguments for and against support of Democratic candidates seeking state or local office in

1. In addition to the items cited in footnote 121 of the preceding chapter, see Alexander Crummell to John W. Cromwell, April 25, 1877, Reel 1, Crummell Papers; P. B. S. Pinchback to Blanche K. Bruce, December 14, 1878, Box 3, Bruce Papers; George T. Downing to Frederick Douglass, May 10, 1883, Reel 12, Douglass Papers; Richard T. Greener in New York *Globe*, November 10, 1883, p. 1; George W. Williams, *The Negro as a Political Problem* (Boston: Alfred Mudge & Son, 1884), p. 33; Hirshson, *Bloody Shirt*, pp. 105–15; Vincent P. De Santis, "Negro Dissatisfaction with Republican Policy in the South, 1882–84," *Journal of Negro History*, XXXVI (April, 1951), 148–59.

On the general theme of Negro political independence, see August Meier, "The Negro and the Democratic Party, 1875–1915," *Phylon*, XVII (1956), 173–91.

2. New York *Globe*, October 20, 27, 1883, both p. 2; Cleveland *Gazette*, November 17, 1883, p. 2; Washington *Bee*, November 10, 1883, p. 2; *People's Advocate* (Washington, D.C.), October 20, 1883, p. 2; H. O. Wagoner to Frederick Douglass, October 29, 1883, Reel 12, Douglass Papers.

the North filled the columns of Negro newspapers. The case for ticket-splitting was most eloquently made by T. Thomas Fortune, the young editor of the New York *Globe*. He wrote that though a black man could not be a "Bourbon Democrat," he might be "an independent, a progressive Democrat." Fortune believed that if the Northern Democracy saw that Negroes could provide the votes to elect Democrats in close Northern contests, the organization would force Southern Democrats to ameliorate the lot of Negroes in that section. Unconvinced, faithful black Republicans countered that a Democratic victory anywhere in the nation encouraged Southern white intransigence; Dixie Democrats, not Northerners, guided the party's national race policy.[3]

If Negro motivation for considering alliances with Northern Democrats was manifest, Democratic interests in such alliances is harder to explain. The new departure of 1871 had merely dropped official Democratic opposition to the Reconstruction amendments, and open use of racism as a political weapon continued to 1874 in parts of the North. As earlier noted, Democratic attempts to attract black votes in 1872 were based on threats, not promises. Why a change in the 1870's and 1880's to pro-black legislation and Negro patronage? The matter is obscure, because the shift in racial policy was not the result of formal party decisions, and it received little coverage in the Democratic press.[4] It arose spontaneously, and perhaps therefore aroused no vocal opposition within party ranks. Advocates of racial liberalism

3. T. Thomas Fortune, *Black and White: Land, Labor and Politics in the South* (New York: Fords, Howard and Hulbert, 1884), pp. 98–129, 144, 174–75. In 1884 Fortune's *Globe* was renamed the *Freeman*, and three years later it became the *Age*. A recent biography which gives scant attention to the pre-1890 period is Emma Lou Thornbrough, *T. Thomas Fortune: Militant Journalist* (Chicago: University of Chicago Press, 1972). Of the other major black newspapers, the Cleveland *Gazette* was firmly Republican, though sometimes critical of the organization, while the Washington *Bee* tended to praise whichever party controlled the White House.

4. Ironically, the only white writer who thought the phenomenon important was Louisiana novelist George W. Cable, a maverick from Southern racial orthodoxy. He wanted Dixie Democrats to emulate their Northern counterparts. See Cable, "The Silent South," in *The Negro Question: A Selection of Writings on Civil Rights in the South*, ed. Arlin Turner (Garden City: Doubleday, 1958), pp. 121–22. The essay was first published in *Century*, September, 1885.

came from every element in the Democratic organization: old Copperhead and veteran abolitionist, life-long Democrat and convert from Republicanism, machine wire-puller and civil service reformer, lower-class politician and upper-class patrician, all combined to change the Northern Democracy's racial stand. Explaining this phenomenon either as a simple grab for black votes or as the high-minded program of a party repenting its racist past risks oversimplification. Motives of Democratic leaders in satisfying Negro demands, like the motives of politicians most of the time, were mixed, and the proportion of expediency to principle varied from one man to another. Examination of developments in each Northern state where significant Negro-Democratic rapprochement occurred shows both the scope of such activity and the complexity of its underlying causes.

Eastern States

New York was a bastion of Democratic moderation in Reconstruction days. The pragmatic New York Democracy dropped appeals to racism in 1869–70 when it became obvious that a white supremacist crusade was futile. By 1873 the state's Democrats even caved in on civil rights. After the election of 1872 the Republicans, boasting huge majorities in the state legislature, sponsored and passed a bill outlawing racial discrimination in places of public accommodation. Despite previous hostility to civil rights, Democratic legislators divided on the measure: two Democratic senators supported it, while three were opposed; Democratic assemblymen voted for it eleven to nine. Equally surprising, party newspapers hardly mentioned the issue.[5] Later in the year the Democracy went beyond acquiescence in Republican initiatives and invited Isaac L. Hunter, a Negro who had supported Greeley, to speak at a Tammany Hall gathering on July 4. Claiming that no black had ever been asked to address a Republican Independence Day celebration, Hunter recalled the

5. Above, pp. 19–20, 21–22; New York, *Journal of the Senate*, 1873, p. 507; *Journal of the Assembly*, 1873, pp. 615–616; Albany *Argus*, March 21, 1873, p. 2. The New York *World* ignored the law entirely.

Republicans' unfulfilled promises of patronage to Negroes. In addition, the Republican state civil rights act had proven unenforceable. After denouncing corruption in the Grant administration and promising many black votes for the Democracy, Hunter ended with praise for Tammany leader John Kelly. This address triggered complaints from other New York Negroes about Republican perfidy.[6] A year later, after the 1874 elections, some New York Democrats advocated an official party repudiation of the "negro-haters" who gave the Democracy a bad name.[7]

But it was not until after Reconstruction that the New York Democrats' new approach to race transcended rhetoric. A relatively minor incident in 1877 presaged future developments. Democratic Congressman Nicholas Muller of Manhattan sponsored a competitive examination for all young men of his district who were aspiring to enter West Point. When a black teenager received the highest grade, resentful whites demanded that the Negro be passed over, but Muller insisted on standing by the winner as a matter of principle, refusing to worry about "losing any constituents." When the black youth said that his limited financial resources would not allow him to accept the appointment, Tammany State Senator John Morrissey, "although a perfect stranger, most generously furnished him money with which to procure a cadet outfit."[8] New York Democrats would hardly have behaved this way a decade earlier. By 1880 there was a Negro Democratic newspaper in the city called the *Suffragist*, and black Democratic clubs campaigned for Hancock in the presidential election. The next year a Democratic member of the legislature from New York City introduced a bill strengthening the 1873 civil rights law. It passed the Senate unanimously,

6. Hunter's speech is in New York *Sun*, July 8, 1873, p. 3, and its repercussions *ibid.*, September 29, 1873, p. 2, October 9, 1873, p. 3, November 26, 1873, p. 1.

7. Albany *Argus*, December 5, 1874, p. 2; Daniel R. Lyddy to John Pope Hodnett, November 9, 1874, in "John Pope Hodnett on the Elections," Box 82, Tilden Papers.

8. New York *Tribune*, August 23, 1877, p. 2; New York *Times*, January 26, 1878, p. 5. Ostracized by white classmates, the young Negro dropped out after a few months. *Ibid.*

and only two upstate assemblymen, one from each party, opposed it.[9]

In 1882 the Democrats captured the statehouse, electing Mayor Grover Cleveland of Buffalo to the governorship. Though when elected Cleveland had no public record on racial issues, he would, as governor and president, come to symbolize the positive Northern Democratic attitude toward blacks; therefore the meager data on his early years must be searched for insight into his later friendship for the race. His family was straitened financially but could trace its lineage back to prominent Puritan forbears. The Reverend Richard Cleveland, Grover's father, raised his children in an atmosphere of piety and godliness; despite abandoning the family's intense religiosity, Grover never lost a sense of moral austerity. A conservative patrician in outlook, young Cleveland stood for respectable nonpartisan causes of principle like civil service reform and governmental economy; such attitudes made him attractive to Mugwumps (independent Republicans opposed to machine politics), who shared with him a paternalistic aloofness toward the masses. Cleveland's racial attitude fits into this framework. He was well aware that two Puritan ancestors had fought for Negro rights: a great-grandfather introduced the first bill to abolish slavery in Connecticut, and a great-uncle tried to prosecute two Massachusetts shipowners for involvement in the African slave trade. Living in Buffalo in the 1850's, Grover nevertheless disappointed his Republican uncle by remaining a Democrat—a decision attributable to the young man's innate conservatism and the accident that his employers and closest friends were Democrats. According to later tradition, Cleveland was a War Democrat and probably voted for Lincoln in 1864. Apologists explain the hiring of a substitute to take his place in the Union army with the assertion that Cleveland was his family's sole means of support. Attaining prominence as a lawyer after the war, Cleveland joined the ex-

9. *People's Advocate*, January 17, 1880, p. 2; Trenton *Sentinel*, September 18, 1880, p. 2; Albany *Argus*, July 7, October 29, 1880, both p. 6; New York, *Journal of the Senate*, 1881, pp. 563, 716; *Journal of the Assembly*, 1881, pp. 1526–27. The law is in New York, *General Statutes*, 1881, Ch. 400.

clusive Buffalo City Club. He struck up a friendship with the club's mulatto steward and took the steward's son under his wing, later bringing him to Albany and Washington to run his official households. Here was an early indication of the upper-class benevolence that Cleveland would display toward the race; his racial attitude resembled the approach of Southern Redeemers, although Cleveland proved more favorable to blacks in practice than any Southern Democrat.[10]

While governor of New York in 1883 and 1884, Cleveland gave public evidence of good will toward the race. In addition to extending the usual menial patronage jobs to Negroes, he appointed D. Garnett Baltimore, a black engineer, to the state engineer and surveyor's staff. Baltimore was the first of his race to achieve a respectable position in the state government.[11] Cleveland also dealt with the issue of school integration. According to state law, a Negro child could attend any public school, but colored public schools remained in New York City. By 1884 only two were left, and the municipal board of education ordered them closed for reasons of economy. The Negro principals and teachers in these schools objected that since blacks were not allowed to teach in the white schools, elimination of colored institutions would close off the teaching profession to them. They also claimed that some Negro children could not cope with integration and benefited from an all-black educational environment. James C. Matthews, a Democratic Negro attorney from Albany, explained the teachers' viewpoint to Cleveland and drew up a bill insuring the continued existence of the black schools by officially merging them into the city system as ward schools open to all, though the two schools would surely remain colored in fact. The Democratic legislature passed the measure and Cleveland signed it into law.[12] While the bill could be interpreted either as a move to integrate the schools

10. Allan Nevins, *Grover Cleveland, a Study in Courage* (New York: Dodd, Mead, 1932), pp. 6–15, 44, 48–52, 74, 127, 212, 521.

11. New York *Globe*, January 13, 1883, p. 4, July 26, 1884, p. 1.

12. New York *World*, April 2, 1884, p. 8, May 6, 1884, p. 5; Anthony R. Mayo, "Charles Lewis Reason," *Negro History Bulletin*, V (June, 1942), 215;

de jure or to insure segregation *de facto,* Cleveland was not, in principle, either an integrationist or a segregationist. Though his support of the proposal was grounded in a desire to satisfy the Negro teachers, a doctrinaire integrationist who discussed the matter with him in 1884 concluded that Cleveland had an open mind and "would approach the consideration of the question without any prejudice against men of color."[13]

When Cleveland resigned the governorship to become president in 1885, he was succeeded in Albany by Lieutenant Governor David Bennett Hill, a Democrat who stood for everything that Cleveland despised, but who nevertheless continued his predecessor's racial policy. Hill was from a poor family boasting no illustrious progenitors, and he clawed his way to political power. Unprincipled and cynical about politics, Hill was a spoilsman of the old school, an opportunistic manipulator allied with the Tammany Hall machine. His search for votes wherever he could find them led Hill to insure his election as alderman of Elmira in 1881 "by paying off the mortgage on the Negro church. . . ."[14] As governor, Hill showed that favors to blacks were available from his wing of the Democracy as from Cleveland's. He placed D. Garnett Baltimore in charge of all state engineering work on Long Island; running for another term in 1885, Hill accumulated substantial Negro support by distributing far more minor patronage to the race than any Republican administration. One New York Negro newspaper, the *Progres-*

Seth M. Scheiner, *Negro Mecca: A History of the Negro in New York City, 1865–1900* (New York: New York University Press, 1965), pp. 175–76.

13. George Hoadly to Daniel S. Lamont, March 28, 1885, Reel 9, Grover Cleveland Papers, Library of Congress. In later years, when white supremacist Tom Watson recalled Cleveland's support for this law, the latter professed not to remember clearly what the legislation was meant to do. In the uproar over Theodore Roosevelt's dinner with Booker T. Washington at the White House, Cleveland's racial record became a subject of congressional debate. See Cleveland to C. L. Bartlett, March 14, 1904, in Albert Ellery Bergh, ed., *Grover Cleveland: Addresses, State Papers and Letters* (New York: Sun Dial Classics, 1908), p. 432, and *Congressional Record,* 58 Cong., 2 sess., pp. 2565, 2742, 4708–11, 4722–23 (February 29, March 3, April 12, 1904), esp. letter cited on p. 4723 from Cleveland to G. A. Sullivan, August 27, 1887.

14. Herbert J. Bass, *"I Am a Democrat": The Political Career of David Bennett Hill* (Syracuse: Syracuse University Press, 1961), p. 9.

sive American, endorsed the victorious Hill.[15] In 1891, with Hill still in the governor's chair, black discontent with Republicanism and Democratic wooing of the race accelerated. New York Negroes had long complained that life insurance companies charged them higher premiums and paid them lower benefits than was the case with white policyholders, a discrimination which cost the state's blacks $50,000 a year. When a bipartisan bill to outlaw this practice was introduced in the legislature, the insurance lobby tried to have it killed, but it passed both houses with no negative votes, and Hill signed it into law. Negroes noted the abstention of Jacob Sloan Fassett, an important Republican state senator from Elmira with links to the insurance interests, and a few months later the Republican nomination of Fassett for governor set off a Negro revolt. Many black voters, whatever their political affiliation, were outraged at this Republican affront and refused to vote the ticket. Exploiting the situation, the Democratic state platform contained the following unprecedented plank, passed by acclamation: "This convention views with gratification the growing friendly feeling toward the Democratic party of our colored fellow citizens in this State, and they are welcomed to our ranks with the assurance that within our party discrimination on account of race is discountenanced." The party had progressed far since Reconstruction days.[16] After a sweeping Democratic victory in November, the Negro New York *Age* blamed the Republican party for its anachronistic assumption that all blacks must vote Republican, and its treatment of Negroes "as if they were the scum of the earth." The Demo-

15. New York *Freeman,* October 17, November 7, 1885, both p. 2; Alton B. Parker to David B. Hill, October 12, William E. Gross and others to Hill, November 4, 1885, Box 6, George S. Bixby Papers, New York State Library.

16. The grievance is stated in William H. Johnson, *Autobiography of Dr. William Henry Johnson* (Albany: Argus, 1900), p. 18. Legislative action can be traced through New York *Times,* March 8, 1891, p. 11; New York, *Journal of the Senate,* 1891, p. 284; *Journal of the Assembly,* 1891, p. 774; New York *Age,* April 11, 1891, p. 2. Black support for the Democrats is evident in New York *World,* October 4, 1891, p. 3, and T. McCants Stewart, *The Afro-American in Politics* (Brooklyn: Citizen Print, 1891). The Democrats' pro-Negro plank is reprinted in New York *Times,* September 17, 1891, p. 1; for the strategy behind it, see Henry F. Downing to Grover Cleveland, September 25, 1891, Reel 69, Cleveland Papers.

crats had capitalized on "this condition of affairs, and the Republicans have suffered in consequence at the ballot box."[17]

On the municipal level Empire State Democrats showed a similar interest in the Negro. The New York City Tammany machine, "never known to spare a vote, from whatever source it comes,"[18] courted black support in the 1870's, and in the next decade Democratic mayors put one Negro on the municipal civil service commission and named another to the post of street inspector, later promoting him to inspector of meters in the public works department.[19] In 1891 the city Democracy invited the first black juror to serve at the court of general sessions. When the man tried to excuse himself from service with the claim that he had to visit a sick mother in the South, the city recorder insisted that he return soon because "we want men of your color and of your apparent intelligence to serve on juries in this county."[20] Democrats in neighboring Brooklyn were equally friendly. In 1888 a temporary law integrating the city public schools lapsed, and a black child was denied admission to the school of his choice. T. McCants Stewart, a Negro lawyer and Democrat, used his influence with the Democratic majority on the school board to have "the color line. . . . wiped out from our schools." Stewart led a Negro organization supporting Democrat Alfred Chapin for mayor in 1889, and the successful Chapin then named Stewart to a vacancy on the school board. Also, the Chapin administration, under Stewart's influence, appointed the first black policeman in Brooklyn's history. When white officers resisted the innovation, the police commissioner silenced the grumblings with threats of disciplinary action.[21] A Democratic mayor of

17. New York *Age*, December 12, 1891, p. 2.

18. Quotation *ibid.*, March 28, 1891, p. 2.

19. On Tammany efforts to win black support in Boss Tweed's time, see *New Era*, May 12, 1870, p. 3; New York *Day Book*, February 18, 1871, p. 4; Ottley, "*New World A-Coming*," p. 209. Democratic patronage for Negroes in the 1880's is noted in Huntsville (Ala.) *Gazette*, October 31, 1885, p. 2; New York *Freeman*, July 3, 1886, January 15, 1887, both p. 2.

20. Cleveland *Gazette*, June 13, 1891, p. 2.

21. On the school integration matter, see New York *Age*, September 15, 1888, p. 2, July 19, 1890, p. 1. The black role in the 1889 election and its consequences are chronicled *ibid.*, November 2, 1889, p. 4; T. McCants Stewart to Grover Cleveland, November 7, 1889, Reel 68, Cleveland Papers; New York *Age*, April

Albany was also sensitive to Negro desires. When the Albany Homeopathic Hospital refused to admit a black pauper sent by the city superintendent of the poor, Mayor John B. Thacher ordered that no city patients or municipal funds go to the institution, and only revoked the ban when the hospital agreed to end discrimination.[22]

The Democrats of nearby New Jersey began to flirt with the black vote in 1880 when a Democrat sent a letter to the state's leading black newspaper, the Trenton *Sentinel*, asking New Jersey blacks to abandon the Republicans who "put them off into colored clubs by themselves, and laugh at them and call them names oftener than the Democrats do." Despite this appeal, a check of the Trenton black vote in the fall election could turn up only five men "accused or suspected of voting the Democratic ticket."[23] In 1881 the state legislature outlawed the exclusion of children from any public school on racial grounds. Republican legislators supported the bill as a bloc. The Senate's four Democrats split evenly on the measure, while six Democratic assemblymen voted yea, and seventeen nay. The bill became law when the Democratic governor declined to exercise his veto. Combined analysis of the vote in both houses reveals that Democratic members representing areas with relatively large numbers of blacks, and those from urbanized districts, tended to favor the legislation more than Democrats elected from lily-white and rural constituencies. These roll calls suggest that a concentration of blacks, especially in an urban area, could wield substantial leverage with politicians, even Democratic ones.[24]

25, 1891, p. 1; Leslie H. Fishel, Jr., "The North and the Negro, 1865–1900: A Study in Race Discrimination" (Ph. D. dissertation, Harvard University, 1954), II, 336; New York *Times*, March 7, 28, 1891, both p. 8, April 4, 1891, p. 4, April 5, 1891, p. 16.

22. Albany *Argus*, December 31, 1887, and Albany *Times*, February 20, 1888, clippings in Vol. 3, John Boyd Thacher Scrapbooks, New York State Library.

23. Trenton *Sentinel*, August 7, 1880, p. 2, November 6, 1880, p. 3.

24. New Jersey, *Journal of the Senate*, 1881, p. 612; *Minutes of Votes and Proceedings of the General Assembly*, 1881, pp. 952–53. Demographic data on the counties is from Bureau of the Census, *Tenth Census*, I, 401–2. The law is

A remarkable Democrat named Leon Abbett was elected governor of New Jersey in 1883. Exploiting his lower-class origins, Abbett attained a reputation as "the Great Commoner of the State," the people's defender against the railroads. He was a spoilsman like his friend and yachting partner Governor Hill of New York, but, unlike Hill, Abbett had a past to live down: he had entered politics during the Civil War as a Negro-hating Copperhead. By the time he entered the statehouse, Abbett was singing a different tune, recognizing blacks in appointments and serving as sponsor at the baptism of the Negro son of the Newark city messenger, a display of interracial friendship remarkable at the time. He also encouraged a New Jersey civil rights law in place of the invalidated federal statute. It passed the state senate unanimously and received just five negative votes, all Democratic, in the assembly.[25]

Governor Abbett did something even more astonishing for a former race-baiter. When the mulatto sexton of Hackensack's First Baptist Church died, the Hackensack Cemetery Company refused to allow burial on its property. Governor Abbett dispatched a special message to the legislature, noting that cemeteries had the legal right to refuse burial only on "reasonable" grounds, and that

> the regulation that refuses Christian burial to the body of a deceased citizen upon the ground of color is not, in my judgment, a reasonable regulation. . . . The State should not attempt to control individuals in their private and social relations as long as they do not interfere with the rights of others. But the Legisla-

---

codified in New Jersey, *Acts*, 1881, p. 186. Also see Marion M. Thompson Wright, *The Education of Negroes in New Jersey* (New York: Teachers College, Columbia University, 1941), pp. 167–68.

25. On Abbett consult William Edgar Sackett, *Modern Battles of Trenton* (Trenton: John L. Murphy, 1895), pp. 144, 408. Information on his early racial attitude was provided by Professor Richard Hogarty, while his liberal policy as governor is seen in New York *Globe*, April 26, 1884, p. 1, New York *Freeman*, August 22, 1885, p. 4; New York *World*, January 1, 1885, p. 4. Roll calls on the civil rights bill are in New Jersey, *Journal of the Senate*, 1884, pp. 142–43; *Minutes of Votes and Proceedings of the General Assembly*, 1884, pp. 816, 1115, and the law is codified in *Acts*, 1884, Ch. 219. There are no apparent demographic patterns to the Democratic vote.

ture should see that the civil and political rights of all men, whether white or black, are protected. . . . It ought not to be tolerated in this State, that a corporation whose existence depends upon the legislative will and whose property is exempt from taxation because of its religious uses should be permitted to make a distinction between the white man and the black man.

Abbett demanded immediate remedial legislation, but there was much hostility to the desegregation of cemeteries. The secretary of the corporation which had so incensed Abbett argued that only a few white agitators were raising the issue: Negroes preferred their own burial grounds. Trustees of his organization, no matter what their own views might be, had to respect the prejudice of the white families owning cemetery plots. When Democrats introduced a bill embodying the governor's request, the Republican leader in the state senate privately asked Abbett to allow an amendment exempting religious corporations, which would have rendered the legislation almost meaningless because most cemeteries were associated with church groups. Abbett replied sharply to the Republican, who left his office in a fury. Abbett explained to reporters: "I do not see why religious corporations should be permitted to refuse to bury a colored man any more than any other kind of corporation." Two days later Senate Republicans cited Abbett's old hostility to Negro rights and attacked New Jersey Democrats for hypocrisy in sponsoring the cemetery bill. The Democratic version, however, with no exemptions, was passed by the Republican-controlled upper house with eighteen votes in the affirmative and one Democrat voting nay, and it then passed the Democratic lower house with no opposition. The Democratic New York *World* hailed the result, remarking: "The stupid proposition that men of a particular hue shall not lie in the same earth with other men needed just such a legislative squelching."[26]

Two wealthy and prestigious Negro businessmen took the

26. *Journal of the Senate*, 1884, pp. 121–22; New York *Times*, January 21, 1884, p. 3, January 26, February 5, 7, 1884, all p. 2; *Journal of the Senate*, 1884, p. 224; *Minutes of Votes and Proceedings of the General Assembly*, 1884, pp. 748–49; New York *World*, February 8, 1884, p. 4. The law is in *Acts*, 1884, Ch. 56.

initiative in breaking with their race's traditional political affiliation in Pennsylvania. In 1874 Robert Purvis and William
Still supported for mayor of Philadelphia an independent candidate who was running with Democratic support against the
Republican machine nominee. Notwithstanding the long and
distinguished service which both Purvis and Still had given to
the cause of Negro rights, black Republicans greeted news of
this political apostasy with denunciations and threats of violence. Still took the unusual course of vindicating his actions in
a public speech. After arguing that blacks should turn their
energies toward economic advancement and moderate their
demands for political influence, he declared:

> If a colored voter chooses, upon due consideration, to vote an
> independent, or nonpartisan, or even Democratic ticket, I think
> he should be free to do so, and, still further, I think that colored
> men who have been so long bound under the yoke, and have
> been so long compelled to think and act only at the bidding of
> the dominant race, should be the last people on earth to institute
> or encourage this kind of political tyranny.

Admitting that Negroes owed gratitude to the Republican party,
Still insisted that this did not extend to Philadelphia's local cor-
ruptionists who had never aided the black man. Since new issues
were taking the place of the race question, "it would not be un-
wise to carefully watch the changes in parties and movements, as
there are many Democrats. . . . who are no longer in sympathy
with old pro-slavery doctrines and ideas." Still had recently been
unable to find "in any of the Democratic papers any sneers
against the colored man." This address won Still and Purvis
some sympathy among Negroes.[27]

The Republican candidate won that year, and it was not until

27. The campaign of 1874 is described by the independent candidate Alexander K. McClure in *Old-Time Notes of Pennsylvania* (Philadelphia: John C.
Winston, 1905), II, 363–75. Black attacks on Still and Purvis are Anonymous to
Still, March 14, 1874, Elizabeth Williams to Still, March 24, 1874, M. A. S. Curry
to Still, May 11, 1874, Still Papers; *New National Era*, March 19, 1874, p. 1. Still
defended himself in *An Address on Voting and Laboring* (Philadelphia: James B.
Rodgers, 1874). Favorable Negro comment came in J. A. Newby to Still, March
11, 1874, F. J. Grimké to Still, March 18, 1874, Reuben Tomlinson to Still, April
14, 1874, Still Papers; *New National Era*, April 16, 1874, p. 1.

1881 that a Democrat, Samuel King, was elected mayor of Philadelphia. King, like Cleveland, was a relative newcomer to politics, belonging to the moralistic civil service reform wing of the Democracy. He received negligible black support but stunned everyone by appointing the first Negro policemen in the city's history. This "radical act. . . . raised a storm of indignation, such as no previous mayor ever encountered," but King persisted, and a white officer was fired for refusing to sit next to one of his new black colleagues in a police van.[28] When King ran for reelection in 1884, Robert Purvis chaired a meeting of two hundred Philadelphia Negroes that endorsed King, but most members of the race remained Republicans on the assumption that a new Republican mayor would have to be at least as forthcoming as the Democrat. "But," warned the Harrisburg *State Sentinel*, an influential Negro newspaper, "this constant recognition of colored men by Democrats in office . . . is a threatening menace to the continuance of Republican rule by the assistance of colored votes. . . ." King lost, and the Republican victor had another surprise for Negroes: he gradually removed most of the black policemen. The *State Sentinel* admitted, too late, that King was "the best mayor in the interest of the colored citizen that has ever held office in this city," and the paper wondered "whether it would not serve our interests better to pay a little attention" to the Democracy.[29] In subsequent years Philadelphia Democrats built up a network of Negro clubs, and in 1891 they nominated a relative of William Still for the common council.[30]

28. *National Cyclopaedia of American Biography* (New York: James T. White, 1906 —), VI, 196; Baltimore *American*, reprinted in New York *Times*, August 29, 1881, p. 2. King's education in a Quaker school might help explain his advanced racial policy.

29. Harrisburg *State Sentinel*, January–June, 1884. The quotations are from the issues of February 9, 1884, p. 2, April 12, 1884, p. 1, May 10, 1884, p. 2. At the same time Democrats in other Pennsylvania cities pursued policies similar to King's: Democrats appointed the first black policeman in Pittsburgh and nominated a Harrisburg Negro for judge of elections. *Ibid.*, February 9, 1884, p. 4, February 23, 1884, p. 2.

30. Lewis Wesley Rathgeber, "The Democratic Party in Pennsylvania, 1880–1896" (Ph.D. dissertation, University of Pittsburgh, 1955), pp. 216–17, 233–34, 258; G. W. Gardiner to Isaiah Wears, April 30, 1891, Wears Papers, Box 9G, Leon Gardiner Collection; Indianapolis *Freeman*, January 17, 1891, p. 2.

While King was impressing Philadelphia blacks, Democrats were making similar strides on the state level. In 1882 Purvis and Still campaigned for the victorious gubernatorial candidate Robert Pattison, another reform Democrat in the Cleveland mold. Pattison was a prominent lay leader of the Methodist Church; he received much favorable publicity when he backed the following resolution which was enacted at a conference of his denomination: "No member of any society within the Church shall be exluded from public worship in any and every edifice of the denomination, and no student shall be excluded from instruction in any and every school under the supervision of the Church, because of race, color, or previous condition of servitude."[31] Governor Pattison appointed blacks to jobs in the executive department and the state arsenal never before held by members of the race, and the *State Sentinel* editorialized: "Every appointment of a colored man by the Democratic administration is another nail in the Republican coffin."[32]

Roll call votes in the Pennsylvania legislature on issues of interest to Negroes also reflected changing Democratic attitudes. In 1881 Pennsylvania, like New Jersey, passed a bill outlawing racial discrimination in public school admissions. The proposal was unopposed in the Senate. Thirty-three Democrats in the House of Representatives joined two Republicans in voting nay, while ten Democrats allied with ninety-nine Republicans to provide a huge majority for the bill. Six years later the legislature passed a civil rights statute overwhelmingly. While the 1881 vote shows no correlation between Democratic votes and the racial makeup of constituencies, the only three members who opposed the civil rights bill of 1887 were Democratic representatives from the counties of Carbon, Elk, and Fulton, where a black man was a rarity. As in New Jersey, the presence of Negro voters in a district seemed to liberalize the racial stand of the Democrat representing the district.[33]

31. Washington *Bee*, February 10, 1883, p. 2; Huntsville *Gazette*, May 31, 1884, p. 2.

32. Harrisburg *State Sentinel*, July 26, December 13, 1884, both p. 2.

33. The roll calls are in Pennsylvania, *Journal of the Senate*, 1881, p. 1098;

Connecticut was the first New England state where Democrats made a serious bid for Negro support. Blacks in Connecticut had a long-standing grievance: their privately organized and financed militia units in Bridgeport, Hartford, and New Haven were not recognized as official components of the state national guard. Democrat Jim Gallagher, minority leader of the Connecticut House of Representatives, introduced a bill in 1878 making the black battalions regular militia companies, but Republican majorities in both houses delayed and then rejected the measure without roll call votes. The aggrieved militiamen of New Haven held a protest meeting and invited Gallagher to address them. In what was probably the first attempt by a Northern Democrat to appeal to black voters on an issue of substance, the legislator noted that, while always a Democrat, "he had assisted colored fugitives through to Canada" before the Civil War. Connecticut, he declared,

> now opens the door to any white man who wants to join the guard in any county in the State, but the door is shut in the face of any colored man. We tax the colored man by property tax, poll tax, commutation tax, and all other tax, make him liable to draft in time of war, but will not permit him to learn military science before war comes.

Gallagher thanked God that slavery was dead and claimed that his own Irish ancestry enabled him to empathize with victims of prejudice. Denying any political motive in his crusade for racial justice, Gallagher promised that whether or not he held any office, the Negroes "could rely upon him. . . ." His appreciative audience passed resolutions denouncing the Republican legislature and urging independent voting. Despite this threat, the legislature adjourned without reconsidering the militia question, a course which even a Republican newspaper branded "dense stupidity." Democratic victories in the Hartford and

---

ibid., 1887, p. 1177; *Journal of the House of Representatives*, 1881, pp. 1456, 1464; *ibid.*, 1887, p. 1125. Demographic data is in *Tenth Census*, I, 406. For the texts of the two statutes, see Pennsylvania, *Laws*, 1881, p. 76; *ibid.*, 1887, pp. 130–31. Also note Ira V. Brown, "Pennsylvania and the Rights of the Negro, 1865–87," *Pennsylvania History*, XXVIII (January, 1961), 45–57.

Bridgeport municipal elections soon thereafter were attributed to black rebellion against the Republicans.[34]

Negro demands were met only after the election of a Democratic governor in 1882. The new man, Thomas Waller, had first attracted public attention by his advocacy of the new departure and Greeley in 1872. He was a civil service reform Democrat and later served as President Cleveland's consul in London. In his first message to the legislature Waller said, "The colored troops . . . have not heretofore been encamped with the Brigade. Whatever may be the reason for this exclusion, it should no longer be permitted." Both houses, without formal roll calls, approved a bill directing that Negro units "shall belong to the battalion at large. . . ." The blacks participated in the next maneuvers held by the militia, despite grumblings from white members, and a Hartford Negro informed Frederick Douglass "that for this Act I admired Governor Waller's pluck and independence more than I think I ever felt for any public man this state ever produced." In 1884 a Bridgeport Democrat introduced a civil rights bill in the legislature. It passed unanimously, and Governor Waller signed it into law.[35]

The first Democratic inroads into the Massachusetts black vote were the work of Benjamin F. Butler, a former Radical Republican and always a spoilsman with demagogic, rabble-

34. The fate of Gallagher's bill can be followed in New Haven *Palladium*, March 6, 1878, p. 1, March 13, 1878, p. 4; Connecticut, *Journal of the Senate*, 1878, p. 423; *Journal of the House of Representatives*, 1878, p. 493. For the New Haven protest meeting and its repercussions, see New Haven *Palladium*, March 20, 1878, p. 4, March 21, April 6, 1878, both p. 2.

35. Waller's background is described in William John Niven, "The Time of the Whirlwind: A Study in the Political, Social, and Economic History of Connecticut from 1861 to 1875" (Ph.D. dissertation, Columbia University, 1954), p. 428, and *National Cyclopaedia of American Biography*, X, 343. His request for a militia bill, legislative action on it, and the text of the measure are in *Journal of the House of Representatives*, 1883, pp. 55, 784; *Journal of the Senate*, 1883, p. 670; *Public Acts*, 1883, Ch. 109. For black participation in militia activity and gratitude to Waller, see Springfield *Republican*, September 13, 1883, p. 8, and T. P. Saunders to Frederick Douglass, September 24, 1883, Reel 11, Douglass Papers. Passage of a civil rights bill is seen in *Journal of the House of Representatives*, 1884, pp. 260, 649; *Journal of the Senate*, 1884, p. 624; *Public Acts*, 1884, Ch. 86, New York *Globe*, April 5, 1884, p. 2. In 1891 New Haven Democrats appointed the first Negro policeman in the city's history. New York *Age*, March 21, 1891, p. 4.

rousing tendencies. In 1882, two years after moving into the Democratic party, he was elected governor of Massachusetts, aided by the votes of some blacks who recalled his pro-Negro record as a Republican. Facing a reelection campaign the next year, Butler appointed a politically independent Negro lawyer, Edwin G. Walker, to be judge of the Charleston district court, subject to confirmation by the Republican-dominated common council. Walker was the first black ever nominated to a judgeship in the state, and a Negro newspaper noted that "if Mr. Walker is confirmed, the Democrats will get the benefit of the nomination, and if he is rejected the Republicans will have to explain why and wherefore to the colored voters. Governor Butler is sly, devilish sly." An organization of black Butler men campaigned for his reelection using this appointment as a magnet to draw the race's votes. Veteran abolitionist Wendell Phillips also declared for Butler because of the Walker nomination. Massachusetts Republicans responded with mudslinging: Walker, they said, had been arrested for drunkenness, was financially dishonest, often sold his vote, and had affairs with white women. Ostensibly because of all this scandal, the Republican members of the common council vetoed the nomination. Butler dramatized the issue by a renomination, which was followed by another rejection.[36] Butler lost the election; however, as a lame-duck governor, he showed that his motives in the Walker matter were not entirely political by appointing the distinguished Negro Republican George L. Ruffin to the vacancy on the bench. Ruffin was quickly confirmed. The black community was impressed, and Butler himself in later years referred with pride to the episode.[37]

36. Butler's appeal to black voters and his appointment of Walker are chronicled in Butler to William B. Berry, September 26, 1882, Vol. 10, Butler Papers; John Daniels, *In Freedom's Birthplace* (Boston: Houghton Mifflin, 1914), p. 120; New York *Globe*, October 6, 1883, p. 2; unidentified clipping, September, 1883, Silver Box 4, Butler Papers; Springfield *Republican*, October 11, 1883, p. 5. For Republican opposition and the two rejections, see Henry Edes to John D. Long, October 1, 5, 1883, Box 11, Long Papers, Massachusetts Historical Society; New York *Times*, October 5, 1883, p. 1; New York *World*, October 17, 1883, p. 4.

37. New York *Globe*, November 17, 1883, p. 1; Gladys J. Gray, "George Lewis Ruffin," *Negro History Bulletin*, V (October, 1941), 18–19; J. J. McKinley to

In the three decades following Butler's brief tenure, a growing number of Massachusetts Negroes adhered to the Democracy in local and state elections. The Democrats named the first Negro policeman to the Boston force in 1885. Three years later a Democratic mayor nominated the unfortunate Edwin G. Walker to the post of city assessor at a salary higher than any ever paid to a Negro municipal employee, but history repeated itself: the Republican majority on the Boston board of aldermen rejected him. Boston Democrats nominated a Negro for the legislature in 1891.[38]

George T. Downing, the Newport caterer, touched off Negro political independence in Rhode Island. Long irritated by Republican complacency on racial matters, he lost all patience in 1873 when the overwhelmingly Republican state legislature voted indefinite postponement of a bill revoking Rhode Island's prohibition on interracial marriage, and he tried to organize a black boycott of the polls. Three years later Rhode Island blacks protested their exclusion from government jobs, and the blacks of Newport abstained from voting in 1882 because none of them had been appointed city postman. Later that year fifty representatives of the race met and resolved to support candidates for office, regardless of party, who would most benefit the Negro cause. When former Senator William Sprague ran for governor as an independent with Democratic support, Downing backed him. Rhode Island Republicans proposed a state civil rights bill in 1885, but Downing prevailed upon the Democratic minority

---

George L. Ruffin, November 8, 1883, C. Steward to Ruffin, November 14, 1883, Ruffin Papers, Moorland-Spingarn Collection, Howard University; Butler to W. S. Taylor, June 21, 1886, Vol. 21, Butler Papers; Benjamin F. Butler, *Autobiographical and Personal Reminiscences of Major General Benjamin F. Butler* (Boston: A. M. Thayer, 1892), p. 974.

38. On the black policeman, see New York *Freeman*, December 16, 1885, p. 2, and Daniels, *In Freedom's Birthplace*, p. 103. Walker's second disappointment can be followed in New York *Age*, May 26, 1888, p. 4, June 2, 16, 1888, both p. 1; the nomination of a black man to the legislature, *ibid.*, October 10, 1891, p. 2. Growing black independence in state politics is evident from the following: New York *Freeman*, October 31, 1885, p. 2, December 12, 1885, December 30, 1886, both p. 1; Archibald H. Grimké to John F. Andrew, August 3, 1886, Howard L. Smith to Andrew, October 1, 1886, Andrew Papers, Massachusetts Historical Society; Daniels, *In Freedom's Birthplace*, pp. 97–98, 279–80, 295–98.

in the legislature to offer a stronger measure which passed, and Downing bragged that "Democrats in Rhode Island are more liberal toward the colored man than are Republicans." The Democrats nominated Downing for the state legislature in 1886, and he ran ahead of his ticket in the Republican city of Newport. The next spring a Providence Negro was elected to the legislature with Democratic endorsement, and when the Democrats finally won the statehouse in the fall, Downing became a prison commissioner.[39]

Midwestern States

The Midwestern state that witnessed the earliest, most persistent, and most influential black independent movement was Ohio; what started in 1873 as the bolt of a few disgruntled Negroes mushroomed by the 1880's into a situation where blacks could play the two parties off against each other. Like Downing, Peter Clark, Cincinnati's black schoolteacher, had long complained about Republican indifference to the race's demands. Before the 1873 state election he convened a conference of Ohio Negroes to discuss Republican failure to deliver patronage and the delay on Sumner's civil rights bill. When the presiding officer called the hundred participants to order and described the Republican organization as "the party to which we belong," Clark showed his own political alienation by correcting: "the party to which we are attached." An address by Clark highlighted the convention. He recognized that Republicans had done much for the Negro, but since the party had sold out the race "it is not only our right but our duty to vote against it." Deprivation of

39. Providence *Daily Journal*, February 7, 8, 1878, both p. 1; New Haven *Palladium*, April 11, 1878, p. 2; Albany *Argus*, April 11, 1878, p. 2; *People's Advocate*, April 2, 1881, p. 2; Albany *Argus*, August 3, 1882, p. 4; New York *Times*, October 19, 1882, p. 1; *People's Advocate*, April 14, 1883, p. 2; Rhode Island, *Acts and Resolves of the General Assembly*, 1885, p. 171 (the legislature did not publish journals of its proceedings); New York *Freeman*, March 21, 1885, p. 1, June 6, 1885, p. 2; Downing to Grover Cleveland, April 8, 1886, Reel 52, Cleveland Papers; New York *Freeman*, April 16, 1887, p. 1; New York *Age*, December 17, 1887, p. 1.

patronage was no minor grievance, Clark insisted, "when that denial of office implies . . . a denial of my equality as a citizen." The assemblage resolved that blacks ought "not consider themselves under eternal obligations to a party who disavows us as a class." While supporting the statewide Republican ticket, Ohio Negroes should exercise independent judgment in local races. The Democrats, sensing potential votes, asked for Negro support and dropped all references to the threat of school integration, an issue they had been planning to stress in the campaign. In October the Democrats won both the governorship and the state legislature for the first time since antebellum days. Although the precise impact of black discontent on the result was unclear, Republican leaders tried hard to win back Clark's allegiance.[40]

Ohio Negroes continued to grumble for the next several years about the meager patronage available from Republicans. Black independent and Democratic clubs sprang up before every election, subsidized by white Democrats.[41] Disillusionment with Republicanism led Peter Clark into the Socialist Workingmen's party in 1877, but by 1879 he was back in the Republican fold. Three years later Clark turned Democrat, and the Democratic municipal authorities of Cincinnati reciprocated by naming his son a deputy sheriff and appointing the first black policeman in the city's history. Democratic politicos also supplied the Clark family with enough financial aid to launch a Negro Democratic newspaper published only before elections, the Cincinnati *Afro-American*.[42]

40. On the convention, see Cincinnati *Enquirer*, August 23, 1873, p. 1, and *New National Era & Citizen*, August 28, 1873, pp. 2–3. Its impact on the Democrats is seen by comparing party pronouncements of late 1872—Cincinnati *Enquirer*, November 16, 1872, p. 1, December 15, 19, 1872, both p. 4—with those of the 1873 campaign: *ibid.*, August 4, 13, 1873, both p. 4; Dayton *Herald*, August 28, 1873, p. 2; *American Annual Cyclopaedia*, 1873, p. 610. The election results and Republican efforts to please Clark are in the *Cyclopaedia*, p. 611; *New National Era & Citizen*, November 20, 1873, p. 2; Cincinnati *Enquirer*, March 27, 1874, p. 4.

41. Cincinnati *Enquirer*, July–October, 1877–80.

42. Herbert G. Gutman, "Peter H. Clark: Pioneer Negro Socialist, 1877," *Journal of Negro Education*, XXXIV (Fall, 1965), 413–18; Cincinnati *Enquirer*, September 7, 1879, p. 4; Cleveland *Gazette*, September 29, 1883, p. 1; Wendell P. Dabney, *Cincinnati's Colored Citizens* (Cincinnati: Dabney Publishing,

Ohio Democrats showed a new sensitivity to the race's griev-
ances by their response to an act of blatant discrimination in
1880. George Washington Williams, a Republican and the first
Negro ever to serve in the Ohio legislature, often dined with
colleagues of both parties in Columbus restaurants. One day a
waiter told Williams to sit either at the lunch counter or in the
kitchen; otherwise, he must leave. Two Democratic legislators
witnessed the event and brought it to public attention, and the
Ohio House appointed a committee of inquiry. After investigat-
ing the incident, the Republican committee members called for
dismissal of the waiter, despite the restaurant owner's public
apology to Williams; the Democrats, while considering the apology sufficient, "unite[d] with the majority of the committee in
condemning discrimination against any member of this House,
or other person, on account of race, color, or previous condition
of servitude."[43]

The themes of Republican neglect, Democratic regeneration,
and Negro independence came together in the 1883 election for
governor of Ohio. The Democrats nominated George Hoadly,
a man of upper-class New England ancestry, a former protegé,
law partner, and "loving disciple" of Salmon P. Chase. Hoadly
had been a fervent foe of slavery, a Radical Republican, and had
served with distinction as city solicitor and judge of the superior
court of Cincinnati in the 1850's. He was a Liberal Republican
in 1872 but refused to vote for Greeley because of their difference on tariff policy, and he became a Democrat in the Tilden
campaign of 1876. Identified with the party's Mugwump wing,
he would become a warm friend of civil service reform, good
government, and Grover Cleveland.[44] His Republican opponent

1926), p. 139; David A. Gerber, "Ohio and the Color Line: Racial Discrimination
and Negro Response in a Northern State, 1860–1915" (Ph.D. dissertation, Princeton University, 1971), I, 92. Gerber's dissertation is forthcoming as *Black Ohio
and the Color Line, 1860–1915* (Urbana: University of Illinois Press).

43. Ohio, *Journal of the House of Representatives,* 1880, pp. 982–84.

44. A short account of Hoadly's ancestry and career is George Hoadly, Jr.,
"George Hoadly," *Green Bag,* XIX (December, 1907), 685–88. He described
himself as Chase's disciple in George Hoadly, *Address at Music Hall, Cincinnati,
Ohio, on the Occasion of the Removal of the Remains of Salmon Portland Chase
to Spring Grove Cemetery, October 14, 1886* (Cincinnati: Robert Clarke, 1887),

was Joseph B. Foraker, a brilliant young Cincinnati attorney and Civil War veteran against whom Negroes had two complaints. According to rumor, Foraker had transferred from Ohio Wesleyan University because a Negro student had been admitted. Also, Foraker had often represented defendants against civil rights suits brought by blacks. Appearing for the defense in one of the earliest Cincinnati cases under the federal Civil Rights Act of 1875, Foraker was not satisfied with winning a judgment in favor of his client, a hotel owner; he also wanted to have the black complainant arrested for perjury. More recently, in 1882, Foraker was counsel for the Springfield, Ohio, public schools in a suit brought by a Negro minister who charged that his daughter had been kept out of a neighborhood school because of race. Some people even claimed to have heard Foraker cast aspersions on blacks during the trial.[45]

Ohio Negroes were stunned. While Foraker parried the allegation that he had left Ohio Wesleyan because of prejudice with a plain denial, the idea of a Republican gubernatorial candidate who opposed civil rights in court grated on the ears of blacks, especially when the Democratic alternative was Hoadly, a man of unimpeachable egalitarian credentials. The Clarks' *Afro-American* played up the issue of Foraker's alleged bigotry, and the state Democratic organization sent out free copies of the black Democratic paper to Negroes all over Ohio.[46] Since Foraker and his defenders could not deny the fact that he had argued against civil rights suits on several occasions, they insisted that he had done so only in his professional capacity; a lawyer must defend his client no matter what the lawyer's own private

---

p. 4. Also see Salmon P. Chase to F. P. Blair, June 11, 1856, Box 9, Blair-Lee Family Papers, Princeton University; George Hoadly to Jacob Schuckers, August 16, 1873, Schuckers Papers; Thomas Hendricks to Samuel J. Tilden, September 2, 1876, Box 12, Tilden Papers.

45. Joseph B. Foraker, *Notes of a Busy Life* (Cincinnati: Stewart and Kidd, 1916), I, 176. Whatever the facts of the 1882 case, Foraker's vindictiveness in the earlier episode is obvious in Cincinnati *Enquirer*, March 2, 31, 1875, both p. 8, April 2, 1875, pp. 4, 8.

46. Black feeling is evident in James Poindexter to Joseph B. Foraker, June 7, 1883, Foraker Papers, Cincinnati Historical Society, and New York *Globe*, September 15, 1883, p. 2. Democratic strategy is noted in Cleveland *Gazette*, September 1, 8, 1883, both p. 1.

attitude toward the subject of the litigation. Certainly, loyal Republicans said, there had been no gratuitous anti-Negro remarks at the 1882 trial.[47]

Democrat Hoadly squeaked by Foraker in the election with a 1,318 vote margin. While the major issues in the campaign were temperance legislation and the wool tariff, the Cleveland *Gazette*, a Negro Republican newspaper, observed that "Foraker was scratched like everything by the colored voters" because of the civil rights issue. The victorious Hoadly was sure that Negroes had decided the contest, and since there were about 16,000 black voters in the state, such an assessment was reasonable. Jubilant about breaking the political "color line," Hoadly foresaw great benefits for the entire Democracy if it would encourage blacks to cross party lines in every state.[48]

Once elected, Hoadly, a sincere believer in racial equality, took steps to detach more Ohio blacks from the Republican party through the use of patronage. He made Peter Clark the first Negro trustee of Ohio State University in recognition of Clark's "accomplishments as a scholar" and also to symbolize the governor's own commitment to equal and integrated education for both races. He then placed two more black Democrats on the board of trustees of Miami University and the State Asylum for the Blind, and he encouraged the formation of new Negro militia units. In addition, both Hoadly and the Democratic legislature gave out lesser patronage to members of the race.[49]

Hoadly took office soon after the Supreme Court's decision

47. Foraker, *Notes of a Busy Life*, I, 177; Cincinnati *Commercial Gazette*, June 16, 1883, clipping in Scrapbook 3, Foraker Papers.

48. *Tribune Almanac*, 1884, p. 79; Cleveland *Gazette*, October 20, 1883, p. 2; Hoadly to Daniel S. Lamont, March 28, 1885, Reel 9, Cleveland Papers. Senator John Sherman, the most powerful Republican in the state and a campaigner for Foraker, did not even mention the race issue in his later reminiscences about the election. Sherman, *Recollections of Forty Years in the House, Senate and Cabinet* (New York and Chicago: Werner, 1895), II, 859–67.

49. Hoadly to W. S. Chamberlain, April 7, 1885, Letterbook, Box 3, p. 655, Hoadly Papers, Governors' Correspondence, Ohio Historical Society; Hoadly to Daniel S. Lamont, March 28, 1885, Reel 9, Hoadly to Grover Cleveland, April 25, 1885, Reel 11, Cleveland Papers; Hoadly to Henry W. Forte, January 18, 1884, Letterbook, Box 3, p. 23, Hoadly Papers; Cleveland *Gazette*, February 9, May 31, 1884, both p. 1.

striking down the Civil Rights Act of 1875, and he asked for state action on the subject. His inaugural address requested the legislature to pass a law insuring that "no citizen . . . will be treated as an inferior, or denied the full measure of equal rights accorded to others, merely because he chanced to inherit a black skin." A Democratic bill guaranteeing civil rights in public accommodations, transportation, places of amusement, and jury service passed the state senate thirty to one; twenty-two Democrats voted yea, and one, representing a rural constituency in southern Ohio, opposed the measure.[50] The Republican minority in the House of Representatives anticipated the Democrats and presented a stronger bill of their own. A motion to reject its consideration failed, as thirty-one Democrats joined the Republicans to defeat twenty-three Democrats. Democratic votes on this key roll call vary from the pattern in Eastern states. While in New Jersey and Pennsylvania two variables, substantial Negro constituencies and urbanization, tended to make party legislators more amenable to black desires, a third factor complicated the Ohio line-up: North–South polarization. Democrats from southern Ohio, an area settled before the Civil War by many Southern migrants, white and black, were more hostile to civil rights than were northern Ohio Democrats. Holding constant the Negro population variable by analyzing only the Democratic legislative votes from counties with significant black concentrations, the cross-cutting effects of geography and urbanization come into sharp focus, showing that even Southern opposition was weaker in the cities, and that among urban Democrats antagonism to the bill decreased the further North the city was. Democrats from rural counties with high proportions of Negro residents in the south of the state favored rejection of the Republican bill six to two, while their eight colleagues from Cincinnati, the racially mixed metropolis of southern Ohio, divided evenly. Democrats from Columbus, which had many blacks and was located in the central region, opposed rejection two to one. The cities with large numbers of Negroes in northern Ohio were

50. Ohio, *Inaugural Address of George Hoadly*, 1884, p. 8; *Journal of the Senate*, 1884, pp. 28, 100.

Cleveland and Toledo, and all six Democrats representing these constituencies voted against the motion to quash the bill. After the Republican proposal was voted down, the milder Democratic version passed unanimously.[51] Negroes expressed displeasure at the limited scope of the statute, and they managed to push the legislature into enacting another measure a few weeks later which barred discrimination in restaurants and barbershops. Only two votes were cast against the bill in each house, all by Democrats.[52]

House Democrats tried to squeeze the greatest possible political benefit out of the issue. When a Republican member proposed a joint resolution asking Congress to begin action on a civil rights amendment to the federal Constitution, a Democrat offered an amendment to the bill denouncing the Supreme Court "for its late cowardly decision in depriving colored men of their civil rights." The Democratic majority passed this amendment, while the entire Republican contingent had to vote nay because it denounced a Republican Supreme Court. In the midst of all this legislative attention to the Negro, the Cleveland *Gazette*, Ohio's major black newspaper, commented: "The world moves, and with it even the Bourbon Democratic Party." Ohio Republicans, the *Gazette* suggested, "better be up and doing."[53]

Governor Hoadly made sure that the civil rights statutes did not become dead letters. When notified that a Columbus roller skating rink did not permit Negroes to use its facilities, Hoadly instructed the state attorney general to begin proceedings against the proprietors. The governor apprised the latter of his action and invited them to explain their policy to him personally, but the owners of the rink preferred to go out of business rather

51. *Journal of the House of Representatives*, 1884, p. 18. Demographic data for this and later Ohio roll calls is from *Tenth Census*, I, 404–5. Passage of the Democratic bill and its codification are in *Journal of the House of Representatives*, 1884, pp. 156–58, and *General and Local Laws and Joint Resolutions*, 1884, pp. 15–16.

52. *Journal of the Senate*, 1884, p. 334; *Journal of the House of Representatives*, 1884, p. 631; *General and Local Laws*, 1884, p. 90.

53. *Journal of the House of Representatives*, 1884, pp. 842–43; Cleveland *Gazette*, February 9, 1884, pp. 1, 2.

than admit Negroes.[54] Blacks complained that the civil rights statute provided no minimum fine for violators and that the maximum penalty of only $100 was too small, but the Cleveland *Gazette* nevertheless considered the law "a good one, though not as complete as it might be."[55]

Ohio still had so-called Black Laws which banned miscegenation and encouraged localities to provide separate educational facilities for the two races, though some parts of northern Ohio had voluntarily integrated their public schools. In 1880 and 1883 black legislators tried to have the Black Laws annulled, but both times Republican majorities in the legislature prevented consideration of the matter.[56] In 1884, however, with Democrats threatening their monopoly of the black vote, Republicans introduced a bill ending the legal sanction for school segregation. Blacks were not of one mind on the question. As in New York, teaching was one of the few prestigious and remunerative occupations open to members of the race, and integration would close the profession to them because regular schools would not employ blacks. Supporters of separate schools also claimed that it was important for black children to have contact with adult models of their own color whom they might emulate. Peter Clark said that he could only endorse integration when assured that public schools would accept Negroes, both students and teachers, on terms of equality with whites, but the pro-integration forces believed that better education for the race outweighed all objections, charging Negro teachers with greater concern for their jobs than for the advancement of their people.[57]

Holding a majority on the committee assigned to study the

54. Hoadly to Messrs. Taft and Mooney, February 5, 1885, Hoadly to J. S. Robinson, February 12, 1885, pp. 559–60, 581–82, Letterbook, Box 3, Hoadly Papers.

55. Gerber, "Ohio and the Color Line," I, 97; Cleveland *Gazette*, May 29, 1886, p. 2.

56. *Journal of the House of Representatives*, 1880, pp. 49, 61; John P. Green, *Fact Stranger Than Fiction* (Cleveland: Riehl Printing, 1920), p. 178.

57. *Journal of the House of Representatives*, 1884, p. 22; Gerber, "Ohio and the Color Line," I, 154–60. See the contrasting views of Harry C. Smith, editor of the Cleveland *Gazette*, and Clark, in *Gazette*, March 22, April 26, 1884, both p. 2.

school bill, the Democrats added an amendment meant to satisfy Clark and like-minded Negroes; it permitted integration only if a majority of blacks in a locality petitioned for it. The measure received a fifty to thirty-two majority, but since many members of both parties avoided the roll call, the bill was three votes short of the majority of the total membership necessary for passage. Analysis of the Democratic vote shows that, even with the amendment allowing segregated schools on an optional basis, many party representatives either found the idea of integration anathema or followed the separatist desires of local Negro educators. Democratic legislators opposed the bill thirty-two to twelve. Ten of the thirty-two represented racially mixed rural constituencies in central and southern Ohio, and another four came from Hamilton County, where Cincinnati was located. The twelve Democratic supporters of the proposal included two from Hamilton, and all three of the voting members from Cuyahoga County (Cleveland). The Cleveland *Gazette* blamed Negro teachers for causing the defeat of educational integration. But, it observed, the black teachers were not yet safe. If the school bill could come within three votes of a constitutional majority in a Democratic House of Representatives, the prospects for continuation of separate schools were dim.[58]

Hoadly took a hand in the struggle. When the principal of the Zanesville Negro schools wrote the Democratic governor about the disadvantages of integration, Hoadly replied:

My belief is that the abolition of the separate school system would result in the dismissal of some teachers. It is very clear that greater benefit will flow to the colored race from the abolition of separate schools. True, many overseers and masters lost money by the abolition of slavery, and infrequently slaves had better food and clothing by being in trusty positions. It was no reason, because they profited by it, that emancipation should not be adopted. The present abnormal condition of our schools is based on a prejudice begotten of slavery. This is no reason why the progress of the world should be impeded.

58. *Journal of the House of Representatives*, 1884, pp. 678, 771; Cleveland *Gazette*, April 19, 1884, p. 2, April 26, 1884, p. 3.

Hoadly chastised the principal for working against his own race. "The foundations of distinctions in Ohio," he concluded, "should be correct conduct, good behavior, merit, and not color." In his annual message of 1885 Hoadly praised Buckeye legislators for passing the two civil rights bills, and he bemoaned the continued existence of separate black schools which, as a rule, provided inferior instruction and forced Negro students to walk long distances to get an education. The state had a "duty . . . to furnish to all alike, irrespective of social rank or color, the same fair start, and equal chance in the race of life. . . ." Hoadly convinced Peter Clark to drop his objections to mixed schools, though the black principal stood to lose his employment if such a measure became law.[59]

In 1885, with Hoadly using his influence in the cause of integration, Clark no longer insisting on separate schools, and the fall elections in sight, Democrats in the House of Representatives dealt more favorably with the school bill. It passed fifty-nine to thirteen, as Democrats backed the measure twenty-five to thirteen. Five of the six Hamilton County Democrats supported the proposal, as did all five members from the other urban counties of Cuyahoga (Cleveland), Franklin (Columbus), and Lucas (Toledo). Five of the bill's opponents were from the racially mixed southern counties where both white citizens and black teachers seemed to favor separation. A few Senate Democrats tried to get their colleagues to approve the measure so that their party could claim credit for ending separate schools, and they almost succeeded. Opponents of the bill tabled it by one vote, but its Democratic backers won a reconsideration by the same margin. It was finally defeated twelve to ten, as three Democrats voted yea and twelve nay.[60]

Never had the favor of Ohio Negroes been so zealously courted as in the 1885 state election. The Republicans renominated Fora-

59. Hoadly to James A. Guy, January 2, 1885, Letterbook, Box 3, pp. 450–52, Hoadly Papers; *Annual Message of George Hoadly*, 1885, pp. 7–8; Hoadly to Daniel S. Lamont, March 28, 1885, Reel 9, Cleveland Papers.

60. *Journal of the House of Representatives*, 1885, p. 454; *Journal of the Senate*, 1885, pp. 569, 735–36. No patterns are discernible from the Democratic Senate votes.

ker despite black protests, and Hoadly, running for a second term, accelerated his pro-Negro policy as the election neared. He formed a Colored Democratic Executive Committee, appointed a Negro to be a trustee of Athens College, and begged the Democratic national administration to "appoint Peter H. Clark to as high an office as you can find for him." The Democratic state organization, in the same spirit, nominated a Negro from Cleveland for the state legislature. Clark's *Afro-American* published statistics purporting to show that the race had received far more patronage from Ohio Democrats than from Republicans. This black Democratic newspaper also resuscitated the old charges of racism against Foraker. As for the claim that a lawyer must defend his client no matter how distasteful the case, would Salmon P. Chase, Hoadly's mentor, have defended in court a slaveowner's right to his chattel? "Vote," said Peter Clark, "for the friends of the race, without regard to the party label they bear."[61] Republicans fought back. In letters and speeches to Negroes, Foraker claimed to be a veteran fighter for racial equality. Ohio Republicans circulated special campaign literature in the black community, nominated the unprecedented number of three Negroes to the legislature, and bought the favor of two black newspapers which had criticized Foraker.[62] But the Republican trump card was the bloody shirt. Foraker, Ohio Senator John Sherman, and Mississippi Republican leaders James Chalmers and John R. Lynch asked what good Hoadly's

61. Cleveland *Gazette*, June 30, 1885, p. 3; New York *World*, August 28, 1885, p. 5; Cleveland *Gazette*, May 2, 1885, p. 1; Hoadly to Grover Cleveland, September 9, 1885, Reel 19, Cleveland Papers; Cleveland *Gazette*, September 26, 1885, p. 2; Cincinnati *Afro-American*, September 19, 1885, p. 1; Clark, in New York *Freeman*, July 18, 1885, p. 2. On the influence of these tactics see Milton M. Holland to John Sherman, August 26, 31, 1885, Noah Thomas to Sherman, September 21, 1885, Vol. 348, Sherman Papers, Library of Congress; M. D. Tyrell to Joseph B. Foraker, September 21, 1885, Box 3, Foraker Papers.

62. Foraker, *Notes of a Busy Life*, I, 179–82; Asa S. Bushnell to C. L. Kurtz, July 21, 1885, Box 17, Kurtz Papers, Ohio Historical Society; New York *Freeman*, October 24, 1885, p. 2. On the use of Republican funds to soften the hostility of the Cleveland *Gazette* and the Cleveland *Globe*, see Joseph B. Foraker to Mark Hanna, July 2, 1885, Hanna to Foraker, July 7, 14, 1885, in "Correspondence with Senator Hanna, 1884–1903," pp. 18–19, 21, Foraker Papers, Library of Congress.

racial record was if he condoned the bloody tactics that Southern Democrats used against Negroes. As Foraker observed, Hoadly would be lynched by his own party if he preached integration in Dixie. This was indeed the Achilles heel of Northern Democratic racial liberalism.[63] Placed on the defensive, Hoadly deplored appeals to old sectional animosities, and insisted that Southern blacks had stopped voting Republican not on account of intimidation but because of disillusionment with the party.

Hoadly redirected attention to internal Ohio concerns, telling a black audience that the Republican

> Supreme Court, at Washington, held the Republican Civil Rights Bill unconstitutional. Our Democratic Legislature gave you, my colored friends, equal rights with me, and these white men in Ohio—the Democrats did it. Don't you forget that. (Cry, 'you can't get the colored vote that way!') My friend over here says I cannot get the colored vote. Perhaps not; but I know enough to do the colored people justice, whether they vote for me or not. (Cheers)[64]

In October, Foraker defeated Hoadly by over 17,000 votes, a landslide having little if anything to do with racial matters. But the lame-duck Democrat left his state a memorable legacy in his last annual message. He again recommended repeal of laws

> which permit the condemnation of colored children, without accusation or trial, to the punishment of compulsory non-association in the common schools with white children, to education often inferior, and in places inconveniently remote from the residences of their parents. This is a badge of servitude having the effect to degrade, and keenly felt by many most worthy colored people, as in effect stamping them as unworthy of equal privileges.[65]

63. Sherman, *Recollections*, II, 929; James R. Chalmers, *Open Letter to George Hoadly* (Sardis, Miss.: n.p., 1885); Lynch, in Cleveland *Gazette*, October 10, 1885, p. 1. Foraker's use of the bloody shirt is evident in *Joint Debates between Hon. George Hoadly and Hon. Joseph B. Foraker at Toledo, Ohio, October 8, 1885, and Cincinnati, Ohio, October 10, 1885* (Columbus: Ohio State Journal Job Printing Establishment, 1887), pp. 115–16.

64. *Joint Debates*, p. 102.

65. *Tribune Almanac*, 1886, p. 71; *Annual Message of George Hoadly*, 1886, pp. 6–7.

In his inaugural address, Governor Foraker, now well aware of black power in the state, called for an end to the Black Laws, and Negro Republican legislator Benjamin Arnett from Xenia, Greene County, introduced a bill legalizing interracial marriage and integrating the public schools. As a concession to black educators, the Negro schools would remain intact with their teachers, but both these institutions and the white schools would be open to all children. Before the vote in the Republican House of Representatives, Arnett told his colleagues that the bill was bipartisan: Governor Hoadly had made the Democracy an equal partner in the struggle for racial equality, and both parties were competing "as to who shall do the most" for Negroes. Arnett reminded Republicans that "we promised the men who stood by our standard bearers last fall that we would allow no party to do more for the equal rights of men than this grand old political party of righteousness." Jere Brown of Cleveland, the other black Republican member, echoed the warning. "Defeat this bill," he threatened Republicans, "and the wrath of the colored voters will bury you beneath their ballots. . . ." Some Negro teachers, led by the black principal from Zanesville, lobbied against the proposal. The House of Representatives approved the legislation fifty-nine to twenty-five. Six Democrats—five from white counties in northern Ohio and one from the racially mixed town of Portsmouth on the Ohio River—voted for the Arnett bill. One Republican and twenty-four Democrats opposed it; seven of the latter represented southern counties and sizeable Negro constituencies. Two months later Senate Republicans unseated several Democrats and gained control of that body, but three Republican members refused to back the Arnett measure and it did not reach the floor during 1886. In 1887 the Senate voted the bill into law twenty-four to seven. Four Democrats, all from northern Ohio, favored passage, while seven of their comrades, five from the southern counties, opposed it.[66] Although much bipartisan

66. Everett Walters, *Joseph Benson Foraker: An Uncompromising Republican* (Columbus: Ohio State Archeological & Historical Society, 1948), p. 36; Benjamin W. Arnett and Jere A. Brown, *The Black Laws* (n.p.: n.p., 1886), pp. 7–12, 15, 27; Cleveland *Gazette*, April 10, 1886, p. 2; *Journal of the House of Representatives*, 1886, p. 342; Cleveland *Gazette*, May 15, 1886, p. 2, May 29, October

white resistance remained in southern Ohio, the Black Laws were permanently dead. Even when the Democrats recaptured the legislature in 1890 they took no backward step. On the contrary, through the late 1880's and the early 1890's Ohio Democrats carried on Hoadly's policy of friendship toward blacks. In 1891 there were three Negro Democratic newspapers published during the gubernatorial campaign, in Cincinnati, Columbus, and Cleveland.[67]

In 1887 Peter Clark looked back on the three and a half years since Hoadly's election and claimed that events had proven the value of black political independence. For years, he noted, "there was a sort of notion prevalent, that to ask the Republicans of Ohio to do justice to her colored citizens would embarrass the party in its alleged fight against wrongs in the South." Then Hoadly won the governorship, "aided thereto by the votes of sundry thousands of colored 'kickers,' a man who . . . wasted no space in bewailing a condition of our brethren in the South, a condition beyond the control of the Ohio Legislature." The Democratic civil rights measures had forced Republicans to bid for Negro support by offering extensive patronage and more favorable legislation. "If you ask the question of any 'kicker,'" he concluded, "'who abolished the Black Laws?' he will slap himself on the breast and say, 'I did it, with my free ballot.'"[68] This boast was justified.

Racial politics were hardly as exciting in Illinois. When the state legislature met in 1885 to discuss a civil rights bill to replace the federal law, the Democrats controlled the House while the Republicans held the Senate. The Democratic lower chamber passed the measure first, eighty-three to nineteen, as fifteen Democrats voted yea and nineteen nay, while most party legislators abstained. This Democratic vote shows a pattern similar to Ohio's: the seven Democrats representing Chicago, East St.

9, 1886, both p. 1; *Journal of the Senate*, 1887, p. 255. The statute is in *General and Local Laws*, 1887, p. 34.

67. Gerber, "Ohio and the Color Line," I, 222–40; Cleveland *Gazette*, October 12, 1889, p. 4, December 21, 1889, p. 1, September 26, 1891, p. 2, October 31, 1891, p. 1.

68. Clark, in New York *Freeman*, March 26, 1887, p. 2.

Louis, and Springfield, urban centers with large Negro populations, voted for the proposal. Viewed geographically, all seven Democrats from northeastern counties—Cook, Will, and Lake—supported civil rights. Sixteen Democratic opponents came from white counties, and the other three represented rural southwestern counties on the Mississippi River with high black concentrations. The same picture emerges from the Senate roll call. The bill passed thirty-seven to six, as Democrats backed it fourteen to six. All Democrats from the three big cities and the northeastern counties voted with the majority, while all the dissenters were from white counties or southwest Illinois. Six years later the legislature passed a stronger civil rights bill which passed the House unanimously, and the Senate thirty-two to five. Six Democratic senators voted yea; five of them represented Cook and Will Counties or Springfield. The five Democratic opponents all came from rural areas, four in southern Illinois, and none had many Negro constituents. Three Democrats from Mississippi River counties containing many blacks abstained, apparently unable to decide whether to follow local white prejudice or to please the Negroes. The pattern was consistent: urbanization and heavy Negro population in a district would dispose a Democratic representative to favor Negro rights, and the more so the further north the district was.[69]

Negroes got along well with Democrats on the local scene in Chicago, especially when the city was run by Carter Harrison, elected mayor five times between 1879 and 1893. Harrison was a blueblood patrician but knew how to run a political machine with skill and flamboyance. Born into a prominent Kentucky slaveholding family, Harrison moved to Chicago before the Civil War. While amassing a fortune in real estate, he got elected to the Cook County Commission after the great Chicago fire of 1871. One of his colleagues was John Jones, a mulatto, and Har-

69. Illinois, *Journal of the House of Representatives*, 1885, p. 447; *ibid.*, 1891, pp. 944–45; *Journal of the Senate*, 1885, p. 872; *ibid.*, 1891, p. 1122. Racial makeup of counties is seen in *Eleventh Census*, I, 407–9. The two laws are codified in Illinois, *Laws*, 1885, pp. 64–65, and 1891, pp. 85–86.

rison was surprised to find that "although I am a prominent Democrat and from the South . . . I have more influence with my friend Jones than any man in the board. . . ."[70] Harrison used this talent for attracting black admiration when he ran for mayor. He always appealed to the "folklore or history, condition or aspiration" of the particular ethnic group he was addressing, and would go so far as to claim membership in the group. Harrison told black audiences of his Kentucky background and "was proud to state that he had been nursed by a Negro 'mammy,' and that (quickly twisting a bit of hair on his finger) he had a little kink in his hair."[71] But his popularity among blacks was based on more than charm. He gave the race substantial patronage in the police and fire departments, hired the city's first black public librarian, and appointed a Negro as a city health inspector. Harrison even had the audacity to assign black policemen to guard the doors of the Democratic National Convention of 1884 which was held in Chicago, infuriating Southern delegates who had to show their credentials to these policemen before gaining admittance.[72]

Indiana, a stronghold of Democratic resistance to Negro rights during Reconstruction, continued to lag behind the other Northern states. Through the 1870's Hoosier Democrats charged Republicans with importing Southern blacks to vote in close elections. By the end of the decade this Democratic tactic ballooned into something far more serious: a subtle revival of appeals to white supremacist feeling. In the summer of 1879 some North Carolina blacks filtered into Indiana, explaining that they could not make ends meet in the South. Indiana Democrats put out no welcome mat. On the contrary, they charged a new Republican plot to gain political control of the state by bringing in hordes

70. *National Cyclopaedia of American Biography*, X, 144–45; Carter Harrison to "Dear Will," April 21, 1872, Carter Harrison Papers, Newberry Library, Chicago.

71. *Current Topics*, December, 1893, clipping in Harrison Papers; Claudius O. Johnson, *Carter Harrison I: Political Leader* (Chicago: University of Chicago Press, 1928), p. 98.

72. Cairo *Gazette*, quoted in Washington *Bee*, April 14, 1883, p. 3; Cleveland *Gazette*, March 2, 1884, p. 2; New York *Globe*, July 19, 1884, p. 2.

of Negroes. This would put "the white labor of Indiana . . . into direct competition with negro labor," depressing wages.[73] Greeley's old antagonist, Daniel Voorhees, was now a U.S. senator, and he insisted that a Senate committee, chaired by himself, investigate this "exodus" of Southern blacks. Looking toward the 1880 election, the committee's Democratic majority accused Republicans of a "conspiracy to . . . degrade her [Indiana's] laboring men and women by an association with the pauper blacks of the South." Despite the fact that few Negroes were emigrating to Indiana, state Democrats decided to play up the issue "even if not exactly true."[74] But the Hoosiers were careful to tone down the racial implications of this appeal. Senator Voorhees said several times that his party welcomed any outsider who came freely, only objecting to artificial migration induced for political purposes, and the Indiana Democratic platform of 1880 echoed this distinction.[75] Indeed, there already was a Negro Democratic club in Indianapolis, and in 1879, at the outset of the "exodus" scare, Democrats in that city nominated a black for the office of marshal.[76]

Overt political racism in the state Democracy declined by the mid-1880's. In response to the Supreme Court's decision in the Civil Rights Cases, the Democratic Indiana legislature passed a state civil rights law in 1885. The House approved it unanimously, and the Senate favored it thirty-six to five. All five

73. Indianapolis *Sentinel*, July 30, October 24, November 6, 20, 1879, all p. 4. Quotation from November 20 issue.

74. U.S. Senate, *Report and Testimony of the Select Committee of the United States Senate to Investigate the Causes of the Removal of the Negro from the Southern States to the Northern States*, Senate Report 693, 46 Cong., 2 sess., 1880, pp. ii–viii; Voorhees, in *Congressional Record*, 46 Cong., 2 sess., p. 4146 (June 4, 1880); J. H. Rhea to William H. English, September 7, 1880, English Papers. For proof that even the chairman of the Democratic National Committee did not take the charge seriously, see William H. Barnum to English, August 10, 1800, English Papers.

75. Voorhees, in Cincinnati *Enquirer*, November 27, 1879, p. 5; *Congressional Record*, 46 Cong., 2 sess., pp. 156, 158, 4148 (December 18, 1879, June 4, 1880); *Appleton's Annual Cyclopaedia*, 1880, p. 396. On the entire episode consult John G. Van Deusen, "Did the Republicans 'Colonize' Indiana in 1879?" *Indiana Magazine of History*, XXX (December, 1934), 335–46.

76. Thornbrough, *The Negro in Indiana before 1900*, p. 300; Cincinnati *Enquirer*, April 13, 1879, p. 1.

recalcitrants were Democrats from white counties; party law-makers representing areas of high black population—India-napolis, Terre Haute, and the Ohio River counties—voted yea. Again, the presence of a substantial Negro constituency seemed to soften opposition to a civil rights bill. The North-South factor and urbanization, important in Ohio and Illinois, played a smaller role in this Indiana roll call.[77]

Meanwhile Democrats and Negroes enjoyed good relations in Indianapolis, where the blacks composed 8.5 percent of the population, a far larger proportion than in the other large Northern cities. The politician who did most to bring Negroes into the Democratic camp was Thomas Taggart. Born in Ireland and raised in Xenia, Ohio, he "possessed an unusually striking and magnetic personality, with a marked kindliness, generosity and good-will which gained him a host of friends and life-long admirers in every walk of life." He first campaigned for county auditor in 1886. "Up to this time," notes his biographer, "negro festivals were considered 'pudding' to which the Republicans had sole claim." Republican politicians had just been to a black fair and had brought some "berries and ice cream" when Democrat Taggart walked in. " 'How much ice cream have you got, auntie?' he asked one of those in charge. He bought it all, and all the berries and all the cake as well. 'Now everyone come up and eat,' he called, 'this treat is on me.' "

After his election, Taggart hired many Negro clerks and did countless small favors for members of the race. For example, when a Negro excursion party could not pay a railroad company what it owed, Taggart guaranteed payment and shrugged the matter off: "What of it . . . the colored people have always been very friendly to me, and I merely want security for them."[78]

77. Indiana, *Journal of the House of Representatives*, 1885, p. 1119; *Journal of the State Senate*, 1885, p. 268. Before passage there was a bewildering series of roll calls on various amended versions of the bill which defy analysis. The text of the statute is in Indiana, *Laws*, 1885, Ch. 47, while the state's racial demography is available from *Eleventh Census*, I, 409–10.

78. Black percentage of city population in 1880 can be calculated from *Tenth Census*, I, 416–24. In contrast to the Indianapolis situation, Boston, Brooklyn, New York City, and Chicago were less than 2 percent black, and Cincinnati and Philadelphia a bit over 3 percent. On Taggart's background see *National*

When he ran for reelection in 1890, one of the two Indianapolis Negro papers, the *World*, supported the entire Democratic ticket, while the other, the *Freeman*, came out half-heartedly for the Republicans, while predicting that Taggart "will be elected auditor not only because the men of his party will elect him, but because black men like, and honor him as well. . . . To the colored people of Indianapolis and vicinity, Thomas Taggart is not a Democrat any more than he is a Republican; he is something better, 'A man, A good man.' " [79]

The Democrats swept Indiana in 1890, and for years thereafter Indianapolis Negroes voted with extreme independence, especially in Taggart's three successful campaigns for mayor. He publicly acknowledged in 1896 that he was "indebted to his colored friends for much of his success, and many favors." Negroes, in return, expressed gratitude in 1897 to the man who "has given employment to hundreds of colored men thereby enabling them to earn a living for their families." [80] The Democrats of Indiana, like their counterparts in other Northern states, had come a considerable way since Reconstruction.

Some Generalizations

Though receiving little attention from commentators at the time and even less from historians since, the transformation of Democratic racial policy in several important Northern states was a more significant new departure than Vallandigham's movement of 1871. Here was a party whose basic tactic through the 1860's had been race baiting, a party which had acquiesced in the Reconstruction amendments with reluctance in 1871–72

Cyclopaedia of American Biography, XXII, 430. Xenia had a large Negro community, and Taggart's good relations with the race perhaps had their origin there. The incident of 1886 is recounted by Charles Sallee, in "Tom Taggart: Evolution of the Sandwich Man," p. 12, unpublished typescript, Taggart Papers, Indiana Division, Indiana State Library. For his friendship with Negroes once elected, see Indianapolis *Freeman*, July 12, 1890, p. 5, September 20, 1890, p. 2.

79. Indianapolis *Freeman*, August 23, 1890, p. 8, October 11, 1890, pp. 4, 5.

80. *Ibid.*, December 6, 1890, p. 4; Thornbrough, *The Negro in Indiana before 1900*, pp. 312–13; Indianapolis *News*, October 6, 1896, Indianapolis *Sentinel*, August 30, 1897, clippings in Taggart Scrapbooks, Taggart Papers.

only to hamstring their enforcement thereafter. But by the 1880's this same Democratic organization was competing with Republicans for the favor of Northern Negroes. Whence this change?

Black political leverage played a role. Democrats risked little by exploiting negrophobia when the race was unenfranchised, but after ratification of the Fifteenth Amendment even the most prejudiced politico would think twice before alienating a racial bloc that might decide the next election. All of the states where Negro-Democratic rapprochement occurred were to some degree "close" states: elections in Connecticut, Indiana, New Jersey, New York, and Ohio were hotly contested throughout the period, while politics in Illinois, Massachusetts, Pennsylvania, and Rhode Island become truly competitive only by the late 1880's. In a situation of political uncertainty, when majorities could swing either way, the small black vote, which ranged in 1890 from 1 percent of the total in Massachusetts to 3.3 percent in New Jersey, might mean much. It is no surprise, then, that Democratic state legislators tended to favor civil rights measures in proportion to the number of Negroes residing in their districts, and that Democratic leaders in big cities with substantial black populations befriended the race.[81] Historians interested in tracing the forces behind the twentieth-century civil rights struggle stress the role of black movement from the South to Northern cities which by the 1930's enabled Negroes to exert political pressure on both parties. But in fact Northern blacks enjoyed a measure of this strategic leverage in the 1880's, before the great migration from the South.

Nevertheless, this "black balance of power" idea that Senator Sumner and Negro independents advocated in the 1870's is not by itself adequate to explain the course of events in the late

81. Party balance in these states can be gauged from election statistics in *Tribune Almanac*, 1873–93, while the entrance of more Northern states into the "doubtful" column in the late 1880's is noted in Robert D. Marcus, *Grand Old Party: Political Structure in the Gilded Age,1880–1896* (New York: Oxford University Press, 1971), pp. 19, 151–52. Ohio was an anomaly, staunchly Republican in presidential years, but up for grabs at other elections. Negro percentages of state population are available in Bureau of the Census, *Negro Population, 1790–1915*, p. 51, while note 78 above cites some city statistics.

nineteenth century. The race's vote was decisive in theory only; it did not regularly determine Northern election results during the Gilded Age except in Indiana, where each presidential and gubernatorial contest between 1876 and 1892 was won by a margin smaller than the number of black voters. Republicans carried Ohio in national elections by less than the Negro vote only in 1876 and 1892, and slight Democratic majorities in state elections occurred when Ohio blacks were discontented (1873 and 1883). The only time Illinois Republicans needed the Negro electorate to win was in 1876, and then only for the state ticket, not the presidential contest. In the Eastern states, Pennsylvania Republicans elected a governor in 1875 by less than the Negro vote; New York gave its electoral vote to Cleveland in the presidential race of 1884 by a razor-thin margin that could have been the result of black respect for the man; and Connecticut elections in the late 1880's, state and national, went Democratic by few enough votes to raise the possibility of a decisive black role. The sum total of this is hardly a Negro balance of power.[82] And if, as the statistics show, the Indiana black vote was always crucial, why did the Democracy of that state continue its racist appeals long after such tactics were discarded elsewhere? The Indiana example shows that a competitive political situation, far from automatically inducing Democratic friendliness to Negroes, might impel the party to hold fast to the tried and true strategy of Reconstruction days, exploitation of white prejudice in some form. The closeness of elections, then, cannot stand as a monolithic explanation for Democratic policy.

Statistical data other than election results suggest additional reasons for the decline in Democratic appeals to race prejudice after the new departure. Wartime Democratic politicians in the East and especially the Midwest whipped up negrophobic fears

82. Election results, federal and state, are in *Tribune Almanac*, 1873–93, although presidential votes are more conveniently available by state in Burnham, *Presidential Ballots*, pp. 246–49. The number of black voters per state in any given election is the number of Negroes in that state as of the nearest federal census, divided by five. William Gillette, in an epilogue appended to the second edition of *The Right to Vote*, pp. 182–84, attempts a similar analysis, but his exaggerated estimates of the Northern black vote lead him to overemphasize its importance in deciding elections.

that Northern states would be overrun by Southern blacks if Republican policy prevailed, but this proved a false prophecy. Between 1870 and 1890 the black percentage of the population in Rhode Island, Connecticut, and New Jersey declined, while remaining stable in Massachusetts, New York, and Ohio, and advancing infinitesimally in Illinois and Pennsylvania. Even the proportion of Negroes in Indiana rose only six-tenths of a percent, despite the hue and cry about the "exodus." The number of Southern black migrants to the North decreased in absolute terms during these two decades. Failure of "invasion" predictions took much of the wind out of Democratic white-supremacist sails.[83] Midwestern white demographic patterns perhaps also played some role. Men of Southern origin shaped the prewar Democratic party in Ohio, Indiana, and Illinois. But after 1860 white movement from Dixie slowed, probably diluting the influence of Southern racial attitudes on the state parties. According to the 1870 census, the percentage of Southern-born whites in the total native white population was 5 percent in Ohio and 10 percent in both Indiana and Illinois. Twenty years later these figures dropped to 3, 4.1, and 5 percent.[84] Of course, Dixie influence did remain. As noted earlier, much of the diehard Democratic hostility to Midwestern civil rights bills came from counties settled by Southerners.

Another way to explain the change in Democratic racial policy is through analysis of the backgrounds and attitudes of party leaders. During the 1860's and up to the Greeley campaign of 1872 the race issue was a crucial line of demarcation between Republicans and Democrats. Whatever their inconsistencies and waverings, Republicans as a group were on the side of the Negro, and Democrats were against him. But new departure politics and the end of Reconstruction changed that: by the 1880's Re-

83. On Democratic use of the "invasion" scare, see especially Voegeli, *Free But Not Equal*, and Trissal, *Public Men of Indiana*, I, 70–71. The relative stability of black percentages of Northern state populations and the actual decline in the number of Southern Negroes coming North is evident from Bureau of the Census, *Negro Population*, pp. 51, 65.

84. *Ninth Census*, I, 328–35; *Eleventh Census*, I, 564–67. See the lament of an old-time Indiana Democratic politician in David Turpie, *Sketches of My Own Times* (Indianapolis: Bobbs-Merrill, 1903), p. 261.

publicans had retreated from equal rights, and Democrats had advanced beyond blatant racist tactics. With the cooling of wartime passions came a decline in the partisan importance of the race question; no longer could one generalize about a man's stand on Negro rights simply by examining his party label.[85]

The passage of time affected Democratic leadership in several ways. First, with the national Democracy pledging constant allegiance to black civil and political equality, it was not hard for an old race-baiter like Governor Abbett of New Jersey to change his stripes and become a proponent of civil rights on the state level. Also, several Democratic proponents of racial liberalism in the 1880's rose to high party rank after 1871. For Governors Cleveland and Hill of New York, Pattison of Pennsylvania, Waller of Connecticut, and Mayors Harrison of Chicago, King of Philadelphia, Taggart of Indianapolis, and Chapin of Brooklyn, the Civil War and Reconstruction were ancient history in which they had taken a negligible part, if any. They were men of the new departure generation and had no background of political racism to repudiate.[86]

Equally crucial was the flow of former Republicans into the Democracy after 1872. One of these men, veteran Indiana Free-Soiler George W. Julian, told a friend that as early as the 1876 election "the great majority of the people with whom you and I used to do battle against Slavery were for Tilden and Hendricks." He was exaggerating, but in succeeding years ex-Republicans took an increasingly prominent place in Democratic ranks: Ohio Democrats, for example, adopted an unwritten rule beginning in 1877 to nominate only former Republicans for governor.[87] While

85. Thus veteran Indiana Democrat Thomas Hendricks, a former senator and governor, said privately in 1880 of an old abolitionist: "He was right . . . and we were wrong." Stoll, *History of the Indiana Democracy*, p. 310.

86. Dates of birth for these men and the years they entered politics are available in Allen Johnson and Dumas Malone, eds., *Dictionary of American Biography* (New York: Charles Scribner's Sons, 1928–36), in the articles about them. Mayor Chapin of Brooklyn, not included in that work, is covered in *National Cyclopaedia of American Biography*, I, 525–26.

87. Julian to G. Swisshelm, February 14, 1877, Vol. 6, Giddings-Julian Papers, Library of Congress; Moore, "Ohio in National Politics," p. 281.

Hoadly of Ohio and Butler of Massachusetts, Democrats with Republican pasts, showed special sensitivity to black desires, there were others of the same type. John M. Palmer was a Republican governor of Illinois during Reconstruction and a proponent of Negro rights. He switched parties in the 1870's, taking a leadership role in the state Democracy which elected him to the Senate in 1891. During his Democratic years Palmer provided legal counsel for Illinois blacks trying to desegregate the public schools of Alton and Quincy. In Indiana the change since Reconstruction was demonstrated dramatically. The Democratic governor who signed the state's civil rights law of 1885 was Isaac Gray—the same man who, as a Republican legislator fifteen years earlier, had locked the state senate doors on his Democratic colleagues and pocketed the key to effect ratification of the Fifteenth Amendment.[88] Republican movement into the Democracy was probably self-reinforcing. As some Republicans entered in the 1870's and changed the party's racial image, even more were attracted. Thus a decline in Democratic appeals to white supremacist prejudice might win the favor of white Republicans, not just blacks. This had a national implication as well. By the early 1890's partisan distinctions on race would be so unclear that Republicans, no longer monopolizing the forces of racial justice, would find it impossible to rally the North behind a renewed enforcement of Southern Negro rights, which Democrats consistently fought on states' rights grounds.

Determining motivation in politics is notoriously difficult, and the question of why Northern Democratic leaders favored Negro rights by the 1880's is no exception. To what extent was it a bid for votes on the one hand, or an expression of principle on

88. On Palmer, see *Personal Recollections of John M. Palmer: The Story of an Earnest Life* (Cincinnati: Robert Clarke, 1901), pp. 324–32; George Thomas Palmer, *A Conscientious Turncoat: The Story of John M. Palmer, 1817–1900* (New Haven: Yale University Press, 1941), pp. 225–26; Topeka *Colored Citizen*, October 4, 1879, p. 2. On Gray, consult Trissal, *Public Men of Indiana*, I, 69. Another example of a Republican, this one a radical Massachusetts abolitionist, who switched parties but never attained high office is treated in Tilden G. Edelstein, *Strange Enthusiasm: A Life of Thomas Wentworth Higginson* (New Haven: Yale University Press, 1968).

the other? Democrats did not wear their motives on their sleeves, and in public they explained their action as "right" rather than expedient.[89] George Hoadly was the only racially progressive Northerner whose private correspondence on the matter survives today. Though Hoadly's Free Soil past made him somewhat atypical of the entire group, he admits to a mixture of motives that presumably characterized the rest in varying degrees. In a February, 1885, letter to Grover Cleveland's private secretary, Hoadly urged greater Democratic friendship toward blacks "for the sake of peace and justice, as well as from the motives of mere policy." The next month Hoadly wrote again; after explaining the political benefits of winning Negro support in close states, he added: "I am not, however, unmindful that God has made of one blood all the children of men. This is part of my religion, as well as my politics."[90] Probably Hoadly and other Democrats with the same Republican pro-Negro background, like Palmer, brought more idealism and less opportunism to the search for black favor than did an old exploiter of racism like Abbett. Also, "aristocratic" political types like Cleveland, Hoadly, Palmer, Pattison, and Waller on the state level, as well as Mayors Chapin, King, and Thacher, were influenced more by noblesse oblige paternalism and less by pragmatism than were spoilsmen Abbett, Butler, and Hill, and the big city machines.[91] But, as Hoadly said, both the principle of human equality and practical political considerations pointed the same way: patronage and favorable legislation for the Northern Negro.

Another point of interest is whether Democratic race policy influenced many Negroes. Was black independence a political reality, or was it confined to editorials and letters in the Negro

89. For example, the statement by Carter Harrison that he was good to blacks "because I think it right," and that he did not "care a continental" whether they supported him. New York *Globe*, September 6, 1884, p. 4.

90. Hoadly to Daniel S. Lamont, February 10, March 28, 1885, Reels 5 and 9, Cleveland Papers.

91. The best way to differentiate between the "aristocrats" and the "spoilsmen" is where they stood on William Jennings Bryan in 1896. Virtually all the "aristocrats," according to the *Dictionary of American Biography* sketches, did not back Bryan, while the machines did. Abbett died before that election, but probably, like Hill, he would have supported the ticket. Carter Harrison, assassinated in 1893, is a more doubtful case, because he belonged to both political worlds.

press? Men at the time did not know, except in the vaguest terms. Governor Hoadly believed that in 1883 he received the votes of "from three to seven thousand" out of a black electorate of 16,000, and Negro lawyer T. McCants Stewart reported that a third of Brooklyn blacks voted Democratic in the mayoral election of 1889.[92] Such estimates were nothing more than guesses, and the modern historian is no wiser because there were not enough Negroes in the North before the 1890's to create any "black" election districts. Pulaski County in southern Illinois, one-third Negro, had the highest black concentration of any county in the North; there the margin of Republican victory rose from 410 in the 1882 state election to 717 four years later. In Ohio, scene of the strongest Democratic attempts to win the black vote, the county with the highest percentage of Negroes was Greene, about one-sixth black; here too Republican majorities jumped from 1,892 votes in 1883 to 2,385 in 1885, despite Hoadly's exertions. The Republican gains in both Pulaski and Greene corresponded to statewide trends in Illinois and Ohio during these years.[93] Such statistics must be treated with caution because heavy white transfers from Democratic to Republican ranks might mask Negro movement in the other direction, but the data do not support the assumption of black defections from Republicanism. And yet the evidence of increased Negro independence, though impressionistic rather than statistically verifiable, cannot be ignored. Politicians at the time took it seriously, Democrats seeing opportunity, Republicans fearing danger.

Historians have heretofore missed the significance of the Northern state civil rights legislation enacted after the Supreme Court struck down the federal law in 1883. Not only has no one analyzed seriously how and why these measures were passed, but the importance of the statutes themselves has been downgraded because they allegedly brought few tangible benefits to

92. Hoadly to Daniel S. Lamont, March 28, 1885, Reel 9, T. McCants Stewart to Grover Cleveland, November 7, 1889, Reel 68, Cleveland Papers.

93. For the racial demography of these counties, see *Tenth Census*, I, 388, 404. Election results are in *Tribune Almanac*, 1887, pp. 56–57; *ibid.*, 1886, pp. 70–71.

blacks.[94] Close study of the sources shows that these civil rights acts got on the books largely owing to changes in Northern Democratic race policy. With that party seeking the black voter's favor through legislative and patronage inducements that would have shocked Democrats a generation earlier, the Republicans could not remain complacent. Thus, regardless of how well or badly the civil rights laws were enforced, their bipartisan passage was evidence that by the mid-1880's the Northern Negro electorate had achieved a small but real measure of political power in some states, and could on occasion compel both parties to contend for black support in state and local contests. It was an open question, however, whether the Democratic policy of conciliating the Negro would remain a Northern monopoly, or whether the national organization, with its strong Southern wing, would also adopt it.

94. Valeria Weaver, "The Failure of Civil Rights, 1875–1883, and Its Repercussions," *Journal of Negro History*, LIV (October, 1969), 368–82; August Meier and Elliott Rudwick, *From Plantation to Ghetto*, rev. ed. (New York: Hill and Wang, 1970), pp. 188–89.

4

A Democratic President
1884-89

In 1884, after almost a quarter-century of Republicans in the White House, one of the racially progressive Northern Democratic governors, Grover Cleveland of New York, was elected President of the United States. His first term, coinciding with the passage of much of the Northern state civil rights legislation, was a test of whether the new Democratic friendship for Negroes was transferable to national politics. Specifically, how would Cleveland deal with racial tension in the South? Would he influence Democratic congressmen to support legislation benefiting Negroes? Would the federal bureaucracy become lily-white, or would it continue to employ blacks? Answers to these questions indicate that the Democratic new departure, as it had developed by the mid-1880's, was still limited in its application.[1]

Democrats had reason to treat the race issue with care in the national campaign of 1884. James G. Blaine received the Republican nomination for president, and his questionable financial dealings while a congressman alienated many Republicans who loathed political corruption. These independent Republicans (or Mugwumps) were likely converts to the Democracy; but, since a good number of them came from abolitionist or strong anti-slavery backgrounds, they could only join the Demo-

---

1. Historians have neglected this aspect of Cleveland's administration. Neither Nevins, *Cleveland*, nor Horace Samuel Merrill, *Bourbon Leader: Grover Cleveland and the Democratic Party* (Boston: Little, Brown, 1957), deals with it. The chapter on Cleveland in George Sinkler, *The Racial Attitudes of American Presidents from Lincoln to Theodore Roosevelt* (Garden City: Doubleday, 1972), barely scratches the surface.

cratic camp if the party's nominee to oppose Blaine was free of association with the backward-looking Democracy of Civil War and Reconstruction days. Such a standard-bearer might also win the support of blacks, who were already considering the benefits of political independence at the state and local level. The Democratic national platform pledged "equal and exact justice to all citizens of whatever nativity, race, color, or persuasion," and declared for "a free ballot and a fair count," while mocking the Republicans for preaching racial equality before the law when it was a Republican Supreme Court that had set aside the Civil Rights Act of 1875.[2] The choice of Cleveland, who had entered politics after Reconstruction, to oppose Blaine would muffle the sectional issue and allow Democrats to concentrate on the questions of civil service reform and honesty in government. In listing Cleveland's accomplishments, Democratic campaign literature always mentioned his approval of the bill that "in fact wiped out the color and race line" in New York City schools, a piece of information that did not go down well with Cleveland's white supporters in the South.[3] Blaine subordinated the race issue to the tariff until the closing days of the campaign; this enabled the few black Democrats working for Cleveland to argue that Republicans had abandoned South-

2. A recent study of the Mugwumps is John G. Sproat, *"The Best Men": Liberal Reformers in the Gilded Age* (New York: Oxford University Press, 1968), while Hirshson, *Bloody Shirt*, pp. 126–31, explains their position on the race question in 1884. Black expectation of Democratic blandishments is seen in Frederick Douglass, *Address of Hon. Frederick Douglass delivered in the Congregational Church, Washington, D.C., April 10, 1883* (Washington: n.p., 1883), p. 6, and George L. Ruffin to John D. Long, December 26, 1883, Box 12, Long Papers. The platform is in Porter and Johnson, eds., *Party Platforms*, p. 66.

3. Some Democratic tracts mentioning Governor Cleveland's racial record are *The Political Reformation of 1884: A Democratic Campaign Text Book* (New York: National Democratic Committee, 1884), p. 73; *Grover Cleveland, the Open Record of an Honest Man* (n.p.; n.p., 1884), p. 30; Deshler Welsh, *Stephen Grover Cleveland: A Sketch of His Life* (New York: R. Worthington, 1884), p. 89, [Indiana] Democratic State Central Committee, *An Indiana Democratic Scrapbook for the Campaign of 1884* (Indianapolis: Carlon and Hollenbeck, 1884), p. 198. For Southern Democratic dismay, see Washington *Post*, November 1, 1884, p. 1, clipping in Container 80, Edward McPherson Scrapbooks, Library of Congress, and Nelson J. Waterbury to Grover Cleveland, January 1, 1885, Reel 4, Cleveland Papers.

ern Negroes. Most of the race was uninfluenced by the charge, continuing to believe that, no matter what the Northern Democracy had done for them on the state and local scene, a national Democratic victory meant disaster.[4]

When Cleveland defeated Blaine in November, black leaders and newspapers took the result in stride and hoped for the best. But many lower-class Southern Negroes, certain that their fortunes were bound up with the Republican party, were pessimistic. According to the exaggerated reports of nervous Southern whites, some blacks quit work, fearing disfranchisement and even reenslavement. Wild, unsubstantiated rumors spread that Negroes in the District of Columbia planned to assassinate Cleveland before his inauguration. Passions rose higher when Blaine, after having concentrated on the tariff through most of the campaign, charged in a post-election speech that intimidation of Southern Negroes had cost him victory. Former Confederates, he alleged, were unrepentant rebels who still persecuted the black man.[5]

4. Republican strategy is discussed by Hirshson in *Bloody Shirt*, pp. 124–26. Negro pro-Cleveland activity can be followed in New York *Globe*, September 13, October 4, 1884, both p. 1; Cincinnati *Afro-American*, reprinted in Harrisburg *State Sentinel*, September 27, October 11, 1884, both p. 2; Cleveland *Gazette*, September 13, October 4, 1884, both p. 2; New York State Colored Democratic Association, *To the Qualified Voters of the State and County of New York, and to the General Public* (New York: n.p., 1884), available at Chicago Historical Society. Mainstream Negro Republicanism was expressed in Washington *Bee*, July 26, September 6, 1884, both p. 2; New York *Globe*, October 4, 1884, p. 1; Edwin F. Horn to Benjamin Harrison, April 21, 1884, Reel 5, Harrison Papers, Library of Congress.

5. The attitudes of black leaders after the election are seen in the contributions of Douglass, Pinchback, Fortune, Downing, Clark, Still, and others to a symposium on "The Democratic Return to Power—Its Effect?" *African Methodist Episcopal Church Review*, I (January, 1885), 213–50, and in the Negro press: Huntsville *Gazette*, November 15, 1884, p. 2; New York *Freeman*, November 29, December 6, 1884, both p. 2; Washington *Bee*, November 22, 1884, p. 2; Cleveland *Gazette*, December 6, 1884, p. 2. Southern black fears are noted in John L. T. Snead to Daniel S. Lamont, November 17, 1884, John E. Develin to Grover Cleveland, Arthur Hood to Cleveland, Merrit E. Sawyer to Cleveland, November 19, 1884, Reel 2, Cleveland Papers. The assassination rumor is in James R. Doolittle to Daniel Manning, November 8, 1884, copy, Box 5, Doolittle Papers; Anonymous to F. J. Porter, November 17, 1884, Porter to Cleveland, November 19, 1884, Reel 2, Cleveland Papers. For Blaine's speech see New York *World*, November 19, 1884, p. 1.

To counteract Blaine's inflammatory words and to reassure Negroes, Cleveland granted an interview on the Southern question to an Associated Press reporter. He expressed surprise "that there was an apprehension existing among the colored people, that in some way the rights now secured to them under the laws and Constitution of the United States were in danger from the election of a Democratic President." Cleveland called such fears "absurd" and "foolish," noting that a change in the race's legal status could be effected only through an alteration of the Constitution "which it would be absolutely impossible to make." Even were such a step feasible, he was pledged to maintain the rights of all and intended to do just that. Referring to Blaine's recent utterance, the victorious candidate concluded that it would be better for the country "if mischievous croakings and dark imaginings should give place to an earnest endeavor to inspire confidence and to make universal a cheerful hope for the future." Despite these conciliatory words, Southern Negroes remained apprehensive.[6]

One month after the election, Republicans in the House of Representatives gave the Democrats, who held a majority in the chamber, an opportunity to declare themselves on Negro rights. In the midst of debate on proposed legislation regulating interstate commerce, James O'Hara, a black Republican from North Carolina, proposed the following amendment: "And any person or persons having purchased a ticket to be conveyed from one State to another, or paid the required fare, shall receive the same treatment and be afforded equal facilities and accommodations as are furnished all other persons holding tickets of the same class without discrimination." Though Democrat John Reagan of Texas, who had sponsored the interstate commerce proposal, argued that the amendment was not germane to his bill (which dealt with freight rates and not treatment of passengers), O'Hara's suggestion passed 133 to 98, as

6. Cleveland quoted in Edward McPherson, ed., *Handbook of Politics for 1886* (Washington: James J. Chapman, 1886), pp. 115–16; C. Augustus Haviland to Cleveland, November 27, 1884, Abram S. Hewitt to Cleveland, December 1, 1884, Reel 2, Cleveland Papers.

Northern Democrats supported the amendment by a more than two-to-one ratio. Pointing out that O'Hara's vague phraseology could imply actual integration or separate-but-equal, a Southerner suggested another amendment allowing railroads to differentiate between passengers "for the public comfort and safety." This Breckinridge proposal which in effect authorized segregation passed, 137 to 131; Northern Democrats supported it by a two-to-one margin. Nathan Goff, a white West Virginia Republican, tacked on still another amendment insuring "that no discrimination is made on account of race or color" which passed, 141 to 102. Excluding Far Westerners, over two-thirds of the Northern Democrats approved Goff's suggestion. Ethelbert Barksdale, a Mississippi Democrat, proposed yet another addition to the bill asserting "that furnishing separate accommodations with equal facilities, at the same charges, shall not be considered a discrimination." This separate-but-equal formula passed, 132 to 124; Northeastern and Midwestern Democratic members supported it thirty-nine to nineteen.

TABLE 2. *Democratic Votes on Amendments to Reagan Bill, December 17, 1884*[7]

	O'Hara		Breckinridge		Goff		Barksdale	
	Yes	No	Yes	No	Yes	No	Yes	No
New England	4	0	3	2	4	1	4	1
Middle Atlantic	12	6	9	10	10	6	13	6
Midwest	24	11	29	12	26	11	22	12
Far West	3	3	7	0	0	5	7	0
Border	3	27	32	2	2	28	33	3
South	1	51	57	0	2	51	52	1
Total	47	98	137	26	44	102	131	23

Democratic proponents of the original Reagan bill accused Republicans of initiating these extraneous amendments in order to doom the legislation,[8] and certainly a number of the Democratic and Republican votes in favor of equal treatment of the

7. *Congressional Record*, 48 Cong., 2 sess., pp. 296–97, 317, 321–23, 332–33 (December 16–18, 1884).
8. *Ibid.*, pp. 316–19 (December 17, 1884).

races came from opponents of the bill who hoped to make it unacceptable to Southerners. Nevertheless, these roll calls shed light both on the contrasting racial attitudes of the two parties and on significant variations within Democratic ranks over this issue. The Republicans placed themselves on record as a party against racial discrimination of any kind in interstate transportation. The only Republican to break ranks was a Mississippian who supported the Barksdale amendment. Democrats from the South, border states, and Far West were almost as united in opposition to any federal interference with the discriminatory acts practiced by Southern railroads. Northeastern and Midwestern Democrats held a middle position. About two-thirds of them were ready to outlaw inferior facilities for Negroes while condoning separation of the races, but approximately one-third accepted the Republican position and voted against the separate-but-equal system. This latter group behaved rather consistently as a bloc. Of the nineteen Northern Democrats opposing the Barksdale Amendment, fourteen had voted for the O'Hara proposal and two against it, fourteen had disapproved of the Breckinridge formula while five had favored it, and fifteen had voted yea on the Goff version with none voting nay. The black press applauded the relative independence of Northern Democrats from the Southerners, considering the roll calls an auspicious prelude to the new Democratic administration.[9]

Cleveland's inaugural address delivered on March 4, 1885, also seemed to augur well:

> In the administration of a government pledged to do equal and exact justice to all men there should be no pretext for anxiety touching the protection of the freedmen in their rights or their security in the enjoyment of their privileges under the Constitution and its amendments. All discussion as to their fitness for the place accorded to them as American citizens is idle and unprofitable except as it suggests the necessity for their improvement. The fact that they are citizens entitles them to all the rights due

9. New York *Freeman*, December 20, 1884, p. 2, December 27, 1884, p. 1; Cleveland *Gazette*, December 27, 1884, p. 1; Washington *Bee*, December 27, 1884, p. 2.

to that relation and charges them with all its duties, obligations, and responsibilities.[10]

With a Democrat in the White House, a major concern of blacks was whether the change in administrations would bring with it a change in the racial situation below the Mason-Dixon Line. While Cleveland's Southern policy proved to be squarely within the new departure tradition of barring federal involvement, thus leaving the ruling Conservative white Democrats in control, by the time he took office such an approach differed little from the contemporary Republican attitude. The Hayes administration had ended military intervention in 1877, but encouraged federal district attorneys to prosecute violators of the Civil Rights and Enforcement Acts after the 1878 elections. By the early 1880's Supreme Court decisions had struck down or weakened much of the legislation passed during Reconstruction, and the South, controlled by Redeemer governments, was relatively free from overt violence. President Arthur's attorney general, after an ineffective attempt to prosecute a federal election case, lost interest in such matters, and Arthur himself ignored this aspect of the Southern problem. Democrat Cleveland, adhering to his party's traditional doctrine of home rule for the states, followed the same passive Southern policy. While instructing his attorney general to execute the election laws "so far as these subjects are by the Constitution and laws, under the supervision and control of the Executive branch of the Government," there were no prosecutions.[11] The most serious racial outbreak during Cleveland's term occurred, not at an election, but in a local courtroom at Carrolton, Mississippi, in the spring of 1886: twelve Negroes were murdered in cold blood. When Negro leaders spoke to Cleveland about it, he termed the incident a "blight to our civilization" and expressed surprise that

10. James D. Richardson, ed., *A Compilation of the Messages and Papers of the Presidents, 1789–1897* (Washington: U.S. Government Printing Office, 1897), VIII, 302.

11. On Hayes and Arthur see Hirshson, *Bloody Shirt*, pp. 45–62, 100–103. Supreme Court decisions are summarized in Logan, *Betrayal of the Negro*, pp. 105–18. Cleveland's instructions are in a letter to Attorney General Augustus Garland, October 5, 1886, Reel 156, Cleveland Papers.

state authorities were taking no action to apprehend the guilty parties. Apparently deeming the matter beyond the jurisdiction of the federal government, Cleveland showed no further interest in the case.[12]

Cleveland did deem it within his legal power to prevent men who had engaged in violent acts from holding appointive federal office. He was about to name G. L. Meade postmaster of Copiah County, Mississippi, when he found out that Meade had intimidated Negro voters in 1883; the president revoked the commission he had already signed.[13] A similar incident occurred later in his term. J. B. Harris, a federal district attorney, harassed blacks at the Jackson, Mississippi, local elections. Cleveland immediately instructed Attorney General Augustus Garland to investigate. The latter sent Harris a sharply worded telegram noting newspaper reports that the district attorney had been involved in efforts "to suppress the colored vote . . . and to prevent colored people from running for office by violence and intimidation." Garland insisted that Harris report on his part in such activities "at once." Harris came to Washington; Garland referred him directly to the president, who told Harris that his action had embarrassed the administration and that his resignation would be accepted. Harris complied, justifying his intimidation of Negroes as the natural way "any good citizen should act in a manner so deeply affecting the material interests of the people with whom his lot is cast."[14]

Supporters of Cleveland in 1884 had predicted that violence against blacks in the South would end once a Democratic president was installed; during the Cleveland administration, these

12. Wharton, *The Negro in Mississippi*, pp. 223–24; New York *Tribune*, March 26, 1886, p. 1.

13. *Nation*, XL (June 25, 1885), 512; T. Thomas Fortune, *The Negro in Politics* (New York: Ogilvie and Rowntree, 1886), pp. 56–57.

14. Augustus Garland to J. B. Harris, January 3, 1888, telegram, Department of Justice Instruction Book Y, pp. 505–6, National Archives; U.S. Senate, *Report of the Committee on the Judiciary on the Municipal Election at Jackson, Mississippi*, Senate Report 1887, 50 Cong., 1 sess., 1888, pp. 10–11; Harris to Cleveland, January 16, 1888, Department of Justice Appointment File, National Archives.

men claimed to see the fulfillment of their prophecies.[15] Despite such optimism, the situation during Cleveland's tenure was about what it had been before he took office. "Don't see much difference 'twixt Democrats and 'Publicans,'" one Southern black told a reporter in 1886.[16] The Democratic president did not undermine the position of the Negroes, and he rebuked outright violence against them through his behavior toward Meade and Harris; however, the moderate Northern Democracy, contrary to black hopes but consistent with new departure doctrine, did not push their Southern friends to grant the race greater rights.

Another matter of interest to blacks during the Cleveland years was the fate of a bill introduced by Senator Henry W. Blair, Republican of New Hampshire, providing substantial federal aid to public schools. The money would go to states in proportion to their number of illiterates. While states would have to account to the federal government for their distribution of the grants, separate schools for the two races were allowed. Illiteracy was a serious problem, particularly in the South and among blacks, who stood to gain much from passage of the Blair bill.[17]

When Blair first introduced his proposal before the 1884 election, some Democrats spoke against it as an unwarranted intrusion of federal power into a state matter, while other party legislators justified the bill as constitutionally sound and likely to ameliorate the race problem. The Republican Senate passed the legislation thirty-three to eleven. While most Southern Democrats, whose states stood to benefit, favored it, Northern and border Democrats were more skeptical.

15. New York *World*, September 15, 1886, p. 4; New York *Age*, November 19, 1887, p. 1; New York *Times*, December 9, 1888, p. 4.

16. New York *Evening Post*, January 12, 1886, p. 3. Also see an editorial entitled "The Situation," in *African Methodist Episcopal Church Review*, V (January, 1888), 309.

17. Important studies of the bill are: Allen J. Going, "The South and the Blair Bill," *Mississippi Valley Historical Review*, XLIV (September, 1957), 466–89; Hirshson, *Bloody Shirt*, pp. 192–200; Daniel W. Crofts, "The Blair Bill and the Elections Bill: The Congressional Aftermath to Reconstruction" (Ph.D. dissertation, Yale University, 1968), pp. 1–220.

TABLE 3. *Democratic Senate Votes on Blair Bill, April 7, 1884*[18] *(counting pairs)*

	Yes	No
North	1	4
Border	4	8
South	14	3
Total	19	15

Majority leaders in the Democratic House of Representatives conspired to keep the measure from coming to a floor vote.[19] An early 1885 roll call on a procedural motion indicated the deep sectional cleavage within the House Democracy over federal aid to common schools. Democrat Frank Hurd of Ohio moved that a committee investigate whether the Blair bill was a revenue measure. If so, it would have to originate in the House, and the Senate's prior action was thus improper. A vote was taken on whether to table this motion: a yea vote showed support for the Blair bill, and a nay vote indicated opposition. The roll call shows much Democratic support for the educational measure in the South, outside of Texas; Northern and border state Democrats, however, showed hostility.

TABLE 4. *Democratic House Votes on Tabling Hurd Motion, January 23, 1885*[20]

	Yes	No
New England	0	6
Middle Atlantic	4	18
Midwest	2	38
Far West	1	4
Border	8	20
Upper South	10	2
Deep South (excluding Texas)	19	9
Texas	0	10
Total	44	107

18. *Congressional Record,* 48 Cong., 1 sess., pp. 2066–2689 (March 19–April 7, 1884), gives the debate, while p. 2724 (April 7, 1884) provides the roll call.

19. Crofts, "The Blair Bill and the Elections Bill," p. 103.

20. *Congressional Record,* 48 Cong., 2 sess., pp. 961–62 (January 23, 1885).

No one knew what the incoming president, Grover Cleveland, thought of the Blair proposal. The platform on which he had run was equivocal: while favoring "the diffusion of free education by common schools, so that every child in the land may be taught the rights and duties of citizenship," it also opposed "all proposals which upon any pretext would convert the General Government into a machine for collecting taxes to be distributed among the States, or the citizens thereof."[21] Enemies of the education bill were alarmed when it became known that Cleveland intended to appoint Senators Augustus Garland of Arkansas and Lucius Lamar of Mississippi, both supporters of the measure, as his Southern cabinet members. Garland defended his Democratic orthodoxy to the president-elect: "After all, this is one of those questions about which Democrats, without violating their party allegiance, might differ—as they do in tariff—gold and silver etc.!"[22] Both Garland and Lamar entered the cabinet, but whether this signified presidential approval of the Blair bill is doubtful. Cleveland made no reference to it either in his inaugural address or in his first annual message. When T. Thomas Fortune asked the president where he stood, Cleveland replied that he was undecided.[23]

Blair reintroduced his bill in 1886. The Senate, still under Republican control, passed it thirty-six to eleven. Democratic attitudes had changed little since 1884.

As in the preceding Congress, the Democratic House leadership kept the measure bottled up in committee. Another procedural roll call showed that differences within the House Democracy over the Blair bill had widened since 1884. On a motion to shift the legislation from the hostile education committee

21. Porter and Johnson, eds., *Party Platforms*, pp. 66, 67.

22. Washington *National Republican*, January 3, 1885, clipping in Augustus Garland to Cleveland, January 3, 1885, Reel 4, Garland to D. S. Lamont, December 29, 1884, Reel 3, Cleveland Papers.

23. Fortune in New York *Freeman*, January 2, 1886, p. 2. There is an early draft of the inaugural address dated March 4, 1885, on Reel 6 of the Cleveland Papers, which mentions national responsibility to "qualify" Negroes for intelligent voting, perhaps a reference to federal support for public education. But it was deleted before the inauguration.

TABLE 5. *Democratic Senate Votes on Blair Bill, March 5, 1886*[24] *(counting pairs)*

	Yes	No
North	2	0
Border	3	8
South	13	4
Total	18	12

to the presumably more friendly labor committee, Democratic representatives from below the Mason-Dixon Line, excluding Texas, showed increased enthusiasm for the bill, while Northern Democratic support for it, feeble enough two years earlier, was now almost extinct. Affirmative votes indicate support for the bill, and negative votes show opposition.

TABLE 6. *Democratic House Votes on Transfer of Blair Bill to Labor Committee, March 29, 1886*[25]

	Yes	No
New England	0	2
Middle Atlantic	0	14
Midwest	1	33
Border	11	19
Upper South	17	2
Deep South (except Texas)	30	4
Texas	0	10
Total	59	84

Blair tried again in the next Congress. This time opponents made much of the argument that Cleveland would veto the bill if it passed. Democratic Senator Joseph Brown of Georgia, supporting Blair, discounted this prediction, citing the appointments of Garland and Lamar as proof that Cleveland backed the education bill. The still-Republican Senate passed the measure by a much reduced margin, thirty-nine to twenty-nine. Border state senators were now unanimously against passage.

24. *Congressional Record*, 49 Cong., 1 sess., p. 2105 (March 5, 1886).
25. *Ibid.*, p. 2882 (March 24, 1886). Although the bill was transferred to the labor committee, it languished there as well.

TABLE 7. *Democratic Senate Votes on Blair Bill, February 15, 1888*[26] *(counting pairs)*

	Yes	No
North	2	4
Border	0	12
South	15	4
Total	17	20

Again the Democratic House of Representatives took no action.

In 1890, with Cleveland out of office and the Republicans holding majorities in both houses of Congress, Blair made a final futile attempt to push his bill through. This time the Senate rejected it thirty-seven to thirty-one. Backing for the legislation had eroded in both parties; within Democratic ranks there was a net shift of three votes from support to opposition since 1888.

TABLE 8. *Democratic Senate Votes on Blair Bill, March 20, 1890*[27] *(counting pairs)*

	Yes	No
North	1	5
Border	0	11
South	13	7
Total	14	23

While Republican enthusiasm for the bill steadily declined between 1884 and 1890, Democrats bore a major degree of responsibility for the defeat of federal aid to education. Despite considerable sentiment for the Blair bill among their constituents, some Southern congressmen who feared economic and social change fought the measure. Opposition from below the Mason-Dixon Line increased in 1890 because Southern whites, seeing both houses of Congress in Republican hands, feared any law that might lead to federal interference with race relations. Northern Democrats, whose states stood to gain little from the bill, were even more hostile to it. Low-tariff Democrats suspected

26. Brown's remarks and the roll call, *ibid.*, 50 Cong., 1 sess., pp. 546, 1223 (January 18, February 15, 1888).

27. *Ibid.*, 51 Cong., 1 sess., p. 2436 (March 20, 1890).

that the expenditures mandated by the proposal would dissipate the treasury surplus and provide an excuse for retaining or even raising import duties. Catholics, most of them traditional Democrats, feared that Blair's real intention was to destroy parochial schools. More basic was the long-standing party distrust of "centralization": the Blair bill, if enacted, might encourage Americans to rely on federal paternalism to supply their needs. Northern Democrats were not sufficiently concerned about the problem of Southern illiteracy to sacrifice their old hostility to the central government.[28]

President Cleveland's noncommittal attitude hurt the Blair bill's chances; perhaps a more broad-minded and determined man could at least have persuaded Democratic leaders in the House to let the measure come to a vote. But there is evidence that even such presidential persuasion might not have worked. Though silent on the Blair bill, Cleveland explicitly favored another federal appropriation to benefit Negroes which nevertheless failed to get to the House floor. In his annual message of 1886 the president asked for reimbursement to depositors of the Freedman's Savings Bank. He was the only chief executive ever to make the suggestion, and a Southern black newspaper called it "the only practical word for the Negro in a President's message for a long time."[29] The Senate passed a reimbursement measure thirty-five to six. Eleven Southern Democrats, three from border states, and one from the North voted yea, while six Southern and

28. On the Southerners, consult R. W. Cobb to John T. Morgan, March 11, 1886, Vol. 1, S. F. Burks to Morgan, April 18, 1886, Vol. 2, Levi Lawler to Morgan, February 14, 1887, Vol. 4, Morgan Papers, Library of Congress; Going, "The South and the Blair Bill," pp. 466–89; Crofts, "The Blair Bill and the Elections Bill," pp. 141–42, 181–84. The tariff and Catholic ramifications are clear from Crofts, pp. 120, 212–13, and John Whitney Evans, "Catholics and the Blair Education Bill," *Catholic Historical Review*, XLVI (October, 1960), 273–98. Fear of government power over education is seen in James A. Barnes, *John G. Carlisle: Financial Statesman* (New York: Dodd, Mead, 1931), pp. 137, 152–53, and Congressman Samuel Randall is quoted as saying "the States ought to attend to their own illiterates" in Margaret White Hunt to Randall, January, 1887, Box 149, Randall Papers.

29. Richardson, ed., *Messages and Papers of the Presidents*, VIII, 528; Huntsville *Gazette*, December 11, 1886, p. 2. See also Fleming, *Freedmen's Savings Bank*, p. 128, and Abby L. Gilbert, "The Comptroller of the Currency and the Freedmen's Savings Bank," *Journal of Negro History*, LVII (April, 1972), 139–41.

border Democrats opposed the bill on the grounds that the federal government had no legal obligation to pay, and that most of the bankbooks were in the hands of speculators, not original depositors. The Democratic House of Representatives took no action. In the next Congress Senator Voorhees presented a similar proposal drawn up by the comptroller of the currency, with the personal approval of President Cleveland. The measure passed the Senate with no recorded roll call—but, true to form, the Democratic House of Representatives buried it.[30] Thus Cleveland's endorsement would not necessarily have helped the Blair bill either.

A third issue of great moment for blacks under the Cleveland administration was whether the president intended to sweep Negro employees of the federal government out of office and replace them with whites. While unable to boast of high-level jobs, blacks viewed whatever patronage members of the race did attain as a valuable symbol of political recognition. Under Republican administrations the custom had developed of granting a few visible appointments to Negroes. These were register of the treasury, recorder of deeds for the District of Columbia, and diplomatic posts in three "Negro" countries: the Liberian and Haitian missions, and the consulate in Santo Domingo. Also, blacks held a number of subordinate positions in the various government departments. Sensitive to black apprehensions, the new president told a Negro visitor: "In determining the fitness, etc. of applicants for office, let the same rule apply to white and black alike."[31] This "rule" was influenced by Mugwump demands that Cleveland eschew the spoils system and grant jobs on the basis of merit. Eager to please these independents, he ordered that only two categories of civil servants should be removed: "offensive partisans," who had campaigned actively

30. *Congressional Record*, 49 Cong., 2 sess., pp. 2323–24, 2328 (January 11, February 26, 1887); *ibid.*, 50 Cong., 1 sess., pp. 2684, 2686, 6610 (April 4, July 21, 1888). There is no correlation between the first roll call and Democratic votes on the Blair bill.

31. Cleveland quoted in C. S. Smith to John H. Oberly, March 24, 1885, Reel 8, Cleveland Papers.

against the Democracy while holding office, and incompetents.

Former Mississippi Senator Blanche K. Bruce, the black register of the treasury, and Frederick Douglass, the recorder of deeds for the District of Columbia, were offensive partisans who had worked for Blaine. Cleveland immediately removed Bruce and replaced him with former Union General William Rosecrans, a white.[32] This was the only prestigious position taken out of Negro hands by the Democrats. Douglass received different treatment. For a full year the veteran black leader retained office despite his record of partisanship. Furthermore, though "under a considerable cloud" for his recent marriage to a white woman, Douglass received presidential invitations to White House receptions—a courtesy that President Arthur had not extended. As Douglass later recalled, "We never failed to attend them. . . . under the gaze of the late slave holders, there was nothing in the bearing of Mr. and Mrs. Cleveland toward Mrs. Douglass and myself less cordial and courteous than that extended to the other ladies and gentlemen present." In the face of criticism from Southern whites, the president "never faltered or flinched" in his enlightened conduct.[33]

As far as the diplomatic corps was concerned, Cleveland inherited a problem from the previous administration. Two days before leaving office President Arthur nominated George Washington Williams, the former Ohio legislator and black historian, as minister to Haiti; the Republican Senate confirmed him in the closing hours of the session. However, Williams had neglected to post the required bond, and Cleveland informed him that some objection had been raised to his appointment. After hearing nothing from the new administration for over a month, the aspiring diplomat came to see Thomas Bayard, a long-time opponent of Negro rights who was now secretary of state. According to Williams, Bayard said, "I have nothing against you personally,

32. New York *Freeman*, May 16, 1885, p. 2.

33. Frederick Douglass, *Life and Times of Frederick Douglass* (New York: Pathway Press, 1941), pp. 556–58. Invitations to White House receptions dated February 11, March 4, and June 15, 1886 are available on Reels 11 and 9, Douglass Papers.

you know; but very grave charges indeed, have been made against you . . . and—well, I advise you to resign." Bayard allegedly offered Williams his pay up to that time if he would relinquish the position, but Williams turned him down. Bayard claimed on the contrary that Williams had asked him for the salary because he needed cash, a plea which Bayard had refused because Williams, never having given bond, was not entitled to the pay.[34] While this disagreement was of little interest to anyone, Republican newspapers gave great publicity to the alleged phrasing of Bayard's denial to reporters that he had treated Williams badly. "Those who know me," he supposedly declared, "will relieve me of the imputation that I am disrespectful to inferiors." Williams charged that he was the victim of Democratic race prejudice.[35] President Cleveland disposed of this accusation by naming another Negro, John E. W. Thompson of New York, to the position.[36]

This episode had an interesting sequel. When Thompson reached Port au Prince, he discovered that the Williams controversy was affecting Haitian politics. Certain newspapers there gave much space to Secretary Bayard's record of hostility to Negroes, warning that American policy toward the black republic was now in the hands of a white supremacist. Bayard told Thompson to ignore the newspapers: "The only language or action of mine ever to be explained to a foreign government will

34. George W. Williams to John Sherman, December 23, 1885, Papers Regarding Nominations, 48 Congress, National Archives; New York *Tribune*, April 17, 1885, clipping in Scrapbook, Container 224, Bayard Papers.

35. New York *Tribune*, undated, Scrapbook, Container 224, Bayard Papers; Williams to Grover Cleveland, April 13, 1885, reprinted in William J. Simmons, ed., *Men of Mark* (Cleveland: George M. Rewell, 1887), pp. 563–64. On Williams, see John Hope Franklin, "George Washington Williams, Historian," *Journal of Negro History*, XXXI (January, 1946), 60–90. The objections to his nomination resulted from his dubious financial transactions and alleged abandonment of his wife. See George Hoadly to D. S. Lamont, March 28, 1885, Reel 9, Cleveland Papers; Washington *Bee*, March 14, April 25, 1885, both p. 2; Cleveland *Gazette*, May 9, 1885, p. 2; Pearle Mintz Oxendine, "An Evaluation of Negro Historians During the Period of the Road to Reunion" (M.A. thesis, Howard University, 1947), p. 29.

36. T. Thomas Fortune to Grover Cleveland, April 27, 1885, Container 185, Bayard Papers; New York *World*, May 9, 1885, p. 3; New York *Freeman*, May 16, 1885, p. 2.

be that employed by me in my present office and in connection with its functions." American policy toward Haiti in the ensuing four years was not marred by racism.[37]

Bayard showed by his disposal of the Santo Domingo consulate that the Williams matter had taught him prudence. H. C. C. Astwood, a black Republican from Louisiana, was the incumbent. When the Democratic congressional delegation from Louisiana protested his retention in office, Bayard told them that Astwood had a good record and spoke the native tongue. He informed the congressmen: "I will be glad if you will present to me the name of a colored man of intelligence and good character, fairly educated, and with a knowledge of Spanish and sufficient business ability to perform the duties of the place." Astwood held the job until his removal late in Cleveland's term for fiscal irregularities. Another Negro, Archibald Grimké of Massachusetts, was then nominated for the position, but the Senate did not act on his confirmation.[38]

A third diplomatic post traditionally held by blacks, the Liberian mission, went to Moses Hopkins, a North Carolina Negro, after he assured Cleveland that he did not smoke or drink and had never been arrested. The unfortunate Hopkins died soon thereafter in Liberia. C. H. J. Taylor, a Democratic Negro lawyer from Kansas who had first entered politics as a supporter of Wade Hampton in the South Carolina campaign of 1876, succeeded him but resigned a short time later, unable to stand the country to which he had been sent. Cleveland then offered the place to a prestigious and politically independent black educator, Joseph C. Price, president of Livingstone College in North Carolina. Price was not interested, but he endorsed one of his former students, Ezekiel E. Smith, who was nominated and confirmed.[39] In his second annual message to Congress in December,

37. John E. W. Thompson to Bayard, November 14, 1885, Container 185, Bayard to Thompson, November 23, 1885, Letterbook Vol. 195, p. 7, Bayard Papers; Rayford Logan, *The Diplomatic Relations of the United States with Haiti, 1776–1891* (Chapel Hill: University of North Carolina Press, 1941), p. 410.

38. Bayard to N. C. Blanchard and others, April 17, 1886, Letterbook Vol. 195, p. 284, Bayard Papers; New York *Age*, January 26, 1889, p. 1. Grimké was confirmed to this post in Cleveland's second term.

39. Moses Hopkins to Cleveland, September 10, 1885, Reel 19, Cleveland

1886, Cleveland recommended that since Liberia was threatened by foreign encroachment, the United States should supply her with a surplus naval vessel, a suggestion that pleased American Negroes.[40] The president also stationed another black diplomat in Africa, appointing Henry F. Downing, previously employed in the Brooklyn Navy Yard, as consul at Luanda, Portuguese Angola.[41]

Lower-echelon jobs in the federal bureaucracy were not under Cleveland's direct control, but in the hands of cabinet members and subordinate bureau chiefs. Since office-hungry Democrats now clamored for the patronage denied their party since 1861, many of the new administrators succumbed to the pressure, interpreting offensive partisanship and incompetence rather loosely; a host of minor Republican officials lost their places as a result. While there are no statistics for this period classifying government workers according to race, the initial turnover in the federal departments brought a definite reduction in the number of Negro job-holders because Republican members of the race had been appointed in earlier administrations, and few blacks were active Democrats with legitimate claims to the spoils of office. A few months after the new administration was installed, a black reporter asked Secretary of the Treasury Daniel Manning why Negroes were being discharged. When Manning put him off by citing considerations of economy, the reporter countered with the observation that whites were getting these jobs. The secretary, fed up with office-seekers, blurted out: "Yes, the whites are the worst of the two."[42]

There is no evidence in any of the departments of deliberate discrimination on racial grounds. Some Negro officials who could

Papers; New York *World*, May 14, 1887, p. 4; William J. Walls, *Joseph Charles Price: Educator and Race Leader* (Boston: Christopher Publishing House, 1943), pp. 61, 92–93.

40. Richardson, ed., *Messages and Papers of the Presidents*, VIII, 501; John H. Smyth to D. S. Lamont, December 7, 1886, Reel 42, Cleveland Papers.

41. Cleveland *Gazette*, June 4, 1887, p. 4; New York *Freeman*, June 4, 1887, p. 2.

42. Black firings are noted in New York *Freeman*, July 4, 1885, p. 1, April 27, June 26, 1886, both p. 2, April 9, 1887, p. 1; Washington *Bee*, May 2, June 27, 1885, both p. 2. The Manning interview was published in the *People's Advocate*, reprinted in New York *Freeman*, September 5, 1885, p. 2.

convince skeptical superiors of their efficiency and political in-
activity were retained and promoted.[43] Indeed, blacks who were
relatives or friends of prominent Negro politicians kept their
well-paying jobs in the treasury, war, and justice departments
despite long records of involvement in Republican campaign
activity.[44] Interior Secretary Lucius Lamar, the Mississippi pa-
ternalist, was especially kind to blacks. Besides insuring that
holdover Negro employees in his own department were not discharged, he intervened with other cabinet members to save
blacks from dismissal. John R. Lynch, a Negro who had served
as a Republican congressman from Mississippi and knew Lamar
well, recalls in his autobiography that the secretary offered him
a position as special land agent if he promised not to be "offen-
sively active or boldly aggressive in political matters." Lynch
graciously declined. The war and navy departments also earned
high marks from blacks for their fair treatment of Negroes.[45]
Gradually all the departments experienced an influx of Democratic Negroes, a rare breed indeed. These men received political appointments ranging in importance from messengers and
clerks to a deputy marshal in Ohio, a special examiner of pen-
sions, and the postmaster of Lyle, Indiana.[46] Another avenue to

43. Milton M. Holland to John Sherman, October 1, 1885, Vol. 350, Sherman
Papers; New York *Freeman*, July 3, 1886, p. 1; Washington *Bee*, November 28,
1885, January 30, May 1, 1886, all p. 2, August 13, 1887, p. 1; Nicodemus (Kans.)
Western Cyclone, August 19, 1886, p. 2.

44. James C. Matthews to Daniel S. Lamont, June, 1887, Reel 50, Cleveland
Papers.

45. On Lamar, see Edward Mayes, *Lucius Q. C. Lamar: His Life, Times, and
Speeches, 1825–1893* (Nashville: Barbee and Smith, 1896), pp. 593–94, and
John R. Lynch, *The Facts of Reconstruction* (New York: Neale Publishing,
1913), pp. 236–39, 249. On the war and navy departments, consult New York
Freeman, July 18, 25, August 22, 1885, all p. 2, July 17, 1886, p. 1; Huntsville
(Ala.) *Gazette*, October 31, 1885, p. 2; John W. Kinsella to William C. Whitney,
May 5, 1887, Vol. 44, Whitney Papers, Library of Congress.

46. Evidence of minor federal patronage is available in New York *Freeman*,
June 12, 1886, p. 1; Cleveland *Gazette*, February 19, 1887, p. 1, April 13, 1889,
p. 2; C. H. J. Taylor to Daniel S. Lamont, February 3, 1887, Reel 45, C. P. Irby
to Grover Cleveland, July 11, 1888, Reel 61, Walter S. Brown to Cleveland,
December 3, 1888, Reel 129, Cleveland Papers; Jeffrey R. Brackett, *Notes on the
Progress of the Colored People of Maryland since the War* (Baltimore: Johns
Hopkins University, 1890), pp. 17, 22. The three more responsible positions went
to Richard A. Jones, Joseph Houser, and W. H. Roundtree, respectively. I. Garland Penn, *The Afro-American Press and Its Editors* (Springfield, Mass.: Wiley,

government positions during this period was the nonpartisan civil service examination system which covered several categories of low-level federal jobs. Set up under the Pendleton Act of 1883 and first implemented on a large scale during the Cleveland years, these examinations were generally administered in a color-blind way outside the South; they caused an increase in the number of Negroes holding employment, especially in the post offices of Northern cities. Because of its timing, this phenomenon redounded to the credit of Cleveland's administration.[47]

The Southern situation regarding federal jobs was somewhat different. Newly appointed postmasters in the South found ways of circumventing the civil service regulations and took a variety of attitudes toward the employment of blacks. Five Negro clerks were retained in the Atlanta post office throughout the Cleveland administration. The Democratic postmaster of Columbia, South Carolina, asked a black employee to stay on, but the latter declined to hold a position under a Democratic administration. In Charlotte, North Carolina, the Negro mail clerk was fired on racial grounds.[48] Conservative Democratic leaders in the South encouraged the administration to give menial positions to blacks as a way to win their political allegiance.[49] But diehard racists

1891), p. 294; New York *World*, December 12, 1887, p. 6; Indianapolis *Freeman*, February 16, 1889, p. 4.

47. New York *Freeman*, March 26, 1887, p. 4; Cleveland *Gazette*, April 23, July 16, 1887, September 22, 1888, all p. 1, January 12, 1889, p. 2; Indianapolis *Freeman*, June 28, 1890, p. 1. Unfortunately there are no statistics on the number of black federal employees in the 1880's. On the subject of civil service examinations and black job holders, also see Henry A. Wallace to Carter G. Woodson, October 26, 1922, Folder 107, Box 6, Woodson Papers, Library of Congress; Kelly Miller, *The Political Plight of the Negro* (Washington: Murray Brothers, 1913), p. 8; Constance M. Green, *The Secret City: A History of Race Relations in the Nation's Capital* (Princeton: Princeton University Press, 1967), p. 129. A numerical estimate is made by Laurence J. W. Hayes in *The Negro Federal Government Worker: A Study of His Classification Status in the District of Columbia, 1883–1938* (Washington: Howard University, 1941), p. 22, but his figures are not to be found in the source he cites.

48. Atlanta: Huntsville *Gazette*, August 24, 1889, p. 2, and J. W. Duryea to William Still, April 30, 1889, Still Papers; Columbia: Henry A. Wallace to Carter G. Woodson, July 22, 1920, Folder 107, Box 6, Woodson Papers; Charlotte: J. W. Brown to Grover Cleveland, undated [1886], Reel 44, Cleveland Papers.

49. Wade Hampton quoted in New York *Freeman*, November 6, 1886, p. 2; Fitzhugh Lee to William C. Whitney, March 10, 1887, William Elliott to Hugh S. Thompson, March 14, 1887, Vol. 42, Whitney Papers; John W. Daniel to W. C.

were disappointed that Cleveland did not make the entire government lily-white, and when a Negro pension agent came to La Forge, Missouri, on official business, a white mob almost lynched him, contenting itself "with whipping, pounding and kicking" him into insensibility.[50] The differences between some Southern Democrats and the administration over Negro office-holding were to be dramatized more publicly though less physically when Cleveland found a replacement for Frederick Douglass as recorder of deeds in the District of Columbia.

On March 4, 1886, a Democratic Negro lawyer from Albany, New York, named James C. Matthews was informed by President Cleveland's private secretary: "You have been nominated to succeed Douglass."[51] Thus began the most important episode involving blacks in Cleveland's first administration. The fate of this appointment would transcend the bounds of mere patronage, becoming a focus of racial politics and embarrassing Republicans. Also, by infuriating Democratic white supremacists, it would demonstrate at the national level the divergent attitudes toward political recognition of Negroes held by Northern Democrats and many of their more prejudiced colleagues from Southern and border states.

James Campbell Matthews, the man Cleveland chose to be the new recorder of deeds, was born in New Haven, Connecticut, in 1846. His family soon moved to Albany, where his father worked as a barber. Despite losing both parents while he was still a boy, Matthews excelled in school, winning a scholarship to the prestigious Albany Boys' Academy and graduating with honors in 1864. While working as a bookkeeper, the young man attended Albany Law School and passed the bar in 1870. Matthews was a delegate to the 1872 Liberal Republican state con-

Endicott, January 11, 1888, Reel 119, Cleveland Papers; Woodward, *Strange Career of Jim Crow*, p. 59.

50. Anonymous (from Georgia) to Cleveland, October 8, 1885, Reel 21, Cleveland Papers; Congressman George D. Tillman of South Carolina, in New York *Freeman*, November 6, 1886, p. 2. The Missouri incident is in New York *World*, December 12, 1887, p. 6.

51. Daniel S. Lamont to James C. Matthews, March 4, 1886, copy of telegram, Container 88, Lamont Papers, Library of Congress.

vention in Syracuse and, after the Liberals and Democrats merged their conventions and nominated a joint ticket, he addressed the delegates, arguing "that the negro race should divide on the two great parties and make its influence felt in both."[52] Matthews campaigned for Democratic candidates thereafter. As a prominent lawyer he accumulated political influence; whenever the Democrats controlled the Albany statehouse, Matthews dictated Negro patronage. The high point of his power came early in 1884, when he framed the legislation protecting the positions of New York City's black teachers and convinced Governor Cleveland and the Democratic legislature to support it. In 1886 Matthews had a reputation as "one of the shrewdest political manipulators in Albany County." At the same time he was described as a "gentleman of ability, education and refinement," with "a professional standing and record that are an honor to any man that achieves them."[53] His long acquaintance with leading New York Democrats made Matthews the logical choice for the recordership once Cleveland decided to appoint a Negro Democrat in place of Douglass.

Washington Democrats were outraged by the appointment because they expected the president to name a white man. One resident complained: "What another 'nigger!' Why, in my time I have bought 'Liklier niggers' for a thousand dollars a head, and this one is given a five-thousand dollar office by a President who calls himself a Democrat." The racial issue was often veiled by the objection that Matthews, not a native of the District, was not qualified to fill a local office. Washingtonians urged Cleveland to withdraw the nomination; when the president ignored them, they resolved to get the Senate to reject Matthews.[54] The

52. On Matthews's life, see New York *Freeman*, December 6, 1884, p. 1, and Simmons, ed., *Men of Mark*, pp. 964–77. His 1872 speech was recalled in New York *Herald*, March 6, 1886, p. 4.

53. The school bill is discussed above, pp. 66–67. The descriptions of Matthews are from Albany *Argus*, March 5, 1886, p. 4, and George R. Howell and Jonathan Tenney, eds., *Bi-Centennial History of Albany: History of the County of Albany, New York, from 1609 to 1886* (New York: W. W. Munsell, 1886), p. 725.

54. New York *Tribune*, March 6, 1886, p. 2; G. W. Conn to Grover Cleveland, March 6, 1886, Reel 102, Cleveland Papers; Washington *Post*, quoted in New York *Evening Post*, March 9, 1886, p. 2.

Washington *Republic* carried banner headlines on every page reading: "DEFEAT THE NOMINATION OF THE CARPETBAGGER."[55]

Matthews took for granted the support of the handful of Northern Democratic Senators and the opposition of many of their white supremacist Southern and border state colleagues. He therefore encouraged his friends of both races to send petitions favoring him to Republican senators, who held a majority in that body. These petitions asked Republicans to confirm the Negro Democrat as a way of demonstrating that only the Democracy opposed Negro advancement.[56]

Senate action seemed to substantiate the assumption that this Democratic nominee would get his job through Republican votes. The Senate committee on the District of Columbia, to which the matter was referred, voted on March 19. Four senators favored Matthews—Republicans John J. Ingalls of Kansas, Thomas Palmer of Michigan, and Austin Pike of New Hampshire, and Democrat Joseph Brown of Georgia. An equal number of Senators were opposed—Democrats Isham Harris of Tennessee, Joseph Blackburn of Kentucky, and Zebulon Vance of North Carolina, and Republican Harrison Riddleberger of Virginia. The ninth committee member, a California Republican, was absent. The tie vote resulted in an unfavorable report to the Senate, which in turn recommitted the nomination to the committee.[57] Still, prospects were good for eventual confirmation. The committee vote showed that Northern Republicans and moderate Dixie Democrats like Brown would back Matthews. At this point only extreme negrophobic Southern and border state men were likely to fight the nomination. Pro-Cleveland Northern Demo-

55. Cited in New York *Tribune*, March 15, 1886, p. 5. Also see the anti-Matthews petitions in Papers Regarding Nominations, 49 Congress, National Archives, hereafter cited as Nomination Papers.

56. Matthews to Daniel S. Lamont, March, 1886, Reel 32, Cleveland Papers. Most of the petitions are in the Nomination Papers. Others are reprinted in U.S. Senate, *Journal of the Executive Proceedings of the Senate of the United States of America*, 1886, pp. 349, 392, and *Proceedings Relating to the Nomination and Rejection of James C. Matthews, of New York, to be Recorder of Deeds in the District of Columbia*, Senate Miscellaneous Document 85, 49 Cong., 2 sess., 1887, pp. 35–37, hereafter cited as *Proceedings*.

57. *Proceedings*, pp. 1–2.

crats feared not that confirmation would fail, but that many negative votes from Southern Democrats would tarnish the party's new color-blind image.[58]

But rumors of Republican opposition took shape. Some Albany Republicans of both races, who had suffered from the nominee's political skill in the past, urged Republican senators not to help Matthews. If his fellow Democrats from the South rejected him, argued the Albany *Evening Journal*, why should Republicans support him? The leading Negro Republican of Albany, William H. Johnson, charged that Matthews often used his political influence to get Republicans discharged from government jobs in New York State. "Every Republican that supports him," warned Johnson, "uses a club to crack his own head, and I stand from under the club." This personal enemy of the nominee wrote to New York's Republican Senator William Evarts that "Matthews' character both private and political ought to be looked into at home before a Republican Senate confirms him. He is in every way except by education *unfit* for a public trust."[59] The anti-Matthews faction in Albany produced specific charges. At the recent local election Matthews allegedly approached a Negro laborer who held a job in the state capitol and warned him that, if he voted Republican, he would soon be unemployed. The man cast a Republican ballot and then lost his job. Here was proof that Matthews was a political scoundrel.[60]

President Cleveland remained firm in support of Matthews against both the attack of the Albany Republicans and the racism of Washington Democrats. When the Republican charges against his nominee became known, Cleveland told reporters:

58. New York *Times*, March 23, 1886, p. 1; New York *World*, March 23, 24, 1886, both p. 4; D. Cady Herrick to Daniel S. Lamont, March 24, 1886, Reel 32, Cleveland Papers; Arthur P. Gorman to David B. Hill, April 6, 1886, Box 5, Bixby Papers.

59. Albany *Evening Journal*, March 12, 1886, clipping, William H. Johnson to William Evarts, March 15, 1886, both in Nomination Papers.

60. Albany *Evening Journal*, April 15, 1886, Albany *Express*, April 17, 1886, both quoted in *Proceedings*, pp. 42, 43; William II. Johnson and others to the Senate, April 23, 1886, Nomination Papers; John Schleicher to William Evarts, April 24, 1886, George Stuart Gregory to Evarts, May 6, 1886, Vol. 38, Evarts Papers, Library of Congress.

That is one of my personal appointments. I have examined the allegations of actions of offensive partisanship against this man. As I lived in Albany, when most of them are said to have occurred, I know nearly all of them to be untrue. The rest, true or not, concern only the action of a private citizen, who then had a right to be as partisan as he pleased.

Asked about the Democratic objections to Matthews, the president was equally blunt:

There are nearly as many colored people as white ones in this District. There are more colored than white people in some Democratic States. Those States are Democratic, because the negroes have largely voted with the Democrats. You can't ask them to take some of the odium and incur some of the danger of being Democrats and then deny them all official recognition. The Republicans would like nothing better than that. Democrats who ask me to do that are short sighted.

Cleveland, a Democratic president, was challenging the Southern wing of his own party on racial policy.[61]

On June 1 a subcommittee consisting of Republican Ingalls and Democrat Harris held hearings on the Matthews case. After listening to the Albany charges against him, they dismissed the accusations as baseless. Nevertheless, three weeks later the full committee voted seven to two against the nomination. Northern Republicans Ingalls, Pike, Palmer, John C. Spooner of Wisconsin, and Jonathan Chace of Rhode Island joined with Democrats Blackburn and Vance against Matthews. Only Democrats Harris and Brown voted for a favorable report. It had become Republican policy to defeat the black Democrat.[62]

Senator Ingalls explained Republican strategy in a private conversation with a black friend of Matthews, who then let the secret out. Ingalls admitted that nothing could be said personally against Matthews. Nonresidency was also a phoney issue.

61. Brooklyn *Eagle*, May 8, 1886, p. 4.

62. *Proceedings*, pp. 6–29. There had been a reorganization of the committee's membership since March. Rumor had it that Democrat Harris shifted from opposition to support after Cleveland threatened to cut off his patronage. New York *Sun*, August 28, 1886, p. 2.

Republicans intended to block the nomination because "it would be bad politics to take a man like Matthews— of his ability and character and standing among his people—and place him in a prominent position." Republicans wanted to show that a Negro Democrat was a "monstrosity." Ingalls never denied having said this, and Negroes were shocked upon hearing it.[63]

On July 31 the full Senate dealt with the nomination in secret session. According to information leaked to the press, before the vote Ingalls explained Republican opposition on the grounds of nonresidency. This complaint, first used to make Democratic racist antagonism to Matthews respectable, was now doing double duty as a mask for the politically motivated hostility of Republicans. Brown and Harris spoke for Matthews, arguing that the president wanted to recognize the Negroes through this appointment, and, unable to find a suitable black Washingtonian, had to name an outsider.[64] But since nonresidency was only a facade put up by the anti-Matthews coalition, such words had no impact: the Senate rejected Matthews thirty-seven to fourteen. Republicans opposed him twenty-nine to one, with two more paired against; only Charles Van Wyck of Nebraska refused to follow party discipline. As expected, all four Northern Democrats backed Matthews. Their colleagues from the former slave states divided: counting pairs, twelve Southern and border Democrats supported their president, and nine defied him. A coalition of calculating Republicans and anti-Negro Democrats prevented confirmation, but the Republican party bore primary responsibility.

President Cleveland delivered a silent rebuke to the Senate by giving Matthews a recess appointment as recorder on August 9, an action that Democratic politicians hoped would increase Cleveland's popularity in the black community and pry mem-

63. Ingalls's explanation is in New York *Times*, June 30, 1886, p. 1. Interestingly, a similar rationale for opposition had been presented in March by a black Republican. See Milton M. Holland to John Sherman, March 16, 1886, Vol. 369, Sherman Papers. Some black reaction to Ingalls's statement is in New York *Freeman*, July 3, 1886, p. 2, and Walter S. Brown to Cleveland, July 3, 1886, Reel 36, Cleveland Papers.
64. New York *Sun*, August 1, 1886, p. 1.

TABLE 9. *First Senate Vote on Matthews Nomination, July 31, 1886*[65] *(pairs added in parentheses)*

	Yes	No
Republicans	1	29 (2)
Northern Democrats	4	0
Border Democrats	4 (1)	2 (1)
Southern Democrats	5 (2)	6
Total	14 (3)	37 (3)

bers of the race away from the Republican party. Even some Southern Democratic newspapers applauded.[66] Indeed, Senate rejection followed by immediate presidential reappointment made the affair symbolically significant to many Negroes. The New York *Freeman*, the leading black newspaper in the country, claimed that though Cleveland was a Democrat "he is worth an army of sentimentalists that preach much and practice little." Another important Negro paper, the Washington *Bee*, printed a "Declaration of Independence" from the Republican party. Republican blacks expressed concern about possible Negro defections to the Democracy because of Matthews—especially in the North, where the race's vote had already begun to divide in state and local elections.[67]

Though surely aware of the political angle, Cleveland, in character, justified his course on grounds of principle. On August 21 the New York *Herald* published a letter in which the president explained to T. McCants Stewart why he named Matthews again. Hoping "that this act will not be regarded as in any way defiant to the Senate or as an attempt to appear heroic," Cleveland wrote:

> I have deemed the question involved in this matter as one rising above politics, and as offering a test of good faith and adherence to pledges—nothing more or less.

65. *Proceedings*, p. 29.

66. Don Dickinson to Cleveland, undated [1886], Reel 56, Cleveland Papers; Congressman Benjamin LeFevre of Ohio in Albany *Argus*, August 15, 1886, p. 7; Selina (Ala.) *Times* and Louisville *Courier-Journal*, quoted in New York *Evening Post*, August 17, 18, 1886, both p. 2.

67. New York *Freeman*, August 28, 1886, p. 2; Washington *Bee*, November 13, 1886, p. 2; New York *Herald*, August 21, 1886, p. 3.

When this thing is put face to face there should be no shuffling.

It is absurd to promise all and perform nothing.

If the colored man is worthy of a promise, he is absolutely entitled to its fulfillment by every honorable man.

I am glad you are pleased, but fail to see how I am entitled to especial credit for being honest.

An enterprising reporter followed the president to his Adirondack vacation retreat and obtained a full interview on the subject of Matthews. Cleveland explained that the recorder's position should go to a Negro, in recognition of the race's remarkable progress since emancipation. After an intensive search, Matthews was found to be the best-qualified black man for the position: "I appointed Matthews solely because I believe him to be the right man for the place, and I feel certain that the people will come to see that I am right."[68]

On December 21 the president submitted Matthews's name once more to the reconvened Senate and imputed some sinister motive to the nominee's opponents. Recalling that the first rejection was only "ostensibly" due to nonresidency, he hoped that the four months of Matthews's recess tenure had mitigated the force of this objection. "Confessing a desire to cooperate in tendering to our colored fellow-citizens just recognition and the utmost good faith," Cleveland hoped for confirmation this time.[69] Matthews himself had not been idle. During the summer he bought new equipment for the recorder's office and increased its services, in the belief that evidence of efficiency would dissolve the complaints against his appointment.[70]

In January, 1887, the District committee reported the Matthews nomination unfavorably by the same seven-to-two margin that it had produced in June, with the same political alignment of supporters and opponents, and the full Senate rejected Matthews again by a vote of thirty-one to seventeen. The political and sectional complexion of this vote was similar to that of July.

68. New York *Herald*, August 21, 1886, p. 2, August 26, 1886, p. 4.
69. Richardson, ed., *Messages and Papers of the Presidents*, VIII, 531.
70. New York *Freeman*, August 28, 1886, p. 1; Matthews to Cleveland, August 31, 1886, Reel 38, Cleveland Papers; Washington *Bee*, November 27, 1886, p. 2; New York *Herald*, December 21, 1886, p. 3.

Matthews's better showing this time was due to the transfer of three Republican votes—those of Henry Blair of New Hampshire, Charles B. Farwell of Illinois, and John Mitchell of Oregon —to his column.

TABLE 10. *Second Senate Vote on Matthews Nomination, January 26, 1887*[71] *(pairs in parentheses)*

	Yes	No
Republicans	3	22 (5)
Northern Democrats	2	0
Border Democrats	5 (3)	3
Southern Democrats	7 (2)	6
Total	17 (5)	31 (5)

"How do the colored voters like it?" asked a Democratic newspaper.[72] They did not like it at all, and were quite vocal about their irritation.[73] Hoping to justify the Republican course in the eyes of Negroes, Senator Ingalls drew up a long resolution to be made public along with the vote on Matthews. This statement, passed by a strict party vote, was really a reply to Cleveland's letter of December 21 resubmitting the Matthews appointment. Ingalls's resolution said:

> Until suggested by the President the Senate was not aware that the question of 'just recognition' or 'good faith to our colored fellow citizens' was involved in the question and it has never been urged that a person's nomination for an office should be confirmed or rejected because he was black or because he was white.
>
> This classification has been abolished by the suppression of the rebellion and by the amendments of the Constitution, and are no longer properly to be recognized in dealing with public affairs. The Senate, however, in view of the message of the President cannot forbear to apprise him, since he has raised the race issue that. . . . 'Just recognition' would have been tendered to our

71. *Proceedings*, pp. 31–32. Van Wyck, Matthews's only Republican supporter in July, had not been reelected.

72. New York *Herald*, January 31, 1887, p. 4.

73. Washington *Bee*, February 5, 1887, p. 2; Horace Talbert to Cleveland, January 27, 1887, Reel 45, Cleveland Papers; W. H. Bonaparte to William Evarts, February 8, 1887, Vol. 43, Evarts Papers.

colored fellow-citizen by the retention of Frederick Douglass, rather than by his enforced retirement in order to reward an unknown and obscure partisan, who had never been a slave and therefore represented the enfranchised race only by the accident of color. . . .

The Senate has no official information other than that contained in the message from the President, whether Matthews is white or black. He is admitted to be a citizen of New York. The office to which he is nominated is strictly local. . . . His confirmation is opposed with substantial unanimity by the citizens of the District. . . .[74]

This renewed Republican attempt to hide behind the fig leaf of nonresidency evoked scorn from administration supporters, especially for its assumption that only a former slave could represent the black race.[75]

The next move was up to the president. Some Democrats felt that Cleveland had exploited the race issue to its fullest; another Negro appointee would be confirmed by the Senate and the entire matter forgotten. He should therefore name a white man, "leaving upon the Republicans the odium they now rest under: of 'going back' upon the colored race." Democratic Senators George Vest of Missouri and Wade Hampton of South Carolina, who had voted for Matthews on both roll calls, suggested that "the point in the case has been sufficiently emphasized already. To send in the name of another colored man would be to jeopardize the obvious advantage you now have in the matter."[76] But Cleveland showed his stubborn streak again. On the advice of Boston Mugwumps, he nominated James M. Trotter, a Negro from Hyde Park, Massachusetts, to the recordership on March 1, 1887. Trotter had been a lieutenant in the Civil War and had then worked as a post office employee for seventeen years, resigning when his superiors discriminated against him on racial grounds. He first left the Republican fold to campaign for Ben

74. *Proceedings,* pp. 32–33.
75. Springfield *Republican,* February 9, 1887, p. 4; New York *Times,* February 8, 1887, pp. 1, 4; New York *Herald,* February 9, 1887, p. 6; New York *Evening Post,* February 8, 1887, p. 2.
76. Anonymous to Cleveland, February 15, 1887, George Vest to Cleveland, January 24, 1887, Reel 45, Cleveland Papers.

Butler in the Massachusetts gubernatorial race of 1883, and he supported Cleveland for president the following year.[77]

As blacks applauded Cleveland and Washington whites vowed eternal enmity to him,[78] Republican senators saw that they were trapped. Having rejected Matthews twice on grounds of non-residency, they could hardly confirm Trotter, another outsider, without transparent inconsistency. But another rejection of a Negro would intensify black discontent with the party. To complicate matters further, the congressional session would end on March 4; because recess appointments expire at the close of the succeeding session, the Senate would have to act swiftly or there would be no recorder of deeds. On March 2 the Senate District of Columbia committee unfavorably reported the nomination to the full Senate, five to three. Republican Person Cheney of New Hampshire joined Democrats Harris and Brown in support of the nominee, while three Republicans united with Democrats Blackburn and Vance in opposition. Facing probable defeat in the Senate, Cleveland made another adroit move. He had Matthews appoint Trotter as his assistant so that, even if rejected, Trotter would automatically take over the office when Matthews left on March 4.[79]

On March 3 the Senate executed an about-face, confirming Trotter thirty to eleven. Only fifteen Democrats participated in the roll call, seven voting yea and eight nay. The seven consisted of two Northerners, two border state men, and three Southerners, while Democratic opposition consisted of four border state senators and four from the South. Southern and border support for a black recorder of deeds had eroded significantly. Twenty-three Republicans supported Trotter, while Ingalls of Kansas,

77. On Trotter's background, see New York *Globe*, February 24, September 29, 1883, both p. 2, November 3, 1883, p. 1; Stephen R. Fox, *The Guardian of Boston: William Monroe Trotter* (New York: Atheneum, 1970), pp. 3–11.

78. Negro approval is expressed in T. Thomas Fortune to Cleveland, T. Mc-Cants Stewart to Cleveland, both March 1, 1887, and W. H. Bonaparte to Cleveland, March 2, 1887, Reel 46, Cleveland Papers. For animosity shown by white Washingtonians, see R. H. Guinnip to Cleveland, March 1, 1887, *ibid.*, and the Washington newspapers quoted in New York *Sun*, March 4, 1887, p. 2.

79. New York *Herald*, March 3, 1887, p. 4.

Palmer of Michigan, and Dwight Sabin of Minnesota were the only Republicans to vote against him.

TABLE 11. *Senate Vote on Trotter Nomination, March 3, 1887*[80] *(pairs added in parentheses)*

	Yes	No
Republicans	23 (4)	3 (4)
Northern Democrats	2 (1)	0
Border Democrats	2 (1)	4 (1)
Southern Democrats	3 (2)	4 (3)
Total	30 (8)	11 (8)

The Senate proceedings were secret, but the next day newspapers published reports of what happened before the vote. Republican Ingalls and Democrat Blackburn, representing the two elements of the anti-Matthews bloc, argued for rejection of Trotter too because of nonresidency. Democrat Harris spoke in favor of the nomination. Then Republican George F. Hoar of Trotter's home state, Massachusetts, broke ranks and pleaded for confirmation, noting that he had received much pro-Trotter mail from constituents of both races. In rejecting Matthews the Senate had already gone on record in favor of home rule for the District, said Hoar, and there could be no harm in approving Trotter, who was surely fit for the post. The roll call followed. Republican backing for Trotter was certainly incongruous with rejection of Matthews, but the party's senators decided to cut their political losses at the cost of consistency.[81]

Negroes were jubilant at the news of Trotter's confirmation. The New York *Freeman* announced: "The Republican Senators Eat Crow—Mr. Trotter Confirmed." Having eaten crow once, editorialized T. Thomas Fortune, the Republicans "will eat more before the end is reached." He urged the Negroes of Kansas to make sure that Senator Ingalls would be denied reelection, and a Detroit Negro journal vowed to do just that to Michigan's Senator Palmer. Boston Negroes of all political persuasions were

80. Senate, *Journal of Executive Proceedings*, 1887, p. 768.
81. New York *Times*, New York *Tribune*, March 5, 1887, both p. 2.

overjoyed. "The most stalwart Republicans of the race—men who never have a kind word for Democracy whenever it did anything that was good, speak in complimentary terms of the President's action all through the Matthews affair down to the nomination of Trotter."[82]

Soon after the vote on Trotter, a reporter observed a casual meeting between Matthews and Ingalls on a Washington street. The black Democrat and the Kansas Republican shook hands politely. When the reporter asked Ingalls his opinion of Matthews, the senator replied:

> Yes, I know Mr. Matthews. He is a bright fellow. I cannot but admire the independent and manly way he acted throughout his contest. He is, strange to say, a Democrat. I would not do him or any man an injustice. The charges made against him were without foundation. I so reported, as the record shows. It was a political fight and Matthews was the victim.[83]

But the Matthews-Trotter affair, carried on for exactly one year in the midst of Cleveland's term, was more than a squabble over a political appointment: certain aspects of the controversy were highly significant. Besides confirming Negro fears that whatever remained of Republican zeal for racial justice was tempered by considerations of expediency, the episode increased black willingness to act as political independents. The cause of Matthews and Trotter mobilized Negro opinion behind the proposition that members of the race should be treated neither as political tools by Republicans nor as second-class citizens by Dixie Democrats, and even blacks remaining staunch Republicans saw the benefits to be gained from the presence of capable Negroes in the high councils of both parties. Trotter's confirmation symbolized the black electorate's potential power, when freed from the straitjacket of party, to further the interests of

82. New York *Freeman*, March 12, 19, 1887, both p. 2.
83. Washington *Star*, quoted in New York *World*, March 10, 1887, p. 4. Matthews continued to wield patronage power in New York and in 1895 was elected to an Albany judgeship on the Democratic ticket. Don Dickinson to Matthews, May 5, 1888, Container 2, Letterbook 2, p. 241, Dickinson Papers, Library of Congress; New York *Tribune*, November 9, 1895, p. 1.

the race, a lesson that some Northern Negroes had already learned in state and local politics.[84]

But if blacks who thought that the struggle over this appointment showed the way toward a promised land of political independence in national affairs had examined the wrangle in perspective, as just one element in the total context of Cleveland's policy, they would not have been so sanguine. Certainly, the decision to name a Negro recorder of deeds and persistence in this course against all opposition indicated that the Northern Democracy of the 1880's, as personified by President Cleveland, was ready to go far to please blacks on the subject of federal as well as state and local patronage, despite considerable Southern objection. The administration's overall handling of the civil service proved that the specific case of Matthews and Trotter, while dramatic, was no aberration in policy. Nevertheless, few American Negroes had a realistic expectation of ever getting a government job. Of far greater practical importance to blacks was the Southern racial situation, and on that score continuity of Democratic policy, not novelty, characterized the Cleveland years.

The cornerstone of Democratic new departure strategy was still, as always, letting the South handle its own affairs. This passivity took a dual form under Cleveland: no executive action on Southern disorders beyond barring federal appointments to two Mississippi whites guilty of outright violence against Negroes, and no attempt to rally Congress in support of the Blair education bill which, if passed, would have benefited blacks and whites in Dixie. The significance of this ideological confinement to new departure constraints was obscured at the time by two factors. First, racial bloodshed was still relatively rare in the Redeemer-controlled South, as compared to Reconstruction days; second, the national Republican administration that preceded Cleveland's had also taken a hands-off approach. With the malady of Southern outbreaks somewhat alleviated and Republican doctors no longer prescribing strong medicine, it is no

84. Simmons, ed., *Men of Mark*, p. 841.

wonder that Cleveland's patronage record, courtesy to Frederick Douglass, and support of reimbursement to Freedman's Bank depositors drew more attention than they in hindsight deserved. If, however, the Southern situation were to deteriorate, and if the Republicans would respond by going back to their pre-1876 interventionist views, the negative side of Democratic new departurism would reappear with a vengeance.

5

"The Southern Tail
Wags the Northern Head"
1888-91

Though Democratic racial policy shifted in the 1870's and 1880's, once Grover Cleveland left office in 1889 the party proved that its new progressive image on the national scene was confined to narrow limits. With Democratic defeat in the 1888 elections came Republican control over Congress and the presidency, and for the first time since Reconstruction the Republicans could redeem their old commitment to the Negro. They tried to do so through legislation giving Southern black voters federal protection. Intent on maintaining a solid Democratic South, the entire Northern Democracy, even while seeking black support in their own states, mobilized against the federal elections measure, lending aid and comfort to Southern white supremacists. This dismayed the black community—but it should not have been surprising, since opposition to a federal role in race relations was always the bedrock of new departure politics. After all, even those Northern Democrats considered to be least prejudiced against Negroes, like Grover Cleveland, drew the line at national intervention in Southern affairs.

Democrats conducted their 1888 presidential campaign on a note of racial liberality. When the party's national convention met in St. Louis to renominate President Cleveland, chairman Patrick Collins of Massachusetts claimed that during the last four years "the negro, whose fears of Democratic rule were played upon by demagogues four years ago [is] not only more protected than by his pretended friends, but honored as his race was never honored before." The Democratic platform claimed that under Cleveland "the rights and welfare of all the people have been guarded and defended, every public interest has been protected, and the equality of all our citizens before the law, without regard to race or section, has been steadfastly maintained." In his letter of acceptance, Cleveland made a "guarantee to our colored citizens of all their rights of citizenship, and their just recognition and encouragement in all things pertaining to that relation."[1] The black vote loomed so large in the minds of Democrats that Cleveland's running mate, the veteran Ohio politician Allen Thurman, tried to explain away his anti-Negro record during the Civil War and Reconstruction with the claim that fear of a black invasion of Ohio, not race prejudice, had motivated his course. Thurman even recounted a story of his childhood friendship with a Negro boy who died young, prompting a black newspaper to jeer: "Judge Thurman has become a public Negro lover."[2]

Democrats tried harder than ever to make inroads into the Republican Negro electorate, citing Cleveland's good record on race and the benefits of Democratic tariff reduction. They convinced prominent blacks like Peter Clark, T. Thomas Fortune, George T. Downing, James M. Trotter, James C. Matthews, and T. McCants Stewart to campaign for Cleveland. The party even subsidized a national convention of Negro independents and Democrats in July. After fierce wrangling at this conference between veteran Negro Democrats and newer converts, the former faction elected Peter Clark as chairman. The intellectual godfather of black rebellion against Republicans, Clark castigated those politicians who "declare in favor of a free ballot and fair count, but know full well that the evils of which they complain is one [*sic*] that cannot be controlled by Federal action." The race should advance its interests on the state level, and drop "the policy of denunciation and hate." The delegates endorsed Cleve-

1. Collins's speech and Cleveland's acceptance letter are in *Official Proceedings of the National Democratic Convention Held in St. Louis, Missouri, June 5–7, 1888* (St. Louis: Woodward and Tiernan Printing Company, 1888), pp. 65, 170. For the platform see Porter and Johnson, eds., *Party Platforms*, p. 77.

2. Thurman, quoted in New York *World*, June 11, 1888, p. 3, September 21, 1888, p. 1; Topeka *American Citizen*, October 12, 1888, p. 1.

land and the Democratic low tariff position. After all, most of the industries protected by tariffs refused to employ blacks.[3] Republican leaders took this convention so seriously that they asked black Republican spokesmen to launch countermeasures.[4]

Though polling more popular votes than Republican candidate Benjamin Harrison, Cleveland lost 233 to 168 in the electoral college as the Republicans carried every Northern state but Connecticut and New Jersey. It is impossible to estimate how many blacks voted for Cleveland or what impact Northern Negroes had on the result. In any case, the Negro Huntsville, Alabama, *Gazette* editorialized that the defeated Cleveland deserved respect from blacks. "He has shown great consideration in his dealings with the colored citizens," it noted, "and taught his party a lesson they will profit by learning."[5]

3. Clark: Indianapolis *Freeman*, October 27, 1888, p. 1; Fortune: Fortune to D. S. Lamont, November 23, 1887, Reel 54, Fortune to Grover Cleveland, June 6, 1888, telegram, Reel 122, Cleveland Papers; Indianapolis *Freeman*, September 22, 1888, p. 1; Downing: New York *World*, September 23, 1888, p. 36; Grimké: Charles R. Codman to Grover Cleveland, January 11, 1889, Reel 66, Cleveland Papers; Trotter: Trotter to John F. Andrew, October 16, 1888, Andrew Papers; Matthews and Stewart: William E. Gross to Grover Cleveland, July 2, 1888, Reel 61, Gross to Cleveland, September 8, 1888, Stewart to D. S. Lamont, September 9, 1888, Matthews to Lamont, September 10, 1888, Reel 63, Cleveland Papers; New York *Age*, September 22, 1888, p. 1, September 29, 1888, p. 2. Similar activity by important but lesser-known blacks Henry F. Downing, R. A. Jones (editor of the Cleveland *Globe*), and C. H. J. Taylor is chronicled in H. F. Downing to Cleveland, June 15, 1888, Reel 60, Cleveland Papers; R. A. Jones to Samuel J. Randall, May 4, 1888, Box 165, Randall Papers; Topeka *American Citizen*, May 25, 1888, p. 1. Official invitations to the black independent convention, signed by Missouri Negro leader J. Milton Turner, came into the hands of the Washington *Bee*'s editor, who sent them on to the Republicans. See William Calvin Chase to Benjamin Harrison, July 9, 1888, and enclosures, Reel 9, Harrison Papers. The *Bee*, August 18, 1888, pp. 1 and 4, presented evidence that the Democrats were subsidizing the event. An additional bit of corroboration for the charge is J. Milton Turner's calling card in Senator Francis M. Cockrell (Missouri Democrat) to Grover Cleveland, May 28, 1888, Reel 122, Cleveland Papers. The Indianapolis convention was reported in New York *Times*, July 25, 26, 1888, both p. 5, July 27, 1888, p. 2.

4. The Negro Republicans decided to issue a public statement against the Democrats rather than hold their own convention. James S. Clarkson to Frederick Douglass, August 21, September 5, 1888, Reel 6, Douglass Papers; William H. Johnson, *Autobiography*, pp. 33–35; W. S. Scarborough to Benjamin Harrison, October 1, 1888, Reel 11, Harrison Papers; New York *Tribune*, September 29, 1888, p. 2.

5. Burnham, *Presidential Ballots*, pp. 246–49; Huntsville *Gazette*, November

Southern Democrats, as if anxious to prove that they had learned no such lesson, made the post-election year of 1889 a disastrous one for Negroes. By this time agrarian threats to the power of Redeemer leadership were causing severe social tensions in several states, and blacks were the available scapegoats. But the immediate trigger to increased racial strife was the election result. Since 1874 Southern whites had been immune to national interference because the Democrats usually controlled at least one house of Congress, eliminating the possibility of federal legislation to protect the black ballot, and with Cleveland in the White House, Dixie Democrats were even more insulated from outside intervention. Suddenly, as of March 4, 1889, a Republican president, Senate, and House confronted the South. Republicans could now implement their traditional allegiance to Negro rights; this prospect evoked white anger, frustration, and fear. A spectacular increase in violence against Southern blacks was the result.[6] Even more ominously, moderate Southern leaders who had previously protected Negroes and frowned on crude racism raised the banner of white supremacy themselves, in an effort to show Republicans that the white South, despite incipient political cleavages, stood united against federal meddling in race relations. Soon after Harrison's election Democratic Congressman William Oates of Alabama, a Conservative, told the president-elect that if the Republicans proposed the official end of Negro suffrage, Southern whites would not protest. He explained: "For my own part, I frankly declare that . . . the negro is incapable of self-government." Governor Fitzhugh Lee of Virginia, another former moderate, chimed in with an open justification for suppressing black votes: "The safety of the Union depends on white sovereignty, not black."

10, 1888, p. 2. For what it is worth, Pulaski County, Illinois, one-third black, showed a net Republican gain of twenty-six over 1884, while the statewide Republican margin declined by about 3,000 votes compared to four years earlier. *Tribune Almanac*, 1889, p. 62.

6. This has been recently noted by Crofts in "The Blair Bill and the Elections Bill," p. 234. It also is obvious from even a cursory reading of the black press following the election. Significantly, 1889 is the first year for which we have statistics on lynchings. Arthur F. Raper, *The Tragedy of Lynching* (Chapel Hill: University of North Carolina Press, 1933), p. 480.

Even South Carolina Senator Wade Hampton abandoned his benevolent paternalism, suggesting that Southern Negroes "go off or settle in New England." In 1890 he stated that "the Constitution was violated when the negro was allowed to vote."[7] Several senators from the Deep South proposed legislation authorizing federal financing for the voluntary deportation of Southern blacks.[8]

The noted Louisiana rebel against Southern racial orthodoxy, George W. Cable, asked "the Democratic party of the wide North and West to withdraw its support from the Southern policy now, as it did in 1860,"[9] but this was an unrealistic suggestion. Northern Democrats were indeed embarrassed by events in the South and urged a return to the racial status quo of the early and mid-1880's. But their opposition to the new Southern temper was vitiated by new departure constraints: states' rights doctrine, the desire that Dixie remain Democratic, and the conviction that whites should exercise political power in the region, albeit through persuasion rather than force. The Northern party press condemned anti-Negro violence while minimizing its extent, opposed the idea of deportation, and denounced Republicans for trying to make political capital out of the situation. Yet no Democratic newspaper could suggest a solution to the race problem beyond the negative approach of leaving the South alone to manage its own affairs.[10]

7. New York *World*, December 29, 1888, February 23, 1889, both p. 4, August 22, 1889, p. 1; Wade Hampton, "The Race Problem," *Arena*, II (July, 1890), 132–38. On the internal South Carolina political situation that influenced Hampton's change of spirit, see Wellman, *Giant in Gray*, pp. 312–13, and Cooper, *Conservative Regime*, pp. 110–11.

8. Senators Wilkinson Call of Florida, Randall Gibson of Louisiana, and Matthew Butler of South Carolina, in *Congressional Record*, 51 Cong., 1 sess., pp. 155, 157, 802 (December 12, 1889, January 7, 1890).

9. Cable, "The Southern Struggle for Pure Government," in *The Negro Question*, ed. Turner, p. 270.

10. This generalization is based upon the following sample: Philadelphia *Record*, October 5, 1889, New York *Herald*, January 2, 1890, Brooklyn *Eagle*, December 30, 1889, Chicago *Herald*, January 9, 1890, Albany *Argus*, January 18, 1890, Brooklyn *Citizen*, January 17, 1890, Boston *Globe*, January 25, 1890, Albany *Times*, January 24, 1890, all reprinted in *Public Opinion*, VIII (October 12, 1889–February 1, 1890), 4, 303, 305, 355, 376–79, 399; Chicago *Times*, January 25, February 15, 1890, both p. 4; Cincinnati *Enquirer*, February 7, 1890, p. 4; New York *World*, February 24, 25, August 23, September 20, October 7,

Governor Hill of New York made the only serious Northern Democratic attempt to soften the increasingly hard line taken by Southern whites on the race question. The ambitious Hill journeyed South late in 1889, hoping to advance his prospects for the Democratic presidential nomination in 1892. In a public speech at Atlanta, Hill denounced "selfish politicians" who encouraged Northern mistrust of Southern whites, but he added that the North had a legitimate interest in Southern attempts to solve the race question. He told his audience that elevation of the black man was both their "interest" and their "duty." When Hill returned to New York, reporters asked for his opinion of the Southern situation. He replied that the racial issue

> is a serious one, but I am inclined to think that it is working itself out well. . . . I saw black men and white men laying bricks and doing carpentry work side by side and working together on the plantations, and I shall not be surprised to see them in a few years employed together upon work which requires more skill and intelligence.

Word leaked out that Hill had also spoken privately to the Democratic leaders of Georgia and advised them to stop terrorizing Negroes, allow them to vote, and win their allegiance with minor patronage as Northern Democrats had done.[11]

Reaction to Hill's activities came quickly. T. McCants Stewart, the black Democrat from Brooklyn, notified Grover Cleveland: "Ah, Sir, there would be no Negro Political Problem if Southern Democrats would square their conduct by the avowed principles of such leaders as yourself, Governor Abbett . . . and Governor Hill *at Atlanta*."[12] But Southern whites rejected Hill's advice as irrelevant to their region. The New Orleans *Times-Democrat* claimed that "the Negro that Governor Hill has seen at the North is not the Negro that is now being discussed; he is not the Negro that must be known by all who desire to speak intelli-

---

21, 27, 1889, all p. 4. The Indianapolis *Sentinel* was exceptional in viewing colonization favorably; see December 30, 1889, p. 2, and February 11, 1890, p. 4.

11. New York *World*, October 17, 1889, pp. 1–2, October 22, 1889, p. 1, October 24, 1889, p. 4.

12. Stewart to Cleveland, November 7, 1889, Reel 68, Cleveland Papers.

gently of the race issue."[13] The inflammatory words and violent deeds of white Southerners continued as before, and in 1890 Mississippi became the first state in Dixie to alter the suffrage provision of its Reconstruction constitution, instituting a literacy and "understanding" requirement for voting clearly intended to disfranchise blacks. As the Negro New York *Age* commented, "the South repudiated the Atlanta position of Governor Hill so quick and with such vengeance that it gave his presidential aspirations the death rattle." Southern whites seemed more determined than ever to keep the Negro down; observed the *Age*, "the Southern tail wags the Northern head of the Democratic party."[14]

The Harrison administration, though at first interested in courting the favor of Southern whites, decided late in 1889 to support legislation protecting Negro voting. The Massachusetts Republican Congressman Henry Cabot Lodge framed a measure providing that a certain number of voters in a district could request federal inspectors to oversee the conduct of congressional elections. A federal board would also review and certify the results of all congressional contests.[15]

When debate opened on the Lodge bill in the House of Representatives, the Democrats behaved as they had in Reconstruction days: the entire Democratic side of the chamber opposed the legislation, but the Southern wing had a monopoly on racist rhetoric. Dixie Democrats vowed never to submit to "Negro domination" and justified their "control" of the black vote on the grounds that the typical Negro "does not know how he is voting," anyway. "Gentlemen," remarked Roger Q. Mills of Texas, "you ought not to forget that we belong to the Anglo-Saxon race."[16] Northern Democrats backed Southern desires for home rule but avoided racist appeals. Claiming that prejudice

13. Quoted in Detroit *Plaindealer*, November 15, 1889, p. 4.
14. Wharton, *Negro in Mississippi*, p. 212; New York *Age*, November 23, December 28, 1889, both p. 2.
15. Hirshson, *Bloody Shirt*, pp. 168–82, 205–11; Crofts, "The Blair Bill and the Elections Bill," pp. 260–61.
16. H. St. George Tucker of Virginia and Mills, in *Congressional Record*, 51 Cong., 1 sess., pp. 6565, 6858 (June 28, July 1, 1890). For similar Southern comment, consult *ibid.*, pp. 6553, 6703, Appendix, p. 446 (June 26, 28, 30, 1890).

against blacks was "fast dying out" in the South, they warned that the Lodge bill could reignite anti-Negro feeling. Since the proposed bill would not aid blacks, its sponsors must have some ulterior motive. Roswell Flower of New York charged that the measure was calculated "to get into the hands of the Republican party the whole election machinery of the States" with the purpose of overturning Democratic majorities in Northern cities. The ultimate Republican goal, according to their Northern rivals, was to pack Congress with fraudulent majorities in order to pass economic legislation favoring the rich.[17] Democratic congressmen irrespective of section voted against the elections bill which passed the House of Representatives in July, 1890.[18] The Senate postponed action until the winter session, and Democrats above and below the Mason-Dixon Line prepared to battle against the Lodge bill and its Republican sponsors in the fall elections.

The state campaigns of 1890 were fought primarily on two issues: the Republicans' protectionist McKinley Tariff Act, and the elections bill. The *Democratic Campaign Book* devoted 129 pages to the tariff and 65 to the Lodge proposal. Every state Democratic platform denounced the federal elections bill as a step toward centralization, a sign of Republican mistrust of the people, a source of sectional and racial strife, and a threat to American prosperity.[19]

But Democrats in the various states placed different degrees of emphasis on the Lodge bill. Border and Southern Democrats hammered away at the proposal, subordinating other issues to it, and openly avowing white supremacist objectives. The Atlanta *Constitution* went so far as to threaten a Southern boycott of Northern products should the bill become law, and the governor of Georgia endorsed the suggestion.[20] The amount of

17. James Covert, Amos Cummings, and Roswell Flower of New York, Elijah Brookshire and John O'Neall of Indiana, *ibid.*, pp. 6599, 6680, Appendix, pp. 405, 415 (June 27, 28, 30, 1890).

18. *Ibid.*, pp. 6940–41 (July 2, 1890).

19. *Democratic Campaign Book: Congressional Elections, 1890* (Washington: Ramsey and Bisbee, 1890), pp. 25–90, 187–316; *Tribune Almanac*, 1891, pp. 42–85 *passim*.

20. On the boycott plan, see Hirshson, *Bloody Shirt*, pp. 218–19. Southern

Northern Democratic stress on the Lodge bill varied; even denouncers of the legislation, anxious to attract black support on the state and local level, avoided racism. Through much of the Midwest, where farmers were thought to oppose the McKinley tariff, party leaders stressed the high duties and soft-pedaled the Lodge bill.[21] New England Democrats avoided the question of federal supervision of elections because voters in this section were sympathetic to the purposes of the measure; the New England conscience was not yet dead, even among Yankee Mugwumps and Democrats. Thus the state organizations of Massachusetts and Vermont framed the only 1890 Democratic platforms coupling denunciation of the Lodge bill with condemnation of election frauds, presumably including those practiced by Southern whites.[22] Elsewhere in the North, especially in large cities, Democrats felt freer to attack the federal elections bill;[23] but nowhere was the issue used as skillfully as in New York, where the Democrats dissociated it entirely from the Southern

---

and border opinion can be sampled in Augusta (Ga.) *Chronicle*, June 14, 1890, Louisville *Courier-Journal*, undated, and July 7, 1890, all reprinted in *Public Opinion*, IX (June 21, 28, July 12, 1890), 238, 263, 311; John G. Carlisle, "Republican Promise and Performance," *Forum*, IX (May, 1890), 254; W. C. P. Breckinridge, "The Race Question," *Arena*, II (June, 1890), 51–52; John T. Morgan, "The Race Question in the United States," *ibid.* (September, 1890), 386, 398; Hilary A. Herbert, ed., *Why the Solid South? Or, Reconstruction and Its Results* (Baltimore: R. H. Woodward, 1890).

21. Midwestern Democratic views are expressed in the following: Chicago *Times* and Cincinnati *Enquirer*, both July–November, 1890; F. A. Johnston to W. C. P. Breckinridge, July 26, 1890, E. C. Wall to Breckinridge, August 7, 1890, Vol. 413, John E. Monnot to Breckinridge, August 27, 1890, Vol. 414, Breckinridge Papers; E. C. Wall to Grover Cleveland, October 6, 1890, J. H. Reigner to Cleveland, October 9, 1890, Lewis Baker to Cleveland, November 15, 1890, Charles W. Sherman to Cleveland, November 26, 1890, Reel 68, Cleveland Papers; Don Dickinson, quoted in New York *Sun*, October 15, 1890, p. 6.

22. The best expression of New England Democratic unease is Edmund M. Wheelright to George F. Williams, October 11, 1890, Box 2, William E. Russell Papers, Massachusetts Historical Society. Also see H. D. Catlin to Grover Cleveland, February 25, 1890, Reel 68, Cleveland Papers; William E. Russell to W. C. P. Breckinridge, July 10, 1890, Vol. 413, O. Lapham to Breckinridge, October 3, 1890, Vol. 415, Breckinridge Papers. The platforms are in *Tribune Almanac*, 1891, pp. 60, 82.

23. Philadelphia *Record*, June 16, 1890, Philadelphia *Times*, June 11, 1890, both reprinted in *Public Opinion*, IX (June 21, 1890), 238–39; Indianapolis *Sentinel*, July 23, 1890, p. 2; Daniel Voorhees to John B. Stoll, undated [1890], in Stoll, *History of the Indiana Democracy*, p. 335; William Singerly to W. C. P. Breckinridge, July 7, 1890, Vol. 412, Breckinridge Papers.

question. Governor Hill's organization opposed reduction of import duties, and therefore wanted to keep the tariff from becoming a partisan matter. However, in the light of national Democratic hostility to the McKinley Act, this would be difficult. The protectionist New York *Sun* pointed out that opposition to the Lodge bill was the only way to unify the Democracy: "the wildest Free Trader and the most inflexible Protectionist can get together in defense of free elections." The Democratic state campaign stressed the Lodge bill more than any other issue, ignoring the South and the Negro while alleging that the federal elections measure was a scheme to subvert the ballot in New York City.[24]

Democrats swept the fall elections, capturing control of the House and winning several governorships. Midwesterners attributed the result to popular revulsion against high tariffs. The New York *World* agreed that the tariff issue had carried the West and Massachusetts, but added that the Lodge bill had "helped everywhere." Governor Hill warned the Republican Senate not to pass the elections bill at its lame-duck session, because the recent returns showed "that such a partisan measure . . . is not approved by the majority of the American people."[25]

Nevertheless, the Senate took up the Lodge bill in December, with the Democratic minority determined to keep it from coming to a vote. Southern and border state Democrats led the fight against the bill with a new barrage of white supremacist oratory.[26] Some Northern Democrats repeated their earlier strategy of fighting the measure without recourse to racism,[27] but for the

24. The quotation is from New York *Sun*, August 25, 1890, p. 4. Also see the statements of Democratic campaign manager Roswell Flower in New York *World*, July 10, 1890, p. 5, August 6, 1890, p. 4, and Flower to David B. Hill, August 3, 1890, Box 5A, Bixby Papers. The official address of the state Democratic committee is in New York *World*, September 24, 1890, p. 2.

25. *Tribune Almanac*, 1891, pp. 274–317; Chicago *Times*, November 5, 1890, p. 4; New York *World*, November 24, 1890, p. 4, November 6, 1890, p. 1, quoting Hill.

26. *Congressional Record*, 51 Cong., 2 sess., pp. 76–77, 122, 365, 453–68, 46–52 (Appendix), 1418–21, 1607–14 (December 4, 5, 12, 15, 31, 1890, January 16, 21, 1891).

27. Rufus Blodgett of New Jersey and Daniel Voorhees of Indiana, *ibid.*, pp. 366–67, 782 (December 12, 22, 1890).

first time since before the new departure two Northerners echoed the Southerners. David Turpie of Indiana, arguing that Republicans promoted the Negro cause for political purposes only, held that all whites, whether admitting it or not, really believed in the supremacy of their own race. Anglo-Saxons had reached a higher point in development than the darker races; Caucasians had a duty to guide Negroes along the path to civilization, and blacks had a corresponding obligation: "a certain deference, submission, and obedience." No matter what abstract "equal rights" might be codified in law, whites must rule. Senator John McPherson of New Jersey evoked the specter of race war should the Lodge bill pass, and he accused Republicans of wanting to revive Reconstruction. He noted that the Negro had been a voter for over twenty years, and asked: "What sort of capacity does he now exhibit for self-government?"[28]

True to their word, Senate Democrats used every possible tactic to prevent a vote on the elections bill. They filibustered tirelessly and, whenever a roll call seemed imminent, left the floor to prevent a quorum. Under the skillful leadership of Arthur P. Gorman of Maryland, the Democrats made a bargain with Republican members who favored the free coinage of silver. After Democrats helped the silverites pass a free coinage bill, the latter faction joined the Democrats in voting to take up an appropriation bill in place of the Lodge measure. The federal elections bill, therefore, never came to a vote in the Senate.[29]

A momentous result of the Lodge bill controversy was the solidification of bonds between Northern and Southern Democrats. The Northern Democracy, which gave up exploitation of racism in the 1870's and 1880's and went far in appealing to the black electorate, decided in 1890 to strengthen its ties to the increasingly violent, racist, and oppressive Southern wing of the

28. *Ibid.*, pp. 50–54, 823 (December 3, 23, 1890).

29. John R. Lambert, *Arthur Pue Gorman* (Baton Rouge: Louisiana State University Press, 1953), pp. 145–66; Hirshson, *Bloody Shirt*, pp. 231–33. Detailed accounts of the political maneuvering that characterized congressional handling of the bill are Crofts, "The Blair Bill and the Elections Bill," pp. 288–343, and Richard E. Welch, Jr., "The Federal Elections Bill of 1890: Postscripts and Prelude," *Journal of American History*, LII (December, 1965), 511–26.

organization. Senators Turpie and McPherson, apparently agreeing with their Dixie colleagues on the matter, had begun to mouth Southern-style racist arguments. Even Northerners who did not go that far abetted the ongoing process of Negro debasement in the South by backing Southern Democrats to the hilt. The respected Massachusetts economist Edward Atkinson, a former abolitionist and Radical Republican turned Democrat, privately assured a Kentucky congressman that, in regard to the Lodge measure, "you have the sympathy and support of a large number of the survivors of the Free Soil party of '48 and their successors, their heirs and assigns." What could the Kentuckian conclude but that the white South was free to subordinate blacks without fear of Northern interference? Governor Hill of New York, who did not himself cater to white prejudice and had advised Southern leaders to win blacks over with kindness, wrote to Senator John W. Daniel of Virginia: "I am sure that every Democrat must admire the masterly manner in which our representatives in the Senate have conducted the opposition to the bill." In view of the white supremacist speeches being delivered in the Senate, such a message from a leading Northern Democratic politician could have meant only one thing: a blank check for the South to do whatever it wanted about the Negro question.[30]

Solid Democratic opposition to the Lodge bill disappointed the black press, which now realized that Northern congressmen of that party, far from influencing their Dixie colleagues, seemed to succumb to the Southern anti-Negro virus as soon as they reached Washington.[31] But to have expected any other stand by new departurists was wishful thinking. From the 1870's through the 1890's Democratic concessions to blacks, first in the form of official acquiescence in the Reconstruction amendments, then through patronage and civil rights laws in the North, and finally crystalized in Cleveland's national policies, whether motivated

30. Atkinson to W. C. P. Breckinridge, January 21, 1891, Vol. 418, Breckinridge Papers; Hill to Daniel, January 27, 1891, Package 1, Vol. 3, pp. 473–74, Bixby Papers.

31. New York *Age*, July 26, 1890, p. 2; Detroit *Plaindealer*, October 24, 1890, p. 4; Indianapolis *Freeman*, June 7, 28, July 19, 1890, all p. 4.

by politics or principle, never extended to federal protection of voting rights in the South. Democrats consistently fought against such intervention because party hopes for electoral success depended on control of a solid South, and party ideology cherished the states' rights creed, even if it meant complicity in the suppression of the Negro. A generation after Reconstruction, Northern public opinion, influenced by persistent Democratic propaganda about the evils of federal interference in race relations and swayed by the new vogue of pseudoscientific racism based on Darwinian biology, was ripe for full acceptance of the new departure.[32]

32. At the time, a black professor delineated most clearly the Darwinian impact on sectional politics. See W. S. Scarborough, "The Negro Question," *Arena*, IV (July, 1891), 220. Fredrickson, *Black Image*, pp. 228–55, is a recent treatment of the topic.

6

The Paradox of Democratic Racial Policy 1892

The 1892 presidential election marked the ultimate triumph of Democratic racial policy. By appealing to white voters' fears of federal control over elections even more than they had in 1890 while continuing to exploit black dissatisfaction with Republicans, the Democrats successfully wielded their double-edged new departure weapon: the leave-the-South-alone strategy used by the national party since Vallandigham, and the win-the-black-vote technique developed in Northern politics. This dual approach was partially based upon expediency but also reflected the conviction of some Democrats that the race problem could best be solved on the state level without federal intervention. Yet the strange posture of enticing black support while propping up Southern white supremacy was open to the same charge of hypocrisy that Republicans leveled against Northern Democratic racial liberalism in the 1880's. However, though lacking in logical consistency, Democratic policy worked. The party's paradoxical stand on the Negro question helped win the election, foreclosing all hope of federal protection for blacks in the nineteenth century.

Republicans disagreed over how to treat the Southern question after their debacle in the 1890 congressional elections and the demise of the Lodge bill in the Senate. President Harrison gave up hope for outright federal protection of the suffrage; at the end of 1891 he called for a nonpartisan commission to investigate the operation of the election laws. But the 1892 Republican national convention renominated Harrison on a platform pledging to protect "the integrity of the ballot and the purity of elections. . . ." Throughout the campaign Republicans remained vague and evasive on the matter.[1]

While all Democratic state platforms continued to denounce the Lodge bill as one of the Republican administration's iniquities, the national Democratic party was divided over what role the issue should play in the upcoming contest. Governor William E. Russell of Massachusetts believed that his state had gone Democratic in recent years because of the tariff question. If the party wished to carry the Bay State, he wrote, the tariff "should be made the one great issue of the presidential campaign." Congressman William L. Wilson of West Virginia privately suggested to Grover Cleveland that tariff reform was "an issue big enough to down the bloody shirt and raise up a great democratic party in all parts of the country."[2] In contrast, those Democrats attuned to the momentous political events in the South had a different perspective. The rapid growth of the Populist party in Dixie meant that Southern whites were dividing politically. Defections from the Democracy to the new party might threaten white supremacy as well as Democratic hegemony in the region by making the blacks a balance of power. Some Democrats saw that the only way to prevent Southern whites from going over to the Populists was to emphasize that every vote for the third party was actually a vote for the Republicans, who stood for the Lodge bill and federal meddling with race relations.[3]

In June the Democrats met in their national convention at Chicago. The delegates approved a platform denouncing the Lodge bill which, they claimed, would "injure the colored citizen even more than the white." Federal interference with elections meant "the subjugation of the colored people to the control of the party in power, and the reviving of race antagonisms,

1. Hirshson, *Bloody Shirt*, pp. 238–39.
2. *Tribune Almanac*, 1893, pp. 42–68; William E. Russell, "Significance of the Massachusetts Election," *Forum*, XII (December, 1891), 440; Wilson to Cleveland, March 22, 1892, Reel 70, Cleveland Papers.
3. Thomas F. Bayard to Grover Cleveland, May 4, 1892, Reel 70, Cleveland Papers; Bayard, "Democratic Duty and Opportunity," *Forum*, XIII (June, 1892), 419–20; George Harmon Knoles, *The Presidential Campaign and Election of 1892* (Stanford: Stanford University Press, 1942), p. 138.

now happily abated." The paradoxical nature of the Democratic position was underlined when Senator Palmer of Illinois, who fought for the right of Negroes in his state to attend white schools, roused the delegates by warning: "As sure as Benjamin Harrision is elected, and the next Congress is Republican, we will have a force bill. . . ." The Democrats nominated Grover Cleveland again.[4] The former president, who hoped to regain the White House by championing a low tariff and the gold standard, had taken no official stand on the Lodge bill, and some Democrats opposed to his candidacy for other reasons asserted that he was soft on the issue. Since leaving office in 1889 Cleveland's only public statement on the Southern situation was his praise for the Mississippi constitution of 1890, with its ostensibly impartial literacy and understanding requirements for voting.[5]

One man, editor Charles A. Dana of the New York *Sun*, determined the direction of the campaign. The *Sun* was at this time an independent journal, though the editor was known to be an ally of the Tammany Democracy. Favoring high tariffs and the spoils system, and receptive to bimetalic coinage, Dana stood for everything Cleveland opposed. But, after the latter's nomination, Dana understood that to withhold his support from the Democratic ticket "would probably mean for himself and his paper financial ruin." He therefore seized upon the Lodge bill as the crucial issue. "Better vote for the liberty and the white government of the Southern States, even if the candidate were the Devil himself," he thundered editorially, "rather than consent to the election of respectable Benjamin Harrison with a Force bill in his pocket!"[6] The *Sun* had used similar tactics in 1890 to unite high and low tariff Democrats on an anti–Lodge bill basis, stressing the possible effects of a federal elections law in New York City. In 1892, however, Dana hammered away at

4. Porter and Johnson, eds., *Party Platforms*, p. 86; *Official Proceedings of the National Democratic Convention Held in Chicago, Illinois, June 21–23, 1892* (Chicago: Cameron, Amberg, 1892), p. 43.

5. Nevins, *Cleveland*, p. 464; Cleveland to Lucius Lamar, May 1, 1892, Reel 70, Cleveland Papers; Wharton, *Negro in Mississippi*, p. 212.

6. Candace Stone, *Dana and the Sun* (New York: Dodd, Mead, 1938), pp. 56–114; Harry Thurston Peck, *Twenty Years of the Republic, 1885–1905* (New York: Dodd, Mead, 1906), p. 296; New York *Sun*, June 24, 1892, p. 6.

the threat of "the horrors of negro domination" in the South.[7]
The shift to a racist battle-cry derived from the Populist threat
to divide the white vote in Dixie. By shining the spotlight on sup-
posed Republican designs to pass the Lodge bill and the result-
ing challenge to white supremacy, the *Sun* found an issue which
could both reconcile Northern anti-Cleveland Democrats with
the national party, and simultaneously scare Southern white
dissidents into voting the regular Democratic ticket.

At first Dana's course seemed to split the party by section.
Many Northern Democrats criticized the subordination of economic issues which a militant crusade against the Lodge bill
necessitated. The Chicago *Herald*, the Chicago *Times*, the Indianapolis *Sentinel*, and especially the New York *World* claimed
that the tariff question would decide the election. It was absurd
to stress the elections bill because, said the *World*, "the Republicans are nowhere openly defending it." Josiah Quincy of Massachusetts, an executive of the Democratic national committee,
also saw the upcoming contest in economic terms: "Plutocracy
against Democracy, the rule of favored special interests against
government by the people."[8] Dixie Democrats, in contrast,
praised the *Sun*'s course. Congressman Hilary Herbert of Alabama and Senators Arthur P. Gorman of Maryland and Matt
Ransom of North Carolina sent messages of encouragement to
Dana. Democratic newspapers in the South echoed the *Sun*'s
editorial line and pressed the argument that a vote for the Populists was a vote for Negro domination. In July a Negro newspaper
commented that the direction of the campaign was making
Southern whites "more brazen than ever."[9]

Ominously, the alliance between the *Sun* and the Democratic

7. New York *Sun*, June 25, 1892, p. 6, repeated monotonously up to election
day.
8. The Chicago *Herald* and Josiah Quincy, quoted *ibid.*, June 28, August
21, 1892, both p. 6; Chicago *Times*, July 24, 1892, p. 4; Indianapolis *Sentinel*,
July 27, 1892, p. 4; New York *World*, July 11, 1892, p. 4.
9. Herbert to Dana, June 28, 1892, Gorman and Ransom to Dana, August 6,
1892, reprinted in New York *Sun*, July 8, 1892, p. 1, August 16, 1892, p. 6; Atlanta *Constitution*, July 23, 1892, Savannah *News*, July 21, 1892, both reprinted
in *Public Opinion*, XIII (July 30, 1892), 396–97; Detroit *Plaindealer*, July 1,
1892, p. 4.

South began to influence the national Democratic effort. With the *Sun* demanding that Grover Cleveland end his silence on the subject of federal supervision of elections, the candidate wrote two private letters which were quickly released to the press; in them he called the Lodge bill "a direct attack upon the spirit and theory of our Government." Cleveland could "not see how any Democrat can think otherwise." He was to accept the nomination in person at Madison Square Garden on July 20, and campaign manager William C. Whitney notified him that Southern leaders "are very anxious that something positive should be said by you on the subject of the Force bill." Cleveland gave them what they wanted. In his acceptance address the nominee went beyond the usual Northern Democratic charges that a federal elections bill meant centralization and was intended to keep Republicans in power. He recalled "the saturnalia of theft and brutal control which followed another Federal regulation of State suffrage." In case of Republican victory, a similar fate might befall Southern states "where peace and hopefulness now prevail."[10] Vice-presidential candidate Adlai Stevenson of Illinois stumped the nation, explaining the evils of federal tampering with elections; he gave Southern audiences detailed descriptions of alleged financial chicanery in Southern state governments during Reconstruction. A vote for the Populists, he said, was an endorsement of a return to that situation.[11] Democratic headquarters issued piles of campaign literature insisting that, though coy on the issue, the Republicans planned to revive the Lodge bill if they won.[12]

As the campaign progressed, the elections bill issue became

10. New York *Sun*, July 9, 1892, p. 6; Cleveland to J. W. Campbell, July 7, Cleveland to Basil B. Gordon, July 9, 1892, both reprinted *ibid.*, July 19, 1892, p. 6; Whitney to Cleveland, July 10, 1892, Reel 70, Cleveland Papers; *Proceedings of Democratic National Convention, 1892*, pp. 224–25.

11. Two Stevenson speeches, one to a Northern audience and one delivered in the South, are printed in Indianapolis *Sentinel*, August 28, 1892, p. 3, September 16, 1892, p. 1.

12. *The Campaign Text Book of the Democratic Party for the Presidential Election of 1892* (New York: M. B. Brown, 1892), pp. 127–65; *The Democratic Party Facts* (Washington: Democratic Congressional Committee, 1892), p. 49; *A Menace to Liberty* (n.p.: n.p., 1892); *Carl Schurz on the Issues of the Campaign* (n.p.: n.p., 1892), pp. 27–29.

ever more prominent in the North despite Republican reticence, but Northern Democrats did not adopt the *Sun's* racist stance. Governor Hill of New York, for example, opposed the Lodge bill because it would "provoke conflicts between races," not because he feared Negro domination. According to Hill, Southern blacks were voting the Democratic ticket willingly. If left alone, the South "will work out its social and other problems in its own way. . . ." The Massachusetts Democracy and the influential Cincinnati *Enquirer*, both of which had downplayed the issue in 1890, now gave it greater prominence, without Dana's racism. Similarly, the Chicago *Times* and the Indianapolis *Sentinel*, which mocked Dana in July, seized upon the Lodge bill in the fall, charging that Republicans planned to grab control of elections in Northern cities. The New York *World*, with its stubborn emphasis on economic questions, was isolated by October.[13] Thus Dana's single-minded campaign against "Negro domination" and Southern white determination to quell the Populist threat by raising the bogey of race were fortified by the willingness of Northerners to press the issue. Republican James G. Blaine, Harrison's secretary of state until June, expressed public pessimism about his party's chances in the face of Dana's barrage, which he called "the most remarkable thing in the Presidential canvass of 1892." With election day near, Democratic national chairman William F. Harrity reported that the Lodge bill, though ignored by Republicans, "like Banquo's ghost, 'will not down.' "[14]

This evidence that the Northern Democracy would follow the Southern lead, when added to the continued degradation of Negroes in the South, confirmed most major black newspapers in their belief that Negroes could hope for nothing from a Democratic victory. It was the lesson of the 1890 Lodge bill struggle

13. Hill and the Massachusetts Democrats, in New York *Sun*, September 20, 1892, p. 2, October 13, 1892, p. 6; Cincinnati *Enquirer*, July 21, October 26, 1892, both p. 4; Chicago *Times*, November 7, 1892, p. 4; Indianapolis *Sentinel*, October 31, 1892, p. 4; New York *World*, October 19, 1892, p. 4.

14. James G. Blaine, "The Presidential Election of 1892," William F. Harrity, "The Democratic Outlook," *North American Review*, CLV (November, 1892), 519, 556.

all over again: "The Northern liberal Democrat, under the pressure of the party South, forgets his liberality and votes with the Negro hating majority which comes from the South."[15]

Even black Democrats had reason for disillusionment. One such man was Archibald Grimké of Massachusetts, a Cleveland supporter who opposed the Lodge bill. In June, 1892, Grimké asked the three Democratic congressmen from his state for a favor. Noting that the seventh congressional district in South Carolina had been set up in 1877 as a black political enclave on the tacit assumption that it would send Negroes to Congress, he complained that in recent years the whites there had manipulated election returns to show majorities for Democratic candidates; whenever that party controlled the House, the Democrat would be awarded the seat despite challenges from black contestants. William Elliott, a white Democrat, now occupied the place, and Negro Thomas Miller was contesting his election. The Democracy held a comfortable majority in the House. Grimké explained:

> Now I do think that we Northern colored men who are willing to work with the Democratic party should be considered by our Northern representatives in Congress in a case like that of Miller vs. Elliott. While I am opposed to the Force Bill I cannot excuse such a bold subversion of the majority principle as has occurred more than once in the Black District of South Carolina. . . . a decision at this time which would give the seat to Miller would be a stroke of very admirable politics. What is Mr. Elliott's vote worth to the Democratic party with its wide margin of power in the present house. . .? But outside of Congress, in Massachusetts for instance, where the colored vote is an increasing power as the balance between the two great parties grows more and more doubtful each year, to seat Miller would be a stroke of good politics.

Grimké added that Northern party leaders should be able to convince Southern Democrats "to conquer their prejudices" in the

15. Detroit *Plaindealer*, September 2, 1892, p. 4. Also see editorials in Cleveland *Gazette*, Huntsville *Gazette*, Indianapolis *Freeman*, and Washington *Bee* during the campaign.

interest of party welfare. Before sending the letter Grimké obtained the endorsements of two powerful figures in the Massachusetts Democracy, Charles R. Codman and Josiah Quincy. But this plea was ineffective. None of the Massachusetts Democrats to whom the letter was sent were on the committee which handled contested election cases. The Democratic majority on the committee, consisting of six Southerners and three Northerners, delayed any action until well after the election; on February 25, 1893, with the session almost over, they unanimously reported that Elliott was entitled to his seat, while the Republican minority supported Miller's claim. Once again Southern Democrats called the tune for the national party. Meanwhile, swallowing his disappointment, Grimké remained a Democrat. He received a consulate after the election.[16]

A more uneasy Negro Democrat was George T. Downing, who did not like the *Sun's* "Negro domination" editorials. Opposed to the Lodge bill and devoted to Cleveland but shocked by Dana's course, Downing asked the editor whether he favored curtailing the rights of any citizen on racial grounds. The *Sun* answered that whatever abstract case might be made for universal suffrage, "the condition and not the theory would determine our judgment," implying that if voting rights for blacks threatened white rule, disfranchisement was justified. Thoroughly alarmed, Downing asked Democratic Governor Abbett of New Jersey, known as a friend of the Negro, whether Dana spoke for the party as a whole. Abbett answered in a conciliatory vein. Cleveland and many other Democratic leaders wanted "to bring about more fraternal relations between the whites and blacks of the South, and, also, of the North." Abbett shrugged off Dana's activities: "The fact that some men, or some papers, are giving expression to views contrary to such a policy is no evidence, in my judgment, that the party as a party, or Mr. Cleve-

16. Grimké to John F. Andrew, George F. Williams, and Sherman Hoar, June 30, 1892, copy, Box 11, Archibald H. Grimké Papers, Moorland-Spingarn Collection, Howard University; U.S. House of Representatives, *Report of the Committee on the Judiciary on the Contested Election Case of Miller versus Elliott,* House Report 2569, 52 Cong., 2 sess., 1893; Angelina Grimké, "A Biographical Sketch of Archibald H. Grimké," *Opportunity,* III (February, 1925), 44–47.

land as its candidate, entertains any views except those friendly to the colored people." This calmed Downing, and he campaigned for the Democrats. Relying on Abbett's assurances, he told Negro audiences that "the mean effort of the New York *Sun*" to exploit racism did not represent mainstream party doctrine. "The Chicago [Democratic] platform, the speeches of the Democratic nominees, in fact of all speakers . . . do not add the insulting exclamation 'No negro domination' . . . they refer to it [the Lodge bill] as a bill designed for political effect . . . to control elections." Candid enough to admit that "neither party at present cares for us," he urged blacks: "Cause both to care for you . . . by letting them understand that you are independent. . . ."[17] Even in the face of Northern Democratic fellow-traveling with Southern racists and with editor Dana, Downing still held to Sumner's advice of twenty years before.

A third black Democrat succumbed to doubts about his party's course. Henry F. Downing (unrelated to the Newport Downing) had held a consulate under Cleveland and now published a Negro Democratic newspaper, the Brooklyn *Messenger*. But in late September, 1892, he informed the party's national committee that he could no longer in good conscience remain a Democrat. Downing explained that he used to think that "party needs would be effective to cause the southern wing of the Democratic party to see the expediency of cultivating friendly political relations with Afro-Americans." Angered by the increasingly militant racism shown by Dixie whites, Downing appealed to the platform committee at the Democratic national convention to approve a plank denouncing violence in the South, but he was told that such a resolution would offend Democrats from that region. When Dana began his propaganda against "Negro domination," Downing warned national chairman Harrity that this would alienate Negro voters, but the chairman replied that there was no way to muzzle the *Sun*. Downing soon learned that the national committee, far from frowning on Dana's

17. New York *Sun*, August 18, 1892, p. 2; Abbett to Downing, October 20, 1892, Downing Papers; Downing, quoted in Brooklyn *Eagle*, November 3, 1892, p. 7.

tactics, had actually requested him to write campaign literature on the subject of the Lodge bill. When Cleveland and Stevenson seemed to echo the *Sun*, Downing decided to support Harrison. The attractiveness of the national Democracy for Northern Negroes who cared deeply about the protection of their Southern brothers was clearly waning, and the *Sun* did not care: "The possible loss of the votes of the few colored men who may share Mr. Downing's opinions in regard to this matter, counts for nothing against the great duty which the Democracy owes to Democratic principles, and to the happiness and fortunes of millions in the South."[18]

While Democratic exploitation of the Lodge bill issue cost the allegiance of blacks like Henry F. Downing, the other side of the new departure paradox had an offsetting impact. President Harrison was unpopular among Negroes. Their resentment against the Republican party had mushroomed during his administration due to the defeat of the Blair and Lodge bills, stinginess with patronage for the race, and failure to provide a black exhibit at the Columbian Exposition of 1892. At the same time, there were complaints about snubs and insults received from state and local Republican politicians.[19] The Democracy played on these resentments, managing to hold or win the allegiance of blacks who, for one reason or another, were willing to overlook the Democrats' anti-"Negro domination" theme. The Democratic-Populist Fusion party in Kansas nominated C. H. J. Taylor, Cleveland's minister to Liberia, for a seat in the legislature. Campaign headquarters in New York City assigned one official to deal specifically with the Negro vote, and he reported in September: "I have gotten the colored contingent into wonderfully good

18. Henry F. Downing to Josiah Quincy, September 27, 1892, in Cleveland *Gazette*, October 22, 1892, p. 1; New York *Sun*, September 29, 1892, p. 6.

19. Blair and Lodge bill discontent: William H. Hart to Frederick Douglass, June 27, 1890, Reel 5, Douglass Papers; Daniel W. Crofts, "The Black Response to the Blair Education Bill," *Journal of Southern History*, XXXVII (February, 1971), 59–61; Detroit *Plaindealer*, January 16, 1891, pp. 1, 4; Indianapolis *Freeman*, February 14, 1891, p. 1. Federal patronage and the Exposition: Indianapolis *Freeman*, June 15, 1889, July 25, 1891, both p. 4; Detroit *Plaindealer*, December 5, 1890, p. 1. State and local complaints: Detroit *Plaindealer*, February 13, 1891, p. 4; Cleveland *Gazette*, August 24, 31, 1889, both p. 2; New York *Age*, February 8, 1890, p. 1. Also see above, pp. 68–69.

shape. . . . They have had no recognition from the Republican party, and they are getting tired of . . . 'Hewing wood, and Drawing water.'" T. McCants Stewart, campaigning for the Democrats in New York, gave his audiences proof that the party was colorblind: he had spoken from the same platform as Governor Hill. Michigan was now a closely contested state, and Democrats there endorsed for governor Allen B. Morse, a judge who had decided for a Negro in a civil rights suit. The state party sent out copies of the decision to blacks; as a result, the presiding elder of the African Methodist Episcopal Church in Michigan came out for Morse, incensing Republicans. A national convention of Negro Cleveland men met in mid-October at Indianapolis. Ignoring the Southern question, the delegates noted that Republican tariff rates made blacks pay high prices for manufactured goods but did not protect the agricultural commodities which the Negro produced. The group also berated Republicans for failing to give the race political recognition. In the campaign's closing days, the Democratic effort to secure Negro support received a boost when the venerable and prestigious A.M.E. Bishop John M. Brown of Washington, D.C., declared his allegiance to Cleveland and urged his race: "If you cannot consistently vote for Mr. Cleveland, then stay away from the voting precinct."[20]

Black Republicans were disturbed and confused at the idea of Negro-Democratic rapprochement in the North while the

20. Kansas City *American Citizen*, September–November, 1892; A. B. Upshaw to Grover Cleveland, September 27, 1892, Reel 72, Cleveland Papers; Stewart, in Brooklyn *Eagle*, September 15, 1892, p. 7. The Michigan situation can be traced in Katzman, *Before the Ghetto*, pp. 96–97; Detroit *Plaindealer*, September 9, 1892, p. 4, October 21, 1892, p. 1; Thomas F. Carroll to Grover Cleveland, October 27, 1892, Reel 72, Cleveland Papers. The Indianapolis convention is covered in Indianapolis *Sentinel*, October 19, 1892, p. 2, while Brown's advice is in *The New York State Cleveland League: Annual Meeting and Convention* (Brooklyn: Citizen Job Print, 1892), pp. 15–16. Also see R. G. Still to Grover Cleveland, September 20, 1892, Reel 72, Cleveland Papers; S. L. Mash to David Bennett Hill, November 14, 1892, Box 2, Hill Papers, New York State Library; Grover Cleveland to James T. V. Hill, August 8, 1892, and Claude Matthews to James T. V. Hill, undated, both in Indianapolis *Sentinel*, August 15, 1892, p. 5; Grover Cleveland to William H. Johnson, August 8, 1892, in Johnson, *Autobiography*, p. 146. This Johnson was James C. Matthews's old antagonist, now, like Matthews, a Democrat.

Southern Democracy and the New York *Sun* preached white supremacy and black subordination. The Cleveland *Gazette* complained that black Democrats "have spent their time in saying what the Republican party has not done, but they give no antidote for the so-called disease." The Detroit *Plaindealer* accused Democrats of sheer opportunism: "In the South, it is no 'force bill' while in the North the managers are proud of the increasing intelligence of the Afro-American, if he but votes the ticket." An editorial in the Washington *Bee* termed every Negro Democrat "an Esau bartering his birthright, or a Judas Iscariot selling his race," but the paper placed ultimate blame on white Republican leaders who, in contrast to Democrats, seemed uninterested in recruiting Negroes to do campaign work.[21]

Racial politics were more confused and Negro allegiance to the Republicans further shaken in 1892 by events in the South, where several Republican state organizations came under the control of lily-whites who banned Negroes from participation in party affairs. To complicate matters, Dixie Democrats had no inhibitions about campaigning for black votes to fend off the challenge of Populists and Republicans. In Alabama, even as Populists and Democrats competed for the white vote with racist appeals, both parties fought for black support. When Texas lily-white Republicans wrested party leadership from black politicians, Democrats were gleeful at the opportunity of recruiting Negroes.[22] Most Georgia Negroes, including the influential Bishop Henry M. Turner, voted the Democratic ticket and helped elect a governor who opposed lynching. The editor of a black newspaper in Valdosta, Georgia, gave another reason why Southern Negroes, whether aligned with Democrats or Populists, had lost faith in Republicanism: "The Negro's vote keeps the Republican party in power yet the party *does not pro-*

21. Cleveland *Gazette*, October 15, 1892, p. 2; Detroit *Plaindealer*, September 2, 1892, p. 4; Washington *Bee*, June 18, 1892, p. 2.

22. Alabama: William Warren Rogers, *One Gallused Rebellion: Agrarianism in Alabama, 1865–1896* (Baton Rouge: Louisiana State University Press, 1970), pp. 217–35; William P. Walsh to Grover Cleveland, October 31, 1892, Reel 72, Cleveland Papers; Texas: Rice, *Negro in Texas*, pp. 44–46; F. G. Schmidt to Grover Cleveland, August 26, 1892, Reel 70, Cleveland Papers.

tect him. He's lynched every day in the South. It should not surprise anybody if *to save his life* and property he goes over to the third party or to the Democrats."[23]

In November the Democrats celebrated a sweeping victory: Cleveland received 277 electoral votes to Harrison's 145. Democrats carried the previously Republican states of Illinois and Wisconsin, while winning one of Ohio's twenty-three electoral votes and five of Michigan's fourteen. The entire South and the swing states of Indiana and New York were safely Democratic, as were both houses of Congress.[24]

Observers interpreted the results in different ways. The New York *World*, which had stressed the tariff, was certain that the election returns were a protest against the McKinley Act, but papers which had pushed opposition to the Lodge bill were equally sure that popular resentment against federal control of elections was at the root of the Democratic landslide. Dana's *Sun* crowed: "There will be no Force bill," while the Indianapolis *Sentinel* asserted that Cleveland's victory was a mandate for the repeal of all federal election laws.[25] There were other issues which hurt the Republicans besides the tariff and the Lodge bill. Several strikes during the summer were put down with the aid of federal troops. Especially the bloody events at the Homestead steel mills aroused public sympathy for the strikers and identified the administration with plutocracy.[26] Also, specific ethnic issues in the Midwest relating to temperance and parochial schools played into Democratic hands.[27]

23. Clarence A. Bacote, "Negro Proscriptions, Protests, and Proposed Solutions in Georgia, 1880–1908," *Journal of Southern History*, XXV (November, 1959), reprinted in *The Negro in the South since 1865*, ed. Charles E. Wynes (New York: Harper and Row, 1965), p. 158; J. H. Blocker to John E. Bruce, October 21, 1892, Reel 1, John E. Bruce Papers, Schomburg Collection, New York Public Library.

24. *Tribune Almanac*, 1893, pp. 138–39.

25. New York *World*, November 9, 1892, p. 4; New York *Sun*, November 9, 1892, p. 6; Indianapolis *Sentinel*, November 10, 1892, p. 4.

26. Hirshson, *Bloody Shirt*, p. 246.

27. Horace Samuel Merrill, *William Freeman Vilas: Doctrinaire Democrat* (Madison: State Historical Society of Wisconsin, 1954), pp. 187–95. A recent trend among historians is the explanation of all Midwestern politics of the late nineteenth century in these local, ethnic, sectarian terms. Such historians, I think, underestimate the role of national issues. See Paul Kleppner, *The Cross of*

Nevertheless, Democrats had carried out a skillful attack on Republican racial policy. Making clever use of the fear of national interference in elections, they won a significant victory which taught Republicans that public opinion opposed any federal effort to protect the rights of Southern blacks. No longer would Republican politicians pursue such an unpopular course.[28] Paradoxically, simultaneous Democratic appeals to Negroes separated many blacks from a Republican party which seemed to care little for them. The Washington *Bee* charged that Republicans had ignored Negroes during the campaign, while Democratic managers had sought them out, causing "a greater division in the colored column than one had any idea."[29]

Indeed, a year after the elections James S. Clarkson of Iowa, an influential Republican leader, explained Republican abandonment of the Southern Negro by arguing that, since Democrats North and South had adopted policies friendly to the race and thereby attracted Negro support, federal intervention was unnecessary.[30] Clarkson was saying that it did not pay for Republicans to continue risking political suicide by pressing for federal protection of a voting bloc no longer solidly Republican. But there is a more subtle point hidden in Clarkson's remarks. Since 1871 the national new departure Democracy struggled to keep the South free of outside interference by telling the North that Southern whites treated their black neighbors fairly, and that federal meddling could only harm matters. While effective, this Democratic position could not by itself end Northern fears that Southern blacks were being subordinated by the old "rebel" party. Therefore the second new departure, on the Northern state and local scene, was a key corollary to the Democratic argument. The manifest function of Democratic friendship for

Culture: A Social Analysis of Midwestern Politics. 1850–1900 (New York: Free Press, 1970), esp. pp. 143–45, and Richard Jensen, *The Winning of the Midwest: Social and Political Conflict, 1888–1896* (Chicago: University of Chicago Press, 1971).

28. Hirshson, *Bloody Shirt*, pp. 249–50.

29. Washington *Bee*, November 12, 1892, p. 2.

30. *Annual Address of James S. Clarkson, President of the National Republican League. Sixth Annual Convention of the League. Held at Louisville, Kentucky, May 10, 1893*, pp. 5–6, in Box 4, Clarkson Papers, Library of Congress.

the Northern Negro was to win his allegiance. But its latent function, never explicitly formulated, was to provide actual evidence to Northern white voters that the difference between Democrats and Republicans was not on the substantive issue of race prejudice, but about federal intervention in Southern state matters. The impression of a bipartisan consensus on race seemed confirmed by the emergence of lily-white Southern Republicanism to match corresponding Democratic attitudes in the region. With party lines on the Negro indistinct, the Democrats could play up the Republican threat to states' rights. And, with Cleveland's victory, the issue was dead.[31]

Thus the Democratic campaign of 1892 both epitomized the new departure as it had developed over twenty years, and marked its successful culmination. Whether the Republicans had sold out the Negro, the Democrats had befriended him, or both, or neither, the race question was no longer a matter for national political debate. The same Democracy which was competing for the Northern black vote had now helped to lift the threat of national involvement in Southern affairs, and the new administration annulled the remaining federal election laws. Southern states had a green light to disfranchise Negroes by statute or constitutional amendment, and the number of lynchings would rise steadily through the 1890's.[32] Just as Chase supporters of 1868, new departurists of 1871, and Greeley Democrats of 1872 had foreseen, the black man's rights might be guaranteed by the federal Constitution and yet remain undefended, unenforced, and almost ignored by both parties, insuring a solidly Democratic South. The new departure which, when first proposed, looked like capitulation, turned out in retrospect to be a strategic retreat instrumental in winning the war.

The Democracy would maintain well into the twentieth century its paradoxical policy of dangling a carrot before the eyes

31. I am using the analytical concepts of "manifest" and "latent" functions developed by sociologist Robert K. Merton in *Social Theory and Social Structure* (New York: Free Press, 1957). Professor August Meier first suggested their applicability to Democratic race policy.

32. Woodward, *Strange Career of Jim Crow*, pp. 82–93; Raper, *Tragedy of Lynching*, p. 480.

of Northern blacks while condoning the policy of the stick against Southern blacks. No matter how satisfactory their relations with Negroes in their own states, Northern Democrats, motivated by political considerations, would allow themselves to be dominated by Southern white racists until the 1930's and 1940's, when new conditions and new attitudes transformed both the party and the nation.

Bibliography

I. PRIMARY SOURCES

A. Manuscripts

Adams Family. Papers, Massachusetts Historical Society, Boston.

Allen, William. Papers, Library of Congress.

Andrew, John F. Papers, Massachusetts Historical Society, Boston.

Atkinson, Edward A. Papers, Massachusetts Historical Society, Boston.

Barlow, S. L. M. Papers, Henry E. Huntington Library, San Marino, California.

Bayard, Samuel J. Papers, Princeton University.

Bayard, Thomas F. Papers, Library of Congress.

Bigelow, John. Diaries and Papers, New York Public Library.

Bigler, William. Papers, Historical Society of Pennsylvania.

Bixby, George S. Papers, New York State Library, Albany.

Black, Jeremiah S. Papers, Library of Congress.

Blair Family. Papers, Library of Congress.

Blair-Lee Family. Papers, Princeton University.

Bradford, Augustus. Papers, Maryland Historical Society, Baltimore.

Breckinridge Family. Papers, Library of Congress.

Bruce, Blanche K. Papers, Moorland-Spingarn Collection, Howard University.

Bruce, John E. Papers, Schomburg Collection, New York Public Library.

Bryant, William Cullen. Papers, Goddard-Roslyn Collection, Microfilm, New York Public Library.

Bryant, William Cullen—Godwin, Parke. Papers, New York Public Library.

Buchanan, James. Papers, Historical Society of Pennsylvania, Philadelphia.

Butler, Benjamin F. Papers, Library of Congress.

Campbell, Lewis D. Papers, Ohio Historical Society, Columbus.

Carroll, Anna Ella. Papers, Maryland Historical Society, Baltimore.
Chase, Salmon P. Papers, Cincinnati Historical Society.
———. Papers, Historical Society of Pennsylvania, Philadelphia.
———. Papers, Library of Congress.
Clarkson, James. Papers, Library of Congress.
Cleveland, Grover. Papers, Library of Congress.
Cooper, Peter—Hewitt, Abram S. Papers, Cooper Union, New York City.
Cox, Samuel S. Papers, Brown University, Microfilm at Rutherford B. Hayes Memorial Library, Fremont, Ohio.
Crummell, Alexander. Papers, Schomburg Collection, New York Public Library.
Davis, David. Papers, Chicago Historical Society.
Dawes, Henry L. Papers, Library of Congress.
Dickinson, Don. Papers, Library of Congress.
Dix, John A. Papers, Columbia University.
Doolittle, James R. Papers, State Historical Society of Wisconsin, Madison.
Douglass, Frederick. Papers, Library of Congress.
Downing, George T. Papers, owned by Reverend Howard De Grasse Asbury.
English, William H. Papers, Indiana Historical Society, Indianapolis.
Evarts, William M. Papers, Library of Congress.
Ewing, Hugh. Papers, Ohio Historical Society, Columbus.
Ewing, Thomas. Papers, Ohio Historical Society, Columbus.
Ewing Family. Papers, Library of Congress.
Fairchild, Charles S. Papers, New York Historical Society.
Foraker, Joseph B. Papers, Cincinnati Historical Society.
———. Papers, Library of Congress.
Fuller, Melville. Papers, Chicago Historical Society.
Giddings, Joshua—Julian, George W. Papers, Library of Congress.
Gorman, Arthur P. Papers, Maryland Historical Society, Baltimore.
Greeley, Horace. Papers, Library of Congress.
———. Papers, New York Public Library.
Grimké, Archibald H. Papers, Moorland-Spingarn Collection, Howard University.
Harrison, Benjamin. Papers, Library of Congress.
Harrison, Carter. Papers and Scrapbooks, Newberry Library, Chicago.
Hassaurek, Friedrich. Papers, Ohio Historical Society, Columbus.

Hewitt, Abram S. Papers, New York Historical Society.

Hill, David B. Papers, New York State Library, Albany.

Hoadly, George. Papers, Governors' Correspondence, Ohio Historical Society, Columbus.

Hoar, George F. Papers, Massachusetts Historical Society, Boston.

James, John. Papers, Ohio Historical Society, Columbus.

Jay Family. Papers, Columbia University.

Johnson, Andrew. Papers, Library of Congress.

Julian, George W. Papers, Indiana Division, Indiana State Library, Indianapolis.

Kurtz, Charles H. Papers, Ohio Historical Society, Columbus.

Lamont, Daniel S. Papers, Library of Congress.

Langston, John M. Papers, Fisk University, Microfilm in Schomburg Collection, New York Public Library.

Laselle, Charles B. Papers, Indiana Division, Indiana State Library, Indianapolis.

Long, Alexander. Papers, Cincinnati Historical Society.

Long, John D. Papers, Massachusetts Historical Society, Boston.

Main, Willet S. Papers, State Historical Society of Wisconsin, Madison.

McClellan, George B. Papers, Library of Congress.

McCormick, Cyrus H. Papers, State Historical Society of Wisconsin, Madison.

McPherson, Edward. Papers, Library of Congress.

Marble, Manton. Papers, Library of Congress.

Miscellaneous Papers, New York Historical Society.

————, New York Public Library.

————, New York State Library, Albany.

————, Ohio Historical Society, Columbus.

Morgan, John T. Papers, Library of Congress.

Paul, George H. Papers, State Historical Society of Wisconsin, Madison.

Pennsylvania Abolition Society. Minutes, Historical Society of Pennsylvania, Philadelphia.

Pennsylvania Equal Rights League. Papers, Leon Gardiner Collection, Historical Society of Pennsylvania, Philadelphia.

Pinchback, P. B. S. Papers, Moorland-Spingarn Collection, Howard University.

Pruyn, John V. S. L. Papers, New York State Library, Albany.

Randall, Samuel J. Papers, University of Pennsylvania.

Reid, Whitelaw. Papers, Library of Congress.

Ruffin, George L. Papers, Moorland-Spingarn Collection, Howard University.

Russell, William E. Papers, Massachusetts Historical Society, Boston.

Schuckers, Jacob. Papers, Library of Congress.

Schurz, Carl. Papers, Library of Congress.

Seymour, Horatio. Papers, New York Historical Society.

————. Papers, New York State Library, Albany.

Sherman, John. Papers, Library of Congress.

Smith, George B. Papers, State Historical Society of Wisconsin, Madison.

Stephens, Alexander H. Correspondence, Manhattanville College, Purchase, New York.

————. Papers, Library of Congress.

Stevenson, John W. Papers, Library of Congress.

Still, William. Papers, Leon Gardiner Collection, Historical Society of Pennsylvania, Philadelphia.

Sumner, Charles. Papers, Houghton Library, Harvard University.

Taggart, Thomas. Papers, Indiana Division, Indiana State Library, Indianapolis.

Thacher, John Boyd. Scrapbooks, New York State Library, Albany.

Thurman, Allen G. Papers, Ohio Historical Society, Columbus.

Tilden, Samuel J. Papers, New York Public Library.

Trimble, John A. Papers, Ohio Historical Society, Columbus.

Trumbull, Lyman. Papers, Library of Congress.

United States Department of Justice. Files and Instruction Books, National Archives.

United States Senate. Papers Regarding Nominations, National Archives.

Vaux, Richard. Papers, Historical Society of Pennsylvania, Philadelphia.

Vilas, William F. Papers, State Historical Society of Wisconsin, Madison.

Watterson, Henry. Papers, Library of Congress.

Wears, Isaiah C. Papers, Leon Gardiner Collection, Historical Society of Pennsylvania, Philadelphia.

Welles, Gideon. Papers, Library of Congress.

————. Papers, New York Public Library.

Wells, David A. Papers, Library of Congress.

————. Papers, New York Public Library.

Whitney, William C. Papers, Library of Congress.

Woodson, Carter G. Papers, Library of Congress.

B. Public Documents

NATIONAL

Congressional Globe, 1868–72.

Congressional Record, 1873–92.

Richardson, James D., ed. *A Compilation of the Messages and Papers of the Presidents, 1789–1897.* 10 vols. Washington: U.S. Government Printing Office, 1898.

United States Department of Commerce, Bureau of the Census. *Negro Population, 1790–1915.* Washington: Government Printing Office, 1918.

United States Department of the Interior. Bureau of the Census. *Census Reports for 1870, 1880, 1890.* Washington: Government Printing Office, 1871, 1883, 1895.

United States House of Representatives. *Report of the Joint Select Committee to Inquire into the Condition of Affairs in the Late Insurrectionary States.* House Report 22, 42 Cong., 2 sess., 1872.

————. *Report of the Committee of the Judiciary on the Contested Election Case of Miller versus Elliott.* House Report 2569, 52 Cong., 2 sess., 1893.

United States Senate. *Journal of the Executive Proceedings of the Senate of the United States of America, 1886–87.*

————. *Proceedings Relating to the Nomination and Rejection of James C. Matthews, of New York, to be Recorder of Deeds in the District of Columbia.* Senate Miscellaneous Document 85, 49 Cong., 2 sess., 1887.

————. *Report of the Committee on the Judiciary on the Municipal Election at Jackson, Mississippi.* Senate Report 1887, 50 Cong., 1 sess., 1888.

————. *Report and Testimony of the Select Committee of the United States Senate to Investigate the Causes of the Removal of the Negro from the Southern States to the Northern States.* Senate Report 693, 46 Cong., 2 sess., 1880.

STATE

Connecticut, *Journal of the House of Representatives*, 1878, 1883–84.
———. *Journal of the Senate*, 1878, 1883–84.
———. *Public Acts*, 1883–84.
Illinois. *Journal of the House of Representatives*, 1885, 1891.
———. *Journal of the Senate*, 1885, 1891.
———. *Laws*, 1885, 1891.
Indiana. *Journal of the House of Representatives*, 1885.
———. *Journal of the State Senate*, 1885.
———. *Laws*, 1885.
New Jersey. *Acts*, 1881, 1884.
———. *Journal of the Senate*, 1881, 1884.
———. *Minutes of Votes and Proceedings of the General Assembly*,
    1881, 1884.
New York. *General Statutes*, 1870, 1873, 1881, 1884, 1891.
———. *Journal of the Assembly*, 1870, 1873, 1881, 1884, 1891.
———. *Journal of the Senate*, 1870, 1873, 1881, 1884, 1891.
Ohio. *General and Local Laws and Joint Resolutions*, 1868–70, 1884,
    1887.
———. *Inaugural Address and Annual Messages of Governor George
    Hoadly*, 1884–86.
———. *Journal of the House of Representatives*, 1870, 1880, 1884–
    90.
———. *Journal of the Senate*, 1870, 1884–90.
Pennsylvania. *Journal of the House of Representatives*, 1881, 1887.
———. *Journal of the Senate*, 1881, 1887.
———. *Laws*, 1881, 1887.
Rhode Island. *Acts and Resolves of the General Assembly*, 1881,
    1885.

C. NEWSPAPERS

GENERAL PRESS

Albany *Argus*, 1868–92.
Atlanta *Constitution*, 1889.
Baltimore *Gazette*, 1871.
Brooklyn *Eagle*, 1886–92.
Chicago *Times*, 1890–92.
Chicago *Tribune*, 1868–72.

Cincinnati *Enquirer*, 1868–92.
Dayton *Herald* (name varies), 1869–74.
Dayton *Ledger*, 1868–69.
Democratic Thunder (N.Y.), 1868.
Indianapolis *Sentinel*, 1868–75, 1879–80, 1890–92.
La Crosse (Wis.) *Democrat*, 1868.
New Haven *Palladium*, 1878.
New York *Day Book*, 1868–75.
New York *Democrat*, 1868, 1870–71.
New York *Evening Post*, 1886–87.
New York *Herald*, 1871, 1886–87.
New York *Sun*, 1873, 1886–87, 1890–92.
New York *Times*, 1868–92.
New York *Tribune*, 1874, 1877–79, 1886–92, 1895.
New York *World*, 1868–92.
Pomeroy's Democrat (N.Y.), 1870–75.
Providence *Daily Journal*, 1878.
Springfield (Mass.) *Republican*, 1883–87.
Washington *Patriot*, 1870–72.

NEGRO PRESS

Cincinnati *Afro-American*, 1885.
Cincinnati *Colored Patriot*, 1883.
Cleveland *Gazette*, 1883–92.
Detroit *Plaindealer*, 1889–92.
Harrisburg *State Sentinel*, 1883–85.
Huntsville (Ala.) *Gazette*, 1881–92.
Indianapolis *Freeman*, 1888–92.
Kansas City (Kans.) *American Citizen*, 1889–92.
New Era (Washington; name varies), 1870–74.
New York *Age*, 1887–92.
New York *Freeman*, 1884–87.
New York *Globe*, 1883–84.
Nicodemus (Kans.) *Western Cyclone*, 1886–87.
People's Advocate (Alexandria, Va., and then Washington), 1876, 1879–84.
Topeka *American Citizen*, 1888–89.
Topeka *Benevolent Banner*, 1887.
Topeka *Colored Citizen*, 1878–79.

Trenton *Sentinel*, 1880–82.
Washington *Bee*, 1882–92.
Washington *Grit*, 1883–84.
Washington *National Leader*, 1888–89.

D. Periodicals

African Methodist Episcopal Church Review, 1884–92.
American Annual Cyclopaedia and Register of Important Events, 1868–74.
Appleton's Annual Cyclopaedia and Register of Important Events, 1875–92.
Arena, 1889–92.
Democratic Almanac, 1868–70.
Forum, 1886–92.
Frank Leslie's Illustrated Newspaper, 1890.
Independent (New York), 1868–92.
Nation, 1868–92.
North American Review, 1868–92.
Old Guard, 1868–70.
Public Opinion, 1886–92.
Tribune Almanac and Political Register, 1868–93.

E. Other Primary Materials

Apptheker, Herbert, ed. *A Documentary History of the Negro People in the United States.* New York: Citadel Press, 1951.
Arnett, Benjamin W., and Brown, Jere A. *The Black Laws.* N.p.: n.p., 1886.
Bancroft, Frederic, ed. *Speeches, Correspondence and Political Papers of Carl Schurz.* 6 vols. New York: G. P. Putnam's Sons, 1913.
Bayard, Thomas F. "Democratic Duty and Opportunity." *Forum*, XIII (June, 1892), 409–20.
Beale, Howard K., ed. *Diary of Gideon Welles.* 3 vols. New York: W. W. Norton, 1960.
Belmont, August. *Letters, Speeches and Addresses.* N.p.: By the author, 1890.
Bergh, Albert Ellery, ed. *Grover Cleveland: Addresses, State Papers and Letters.* New York: Sun Dial Classics, 1908.

Bigelow, John, ed. *Letters and Literary Memorials of Samuel J. Tilden.* 2 vols. New York and London: Harper and Brothers, 1908.

———. ed. *The Writings and Speeches of Samuel J. Tilden.* 2 vols. New York: Harper and Brothers, 1885.

Blaine, James G. *Political Discussions: Legislative, Diplomatic, and Popular, 1856–1886.* Norwich, Conn.: Henry Bill Publishing, 1887.

———. "The Presidential Election of 1892." *North American Review,* CLV (November, 1892), 513–25.

———. *Twenty Years in Congress.* 2 vols. Norwich, Conn.: Henry Bill Publishing, 1884.

———; Lamar, Lucius Q. C.; Hampton, Wade; Garfield, James A.; Stephens, Alexander H.; Phillips, Wendell; Blair, Montgomery; and Hendricks, Thomas A. "Ought the Negro to be Disfranchised? Ought He to Have Been Enfranchised?" *North American Review,* CXXVIII (March, 1879), 225–84.

Brackett, Jeffrey R. *Notes on the Progress of the Colored People of Maryland since the War.* Johns Hopkins Studies in Historical and Political Science, series 8, VII–IX. Baltimore: Johns Hopkins University, 1890.

Breckinridge, W. C. P. "The Race Question." *Arena,* II (June, 1890), 39–56.

Butler, Benjamin F. *Autobiographical and Personal Reminiscences of Major General Benjamin F. Butler.* Boston: A. M. Thayer, 1892.

Cable, George W. *The Negro Question: A Selection of Writings on Civil Rights in the South.* Ed. Arlin Turner. Garden City: Doubleday, 1958.

Carey, Matthew, Jr., ed. *The Democratic Speaker's Handbook.* Cincinnati: Miami Printing and Publishing, 1868.

Carlisle, John G. "The Republican Program." *Forum,* VII (August, 1889), 583–96.

———. "Republican Promise and Performance." *Forum,* IX (May, 1890), 243–54.

Casserly, Eugene. *Speech of Hon. Eugene Casserly on the Fifteenth Amendment and the Labor Question.* San Francisco: n.p., 1869.

Cauthen, Charles E., ed. *Family Letters of the Three Wade Hamptons, 1782–1901.* Columbia: University of South Carolina Press, 1953.

Chalmers, H. H. "The Effects of Negro Suffrage." *North American Review,* CXXII (March, 1881), 239–48.

Chalmers, James R. *Open Letter to George Hoadly.* Sardis, Miss.: n.p., 1885.

Chase, Salmon P. *Diary and Correspondence of Salmon P. Chase.* Vol. II of *Annual Report of the American Historical Association for the Year 1902.* 2 vols. Washington: Government Printing Office, 1903.

Clark, Edward P. *A Bill to Promote Mendicancy.* New York: Evening Post, 1886.

Clark, Peter H. *The Black Brigade of Cincinnati.* Cincinnati: Joseph Boyd, 1864.

Clay, Cassius M. *The Life of Cassius Marcellus Clay: Memoirs, Writings and Speeches.* New York: Negro Universities Press, 1969.

Coleman, Lucretia H. Newman. *Poor Ben: A Story of Real Life.* Nashville: Publishing House of the African Methodist Episcopal Sunday School Union, 1890.

Colloquium: Republican Versus Democratic, The Truth in Regard to the South, and the Duty of the Colored Voter. N.p.: n.p., 1876.

Common Sense for the People, no. 2. N.p.: n.p., 1868.

Conkling, Roscoe. *Speech of Hon. Roscoe Conkling of New York at Cooper Union Institute, New York, July 23, 1872.* N.p.: n.p., 1872.

Convention of Colored Newspaper Men. Cincinnati: n.p., 1875.

Cox, Samuel S. *Grant or Greeley.* New York: S. W. Green, 1872.

————. *Speeches of S. S. Cox in Maine, Pennsylvania and New York during the Campaign of 1868.* New York: Douglas Taylor's Democratic Printing Establishment, 1868.

————. *Three Decades of Federal Legislation.* Providence: J. A. and R. A. Reid, 1885.

Democratic National Committee. *Campaign Text Book* (title varies). New York: Democratic National Committee, 1876, 1880, 1884, 1888, 1892.

The Democratic Party Facts. Washington: Democratic Congressional Committee, 1892.

Derrick, William B. "An Oration." *African Methodist Episcopal Church Review,* II (April, 1886), 445–51.

Douglass, Frederick. *Address of Hon. Frederick Douglass delivered in the Congregational Church, Washington, D.C. April 10, 1883.* Washington: n.p., 1883.

————. "Future of the Race." *African Methodist Episcopal Church Review,* VI (October, 1889), 221–39.

————. *Life and Times of Frederick Douglass.* New York: Pathway Press, 1941.

————. *U. S. Grant and the Colored People.* Washington: n.p., 1872.

————; Scarborough, W. S.; Pinchback, P. B. S.; Fortune, T. Thomas; Green, John P.; Harper, Frances E. W.; Thomas, William H.; Downing, George T.; Smith, C. S.; Clark, Peter H.; Still, William; Lewis, John D.; Turner, Henry M.; and Jackson, Thomas H. "The Democratic Return to Power—Its Effect?" *African Methodist Episcopal Church Review,* I (January, 1885), 213–50.

Ellis, John B. *The Sights and Secrets of the National Capital: A Work Descriptive of Washington City in all its Various Phases.* New York: United States Publishing, 1869.

Fielder, Herbert. *A Sketch of the Life and Times and Speeches of Joseph E. Brown.* Springfield, Mass.: Springfield Printing, 1883.

Fisk, Ethel F., ed. *The Letters of John Fiske.* New York: Macmillan, 1940.

Foner, Philip S., ed. *The Life and Writings of Frederick Douglass.* 4 vols. New York: International Publishers, 1950–55.

Foraker, Joseph B. *Notes of a Busy Life.* 2 vols. Cincinnati: Stewart and Kidd, 1916.

Fortune, T. Thomas. "The African in Our Politics." *Frank Leslie's Illustrated Newspaper,* LXX (March 15, 1890), 122.

————. *Black and White: Land, Labor and Politics in the South.* New York: Fords, Howard, and Hulbert, 1884.

————. *The Negro in Politics.* New York: Ogilvie and Rowntree, 1886.

Godkin, Edwin L. "The Republican Party and the Negro." *Forum,* VII (May, 1889), 246–57.

Green, John P. *Fact Stranger Than Fiction.* Cleveland: Riehl Publishing, 1920.

Grover Cleveland, the Open Record of an Honest Man. N.p.: n.p., 1884.

Hampton, Wade. "The Race Problem." *Arena,* II (July, 1890), 132–38.

Harrity, William F. "The Democratic Outlook." *North American Review,* CLV (November, 1892), 551–59.

Hendricks, Thomas A. *An Address by Governor Thomas A. Hendricks of Indiana.* Philadelphia: Gillin and Nagle, 1875.

————. "Retribution in Politics." *North American Review,* CXXVIII (April, 1879), 337–51.

Herbert, Hilary A., ed. *Why the Solid South? Or, Reconstruction and Its Results.* Baltimore: R. H. Woodward, 1890.

Hill, Benjamin H. *Great Speech of the Hon. Benjamin H. Hill, of Georgia, delivered before the "Young Men's Democratic Union," October 6, 1868.* New York: n.p., 1868.

Hill, Benjamin H., Jr. *Senator Benjamin H. Hill of Georgia: His Life, Speeches and Writings.* Atlanta: H. C. Hudgins, 1891.

Hinckley, Reverend Francis A. *Sermon Preached at the Funeral of Robert Purvis.* Washington: Judd and Detweiler, 1898.

Hoadly, George. *Address at Music Hall, Cincinnati, Ohio, on the Occasion of the Removal of the Remains of Salmon Portland Chase to Spring Grove Cemetery, October 14, 1886.* Cincinnati: Robert Clarke, 1887.

―――. *Governor Hoadly's Address at Painesville, Ohio, Saturday, September 12, 1885.* N.p.: n.p., 1885.

―――. *Governor Hoadly's Great Speech delivered at Hamilton, Ohio, September 5, 1885.* N.p.: n.p., 1885.

Hoar, George F. *Autobiography of Seventy Years.* 2 vols. New York: Charles Scribner's Sons, 1903.

Holcombe, John W., and Skinner, Hubert M. *Life and Public Services of Thomas A. Hendricks with Selected Speeches and Writings.* Indianapolis: Carlon and Hollenbeck, 1886.

Howell, George R., and Tenney, Jonathan, eds. *Bi-Centennial History of Albany: History of the County of Albany, New York, From 1609 to 1886.* New York: W. W. Munsell, 1886.

"The 'Independents' in the Canvass." *North American Review,* CXXIII (October, 1876), 426–67.

[Indiana] Democratic State Central Committee. *An Indiana Democratic Scrapbook for the Campaign of 1884.* Indianapolis: Carlon and Hollenbeck, 1884.

Johnson, Madison Y. *A Political Review, Speech of Hon. M. Y. Johnson of Galena, Illinois.* N.p.: n.p., 1872.

Johnson, William H. *Autobiography of Dr. William Henry Johnson.* Albany: Argus, 1900.

Joint Debates between Hon. George Hoadly and Hon. Joseph B. Foraker at Toledo, Ohio, October 8, 1885, and Cincinnati, Ohio, October 10, 1885. Columbus: Ohio State Journal Job Printing Establishment, 1887.

Julian, George W. *Later Speeches on Political Questions.* Ed. Grace Julian Clarke. Indianapolis: Carlon and Hollenbeck, 1889.

————. *Political Recollections, 1840–72*. Chicago: Jansen, McClurg and Co., 1884.

Kernan, Francis, and Hunter, R. M. T. *Speeches of Hon. Francis Kernan of New York and Hon. R. M. T. Hunter of Virginia at the Mass Meetings in New York on Thursday Evening, September 12, 1872*. New York: John Polhemus, 1872.

Langston, John Mercer. *Freedom and Citizenship: Selected Lectures and Addresses of Hon. John Mercer Langston*. Washington: Rufus H. Darby, 1883.

————. *From the Virginia Plantation to the National Capital*. Hartford: American Publishing, 1894.

Lawrence, William. *Negro Suffrage: Ohio Holds the Casting Vote on the XVth Amendment*. N.p.: n.p., 1869.

Lusk, D. W. *Eighty Years of Illinois Politics and Politicians: Anecdotes and Incidents, 1809–1889*. Springfield, Ill.: H. W. Rokker, 1889.

Lynch, John R. *The Facts of Reconstruction*. New York: Neale Publishing, 1913.

McClure, Alexander K. *Old Time Notes of Pennsylvania*. 2 vols. Philadelphia: John C. Winston, 1905.

————. *Recollections of Half a Century*. Salem, Mass.: Salem Press, 1902.

McCormack, Thomas J., ed. *Memoirs of Gustave Koerner, 1809–1896: Life Sketches Written at the Suggestion of his Children*. 2 vols. Cedar Rapids, Iowa: Torch Press, 1909.

McPherson, Edward, ed. *A Handbook of Politics*. Washington: Philp and Solomons (publisher varies), 1868–92.

————, ed. *The Political History of the United States of America during the Period of Reconstruction*. Washington: Solomons and Chapman, 1875.

A Menace to Liberty. N.p.; n.p., 1892.

Morgan, John T. "Federal Control of Elections." *Forum*, X (September, 1890), 23–36.

————. "The Political Alliance of the South with the West." *North American Review*, CXXVI (March–April, 1878), 309–22.

————. "The Race Question in the United States." *Arena*, II (September, 1890), 385–98.

Mowry, Duane, ed. "Post-Bellum Days: Selections from the Correspondence of the Late Senator James R. Doolittle." *Magazine of History*, XVII (August–September, 1913), 49–64.

Nevins, Allan, ed. *Letters of Grover Cleveland, 1850–1908.* Boston: Houghton Mifflin, 1933.

New York State Cleveland League: Annual Meeting and Convention. Brooklyn: Citizen Job Print, 1892.

New York State Colored Democratic Association. *To the Qualified Voters of the State and County of New York, and to the General Public.* New York: n.p., 1884.

Norris, James D., and Shaffer, Arthur H., eds. *Politics and Patronage in the Gilded Age: The Correspondence of James A. Garfield and Charles E. Henry.* Madison: State Historical Society of Wisconsin, 1970.

O'Connor, Mary Doline. *Life and Letters of M. P. O'Connor.* New York: Dempsey and Carroll, 1893.

Official Compilation of Proceedings of the Afro-American League National Convention Held at Chicago, January 15–17, 1890. Chicago: C. Battles and R. B. Cabbell, 1890.

Official Proceedings of the National Democratic Convention at Tammany Hall, New York City, July 4–9, 1868. Boston: Rockwell and Rollins, 1868.

Official Proceedings of the National Democratic Convention Held at Baltimore, July 9, 1872. Boston: Rockwell and Churchill, 1872.

Official Proceedings of the National Democratic Convention Held in Chicago, Illinois, July 8–11, 1884. New York: Douglas Taylor's Democratic Printing House, 1884.

Official Proceedings of the National Democratic Convention Held in Chicago, Illinois, June 21–23, 1892. Chicago: Cameron, Amberg, 1892.

Official Proceedings of the National Democratic Convention Held in Cincinnati, Ohio, June 22–24, 1880. Dayton: Daily Journal Book and Job Rooms, 1882.

Official Proceedings of the National Democratic Convention Held in St. Louis, Missouri, June 1876. St. Louis: Woodward, Tiernan and Hale, 1876.

Official Proceedings of the National Democratic Convention Held in St. Louis, Missouri, June 5–7, 1888. St. Louis: Woodward and Tiernan Printing, 1888.

Palmer, John M. *Personal Recollections of John M. Palmer: The Story of an Earnest Life.* Cincinnati: Robert Clarke, 1901.

Parker, George F., ed. *The Writings and Speeches of Grover Cleveland.* New York: Cassell Publishing, 1892.

Pendleton, George H. *Speech of Hon. George H. Pendleton at Loveland, Ohio, August 22, 1871.* N.p.: n.p., 1871.

Penn, I. Garland. *The Afro-American Press and Its Editors.* Springfield, Mass.: Wiley, 1891.

Phillips, Ulrich B., ed. *Correspondence of Robert Toombs, Alexander H. Stephens, and Howell Cobb.* Vol. II of *Annual Report of the American Historical Association for the Year 1911.* 2 vols. Washington: U.S. Government Printing Office, 1913.

Pollard, Edward A. *A Southern Historian's Appeal for Horace Greeley.* Lynchburg, Va.: Daily Republican Book and Job Printing Establishment, 1872.

Pomeroy, Marcus M. *A Journey of Life: Reminiscences and Recollections of Brick Pomeroy.* 2 vols. New York: Advance Thought, 1890.

Porter, Kirk H., and Johnson, Donald B., eds. *National Party Platforms, 1840–1964.* Urbana: University of Illinois Press, 1966.

Potter, Clarkson N. *Address Delivered Before the Tammany Society at Tammany Hall, New York, July 4, 1873.* New York: D. Taylor, Law, Book and Job Printer, 1873.

————. *Remarks of Hon. Clarkson N. Potter Delivered at the Celebration at Tammany Hall, July 4, 1871.* New York: Press of Douglas Taylor, Law, Book and Job Printer, 1871.

Proceedings of a Convention of the Colored Men of Ohio Held in the City of Cincinnati on the 23rd, 24th, 25th and 26th days of November, 1858. Cincinnati: Moore, Wilstach, Keys, 1858.

Proceedings of a Convention of the Colored Men of Ohio, Held in Xenia, on the 10th, 11th and 12th days of January, 1865. Cincinnati: A. Moore, 1865.

Proceedings of the Colored National Convention Held in Rochester, July 6th, 7th and 8th, 1853. Rochester: Frederick Douglass' Paper, 1853.

Proceedings of the Colored National Labor Convention Held in Washington, D.C. on December 6–10, 1869. Washington: Office of the New Era, 1870.

Proceedings of the National Conference of Colored Men of the United States. Washington: Rufus H. Darby, 1879.

Proceedings of the State Convention of Colored Men Held in the City of Columbus, Ohio, January 16th, 17th and 18th, 1856. N.p.: n.p., 1856.

Remey, Charles Mason, ed. *Life and Letters of Charles Mason, Chief*

Justice of Iowa, 1804–1882. 12 vols. Washington: By the editor, 1939.

Report of the National Executive Committee of Republicans and Independents: Presidential Campaign of 1884. New York: Burr Printing House, 1885.

Republican National Congressional Committee. *Grant or Greeley —Which? Facts and Arguments for the Consideration of the Colored Citizens of the United States Being Extracts from Letters, Speeches and Editorials by Colored Men and Their Best Friends.* Washington: Republican National Congressional Committee, 1872.

Russell, William E. "Significance of the Massachusetts Election." *Forum,* XII (December, 1891), 433–40.

Scarborough, William S. "The Negro Question." *Arena,* IV (July, 1891), 219–22.

Schuckers, Jacob W. *The Life and Public Services of Salmon Portland Chase.* New York: D. Appleton and Company, 1874.

Schurz, Carl. *Carl Schurz on the Issues of the Campaign.* N.p.: n.p., 1892.

———. "Party Schisms and Future Problems." *North American Review,* CXXXIV (May, 1882), 431–55.

Seward, William H. *Speech of William H. Seward at Auburn, New York, October 31, 1868.* Washington: Philp and Solomons, 1868.

Seymour, Horatio. *The Public Record of Horatio Seymour for 1865–1868.* New York: I. W. Engler, 1868.

Sherman, John. *Recollections of Forty Years in the House, Senate and Cabinet.* 2 vols. New York and Chicago: Werner Company, 1895.

Simmons, William J., ed. *Men of Mark.* Cleveland: George M. Rewell, 1887.

Smith, Hoke. "The Disastrous Effects of a Force Bill." *Forum,* XIII (August, 1892), 682–92.

Spencer, Edward. *Public Life and Services of Thomas F. Bayard.* New York: D. Appleton, 1880.

Stewart, T. McCants. *The Afro-American in Politics.* Brooklyn: Citizen Print, 1891.

———. "Tariff Reduction—The Problem of the Hour." *African Methodist Episcopal Church Review,* V (October, 1888), 83–95.

Still, William, *An Address on Voting and Laboring.* Philadelphia: James B. Rodgers, 1874.

Straker, D. Augustus. *The New South Investigated*. Detroit: Ferguson Printing, 1888.

Sumner, Charles. *The Works of Charles Sumner*. 15 vols. Boston: Lee and Shepard, 1870–83.

Taylor, C. H. J. *Whites and Blacks or the Question Settled*. Atlanta: James P. Harrison, 1889.

Thorndike, Rachel Sherman, ed. *The Sherman Letters: Correspondence Between General and Senator Sherman from 1837 to 1891*. New York: Charles Scribner's Sons, 1894.

Thurman, Allen G. *Speech of Allen G. Thurman at Tiffin, Ohio, September 6, 1872*. Columbus: Columbus Daily Sentinel Office, 1872.

Turpie, David. *Sketches of My Own Times*. Indianapolis: Bobbs-Merrill, 1903.

Vallandigham, James L. *A Life of Clement L. Vallandigham*. Baltimore: Turnbull Brothers, 1872.

Voorhees, Daniel W. *The Political Issues in Indiana: Speech of Hon. D. W. Voorhees delivered in the Academy of Music, Indianapolis, March 31, 1870*. N.p.: n.p., 1870.

Waddell, James D. *Biographical Sketch of Linton Stephens Containing a Selection of his Letters, Speeches, State Papers, etc.* Atlanta: Dodson and Scott, 1877.

Wallace, William A. "The Mission of the Democratic Party." *North American Review*, CXXXII (January, 1881), 96–98.

Ward, Durbin. *Life, Speeches and Orations of Durbin Ward of Ohio*. Columbus: A. H. Smythe, 1888.

Warden, Robert B. *An Account of the Private Life and Public Services of Salmon Portland Chase*. Cincinnati: Wilstach, Baldwin, 1874.

Watterson, Henry. "The Democratic Party Outlook." *North American Review*, CXLV (September, 1887), 267–75.

———. *"Marse Henry": An Autobiography*. 2 vols. New York: George H. Doran, 1919.

———. "A Reunited Union." *North American Review*, CXL (January, 1885), 22–29.

———. "The Solid South." *North American Review*, CXXVIII (January, 1879), 47–58.

Welling, James C. "Race Education." *North American Review*, CXXXVI (April, 1883), 353–63.

Welsh, Deshler. *Stephen Grover Cleveland: A Sketch of His Life*. New York: R. Worthington, 1884.

Williams, Charles R., ed. *Diary and Letters of Rutherford B. Hayes.* 5 vols: Columbus: Ohio State Archeological and Historical Society, 1922–25.

Williams, George W. *The Negro as a Political Problem.* Boston: Alfred Mudge and Son, 1884.

Wilson, William L. "A Campaign for Principle." *Forum,* XIII (April, 1892), 158–68.

Woodson, Carter G., ed. *The Works of Francis J. Grimké.* 4 vols. Washington: Associated Publishers, 1942.

II. SECONDARY SOURCES

A. UNPUBLISHED WORKS

Abramowitz, Jack. "Accommodation and Militancy in Negro Life, 1876–1916." Ph.D. dissertation, Columbia University, 1950.

Bell, Harold Holman. "A Survey of the Negro Convention Movement, 1830–1861." Ph.D. dissertation, Northwestern University, 1953.

Crofts, Daniel W. "The Blair Bill and the Elections Bill: The Congressional Aftermath to Reconstruction." Ph.D. dissertation, Yale University, 1968.

Ellwein, Linda Krane. "The Negroes in Cincinnati: The Black Experience, 1870–1880." M.A. thesis, University of Cincinnati, 1970.

Fishel, Leslie H., Jr. "The North and the Negro, 1865–1900: A Study in Race Discrimination." 2 vols. Ph.D. dissertation, Harvard University, 1954.

Furniss, George M. "The Political Assimilation of Negroes in New York City." Ph.D. dissertation, Columbia University, 1969.

Gambill, Edward L. "Northern Democrats and Reconstruction, 1865–1868." Ph.D. dissertation, University of Iowa, 1969.

Gerber, David A. "Ohio and the Color Line: Racial Discrimination and Negro Response in a Northern State, 1860–1915." 2 vols. Ph.D. dissertation, Princeton University, 1971.

Hare, John S. "Allen G. Thurman: A Political Study." Ph.D. dissertation, Ohio State University, 1933.

Mantell, Martin. "The Election of 1868." Ph.D. dissertation, Columbia University, 1969.

Niven, William John. "The Time of the Whirlwind: A Study in the Political, Social, and Economic History of Connecticut from 1861 to 1875." Ph.D. dissertation, Columbia University, 1954.

Oxendine, Pearle Mintz. "An Evaluation of Negro Historians During the Period of the Road to Reunion." M.A. thesis, Howard University, 1947.

Polakoff, Keith I. "An Institutional Study of the Democratic Party, 1872–1880." Ph.D. dissertation, Northwestern University, 1968.

Rathgeber, Lewis Wesley. "The Democratic Party in Pennsylvania, 1880–1896." Ph.D. dissertation, University of Pittsburgh, 1955.

Roberts, Mary Gretchen. "The Governorship of George Hoadly." M.A. thesis, Ohio State University, 1952.

Sheeler, John R. "The Negro in West Virginia Before 1900." Ph.D. dissertation, University of West Virginia, 1954.

Slocum, A. Terry. "Timothy Thomas Fortune, A Negro in American Society." B.A. thesis, Princeton University, 1967.

Swinney, Everette. "Suppressing the Ku Klux Klan: The Enforcement of the Reconstruction Amendments, 1870–1874." Ph.D. dissertation, University of Texas, 1966.

B. Published Works

Alexander, DeAlva Stanwood. *A Political History of the State of New York.* 4 vols. New York: Henry Holt, 1909.

Bacote, Clarence A. "Negro Proscriptions, Protests and Proposed Solutions in Georgia, 1880–1908." *Journal of Southern History,* XXV (November, 1959), 471–98. Reprinted in *The Negro in the South Since 1865: Selected Essays in American Negro History.* Ed. Charles E. Wynes. New York: Harper and Row, 1965.

Barclay, Thomas S. *The Liberal Republican Movement in Missouri, 1865–1871.* Columbia: State Historical Society of Missouri, 1926.

Barnes, James A. *John G. Carlisle: Financial Statesman.* New York: Dodd, Mead, 1931.

Barrett, James Wyman. *Joseph Pulitzer and His "World."* New York: Vanguard Press, 1941.

Bartlett, Irving H. *From Slave to Citizen: The Story of the Negro in Rhode Island.* Providence: Urban League of Greater Providence, 1954.

Bass, Herbert J. *"I Am a Democrat": The Political Career of David Bennett Hill.* Syracuse: Syracuse University Press, 1961.

Battle, Charles A. *Negroes on the Island of Rhode Island.* Newport: n.p., 1932.

Biographical Directory of the American Congress, 1774–1949. 81 Cong., 2 sess., House Document 607.

Blodgett, Geoffrey. *The Gentle Reformers: Massachusetts Democracy in the Cleveland Era.* Cambridge: Harvard University Press, 1966.

Bogardus, Frank Smith. "Daniel W. Voorhees." *Indiana Magazine of History,* XXVII (June, 1931), 91–103.

Bonadio, Felice A. *North of Reconstruction: Ohio Politics, 1865–1870.* New York: New York University Press, 1970.

Brown, Ira V. *The Negro in Pennsylvania History.* Pennsylvania Historical Studies, no. 11. University Park: Pennsylvania Historical Association, 1970.

———. "Pennsylvania and the Rights of the Negro, 1865–87." *Pennsylvania History,* XXVIII (January, 1961), 45–57.

Buck, Paul H. *The Road to Reunion, 1865–1900.* Boston: Little, Brown, 1937.

Burnham, W. Dean. *Presidential Ballots, 1836–1892.* Baltimore: Johns Hopkins University Press, 1955.

Callcott, Margaret Law. *The Negro in Maryland Politics, 1870–1912.* Johns Hopkins University Studies in Historical and Political Science, series LXXXVII, no. 1. Baltimore: Johns Hopkins University Press, 1969.

Clancy, Herbert J. *The Presidential Election of 1880.* Chicago: Loyola University Press, 1958.

Clark, Dovie King. "Peter Humphries Clark." *Negro History Bulletin,* V (May, 1942), 176.

Clarke, Grace Julian. *George W. Julian.* Indianapolis: Indiana Historical Commission, 1923.

Coleman, Charles H. *The Election of 1868: The Democratic Effort to Regain Control.* New York: Columbia University Press, 1933.

Conway, Alan. *The Reconstruction of Georgia.* Minneapolis: University of Minnesota Press, 1966.

Cooper, William J., Jr. *The Conservative Regime: South Carolina, 1877–90.* Johns Hopkins University Studies in Historical and Political Science, series LXXXVI, no. 1. Baltimore: Johns Hopkins University Press, 1968.

Cox, LaWanda, and Cox, John H. "Negro Suffrage and Republican Politics: The Problem of Motivation in Reconstruction Historiography." *Journal of Southern History*, XXXIII (August, 1967), 303–330.

Crofts, Daniel W. "The Black Response to the Blair Education Bill." *Journal of Southern History*, XXXVII (February, 1971), 41–65.

Cromwell, John W. *The Negro in American History: Men and Women Eminent in the Evolution of the American of African Descent.* Washington: American Negro Academy, 1914.

Curry, Richard O. "Copperheadism and Continuity." *Journal of Negro History*, LVII (January, 1972), 29–36.

————, ed. *Radicalism, Racism, and Party Realignment: The Border States during Reconstruction.* Baltimore: Johns Hopkins University Press, 1969.

Dabney, Wendell P. *Cincinnati's Colored Citizens.* Cincinnati: Dabney Publishing Company, 1926.

Daniels, John. *In Freedom's Birthplace.* Boston: Houghton Mifflin, 1914.

De Santis, Vincent P. "Negro Dissatisfaction with Republican Policy in the South, 1882–84." *Journal of Negro History*, XXXVI (April, 1951), 148–59.

————. "The Republican Party and the Southern Negro, 1877–97." *Journal of Negro History*, XLV (April, 1960), 71–87.

————. *Republicans Face the Southern Question: The New Departure Years, 1877–1897.* Johns Hopkins University Studies in Historical and Political Science, series LXXVII, no. 1. Baltimore: Johns Hopkins University Press, 1959.

Dilla, Harriette May. *The Politics of Michigan, 1865–1878.* Studies in History, Economics and Public Law edited by the Faculty of Political Science of Columbia University, vol. XLVII, no. 1. New York: Columbia University, 1912.

Dilliard, Irving. "James Milton Turner: A Little Known Benefactor of His People." *Journal of Negro History*, XIX (October, 1934), 372–411.

Donald, David. *Charles Sumner and the Rights of Man.* New York: Alfred A. Knopf, 1970.

Downey, Matthew T. "Horace Greeley and the Politicians: The Liberal Republican Convention in 1872." *Journal of American History*, LIII (March, 1967), 727–50.

Drake, Donald E., III. "Militancy in Fortune's New York *Age.*" *Journal of Negro History*, LV (October, 1970), 307–22.

Duberman, Martin B. *Charles Francis Adams.* Stanford: Stanford University Press, 1960.

DuBois, W. E. B. *The Philadelphia Negro.* Philadelphia: University of Pennsylvania, 1899.

Dunbar, Willis F., and Shade, William G. "The Black Man Gains the Vote: The Centennial of 'Impartial Suffrage' in Michigan." *Michigan History,* LVI (Spring, 1972), 42–57.

Dykstra, Robert R., and Hahn, Harlan. "Northern Voters and Negro Suffrage: The Case of Iowa, 1868." *Public Opinion Quarterly,* XXXII (Summer, 1968), 202–15.

Edelstein, Tilden G. *Strange Enthusiasm: A Life of Thomas Wentworth Higginson.* New Haven: Yale University Press, 1968.

Evans, John Whitney. "Catholics and the Blair Education Bill." *Catholic Historical Review,* XLVI (October, 1960), 273–98.

Faulkner, Harold U. *Politics, Reform and Expansion, 1890–1900. The New American Nation Series.* Ed. Henry Steele Commager and Richard B. Morris. New York: Harper and Row, 1959.

Fishel, Leslie H., Jr. "The Negro in Northern Politics, 1870–1900." *Mississippi Valley Historical Review,* XLII (December, 1955), 466–89.

———. "Northern Prejudice and Negro Suffrage, 1865–1870." *Journal of Negro History,* XXXIX (January, 1954), 8–26.

———. "Wisconsin and Negro Suffrage." *Wisconsin Magazine of History,* XLVI (Spring, 1963), 180–96.

Fleming, Walter L. *The Freedmen's Savings Bank: A Chapter in the Economic History of the Negro Race.* Chapel Hill: University of North Carolina Press, 1927.

Flick, Alexander C. *Samuel J. Tilden: A Study in Political Sagacity.* New York: Dodd, Mead, 1939.

Fox, Stephen R. *The Guardian of Boston: William Monroe Trotter.* New York: Atheneum, 1970.

Franklin, John Hope. *From Slavery to Freedom: A History of Negro Americans.* New York: Alfred A. Knopf, 1967.

———. "George Washington Williams, Historian." *Journal of Negro History,* XXXI (January, 1946), 60–90.

Fredrickson, George M. *The Black Image in the White Mind: The Debate on Afro-American Character and Destiny, 1817–1914.* New York: Harper and Row, 1971.

Fuess, Claude Moore. *Carl Schurz, Reformer, 1829–1906.* New York: Dodd, Mead, 1932.

Garraty, John A. *Interpreting American History: Conversations with Historians.* New York: Macmillan, 1970.

Gaston, Paul M. *The New South Creed: A Study in Southern Mythmaking.* New York: Alfred A. Knopf, 1970.

Gerichs, William C. "The Ratification of the Fifteenth Amendment in Indiana." *Indiana Magazine of History,* IX (September, 1913), 131–66.

Gibson, Florence E. *The Attitude of the New York Irish toward State and National Affairs, 1848–1892.* New York: Columbia University Press, 1951.

Gilbert, Abby L. "The Comptroller of the Currency and the Freedmen's Savings Bank." *Journal of Negro History,* LVII (April, 1972), 125–43.

Gillette, William. *The Right to Vote: Politics and the Passage of the Fifteenth Amendment.* Johns Hopkins University Studies in Historical and Political Science, series LXXXIII, no. 1. Baltimore: Johns Hopkins University Press, 1969.

Going, Allen J. "The South and the Blair Bill." *Mississippi Valley Historical Review,* XLIV (September, 1957), 466–89.

Gray, Gladys J. "George Lewis Ruffin." *Negro History Bulletin,* V (October, 1941), 18–19.

Green, Constance M. *The Secret City: A History of Race Relations in the Nation's Capital.* Princeton: Princeton University Press, 1967.

Greve, Charles T. *Centennial History of Cincinnati and Representative Citizens.* 2 vols. Chicago: Biographical Publishing, 1904.

Grimké, Angelina. "A Biographical Sketch of Archibald H. Grimké." *Opportunity,* III (February, 1925), 44–47.

Gutman, Herbert G. "Peter H. Clark: Pioneer Negro Socialist, 1877." *Journal of Negro Education,* XXXIV (Fall, 1965), 413–18.

Hair, William Ivy. *Bourbonism and Agrarian Protest: Louisiana Politics, 1877–1900.* Baton Rouge: Louisiana State University Press, 1969.

Hancock, Harold B. "The Status of the Negro in Delaware after the Civil War, 1865–75." *Delaware History,* XIII (April, 1968), 57–66.

Hart, Albert Bushnell. *Salmon Portland Chase.* Boston: Houghton, Mifflin, 1899.

Hayes, Laurence J. W. *The Negro Federal Government Worker: A Study of His Classification Status in the District of Columbia, 1883–1938.* Howard University Studies in the Social Sciences, vol. III, no. 1. Washington: Howard University, 1941.

Hiller, Amy M. "The Disfranchisement of Delaware Negroes in the Late Nineteenth Century." *Delaware History*, XIII (October, 1968), 124–53.

Hirsch, Mark D. *William C. Whitney: Modern Warwick.* New York: Dodd, Mead, 1948.

Hirshson, Stanley P. *Farewell to the Bloody Shirt: Northern Republicans and the Southern Negro, 1877–1893.* Bloomington: Indiana University Press, 1962.

Hoadly, George, Jr. "George Hoadly." *Green Bag*, XIX (December, 1907), 685–89.

House, Albert V., Jr. "Northern Congressional Democrats as Defenders of the South during Reconstruction." *Journal of Southern History*, VI (February, 1940), 46–71.

Hutchinson, William T. *Cyrus Hall McCormick.* 2 vols. New York: Century, 1935.

Jarrell, Hampton. *Wade Hampton and the Negro: The Road Not Taken.* Columbia: University of South Carolina Press, 1949.

Jensen, Richard. *The Winning of the Midwest: Social and Political Conflict, 1888–1896.* Chicago: University of Chicago Press, 1971.

Johnson, Allen, and Malone, Dumas, eds. *Dictionary of American Biography.* 20 vols. New York: Charles Scribner's Sons, 1928–36.

Johnson, Claudius O. *Carter Harrison I: Political Leader.* Chicago: University of Chicago Press, 1928.

Jones, Charles Henry. *The Life and Public Services of J. Glancy Jones.* 2 vols. Philadelphia and London: J. B. Lippincott, 1910.

Jordan, Philip D. *Ohio Comes of Age, 1873–1900.* Vol. V of *The History of the State of Ohio.* Ed. Carl Wittke. Columbus: Ohio State Archeological and Historical Society, 1943.

Juergens, George. *Joseph Pulitzer and the New York "World."* Princeton: Princeton University Press, 1966.

Katz, Irving. *August Belmont: A Political Biography.* New York: Columbia University Press, 1968.

Katzman, David M. *Before the Ghetto: Black Detroit in the Nineteenth Century.* Urbana: University of Illinois Press, 1973.

Klement, Frank L. *The Limits of Dissent: Clement L. Vallandigham and the Civil War.* Lexington: University Press of Kentucky, 1970.

Kleppner, Paul. *The Cross of Culture: A Social Analysis of Midwestern Politics, 1850–1900.* New York: Free Press, 1970.

Knapp, Charles M. *New Jersey Politics during the Period of the Civil War and Reconstruction.* Geneva, N.Y.: W. F. Humphrey, 1924.

Knoles, George Harmon. *The Presidential Campaign and Election of 1892.* Stanford University Publications, University Series. History, Economics, and Political Science, vol. V., no. 1. Stanford: Stanford University Press, 1942.

Koenig, Louis W. *Bryan: A Political Biography of William Jennings Bryan.* New York: G. P. Putnam's Sons, 1971.

Krug, Mark M. *Lyman Trumbull: Conservative Radical.* New York: A. S. Barnes, 1965.

Lambert, James R. *Arthur Pue Gorman.* Baton Rouge: Louisiana State University Press, 1953.

Lewis, Elsie M. "The Political Mind of the Negro, 1865–1900." *Journal of Southern History,* XXI (May, 1955), 189–202. Reprinted in *The Negro in the South since 1865: Selected Essays in American Negro History.* Ed. Charles E. Wynes. New York: Harper and Row, 1965.

Lindsey, David. *"Sunset" Cox, Irrepressible Democrat.* Detroit: Wayne State University Press, 1959.

Litwack, Leon F. *North of Slavery: The Negro in the Free States, 1790–1860.* Chicago: University of Chicago Press, 1961.

Livesay, Harold C. "Delaware Negroes, 1865–1915." *Delaware History,* XIII (October, 1968), 87–123.

Logan, Frenise A. *The Negro in North Carolina, 1876–1894.* Chapel Hill: University of North Carolina Press, 1964.

Logan, Rayford W. *The Betrayal of the Negro: From Rutherford B. Hayes to Woodrow Wilson.* New York: Collier, 1968.

————. *The Diplomatic Relations of the United States with Haiti, 1776–1891.* Chapel Hill: University of North Carolina Press, 1941.

McElroy, Robert M. *Grover Cleveland, the Man and the Statesman.* 2 vols. New York: Harper and Brothers, 1923.

McJimsey, George T. *Genteel Partisan: Manton Marble, 1834–1917.* Ames: Iowa State University Press, 1971.

McKay, Claude. *Harlem: Negro Metropolis.* New York: E. P. Dutton, 1940.

McPherson, James M. "Abolitionists and the Civil Rights Act of 1875." *Journal of American History,* LII (December, 1965), 493–510.

————. "Grant or Greeley? The Abolitionist Dilemma in the Election of 1872." *American Historical Review,* LXXI (October, 1965), 43–61.

————. *The Struggle for Equality: Abolitionists and the Negro in* the *Civil War and Reconstruction*. Princeton: Princeton University Press, 1964.

Maddex, Jack P., Jr. *The Virginia Conservatives, 1867–1879: A Study in Reconstruction Politics*. Chapel Hill: University of North Carolina Press, 1970.

Marcosson, Isaac. *"Marse Henry": A Biography of Henry Watterson*. New York: Dodd, Mead, 1951.

Marcus, Robert D. *Grand Old Party: Political Structure in the Gilded Age, 1880–1896*. New York: Oxford University Press, 1971.

Martin, Isaac, ed. *History of the Schools of Cincinnati and Other Educational Institutions, Public and Private*. Cincinnati: n.p., 1900.

Mayes, Edward. *Lucius Q. C. Lamar, His Life, Times, and Speeches, 1825–1893*. Nashville: Barbee and Smith, 1896.

Mayo, Anthony R. "Charles Lewis Reason." *Negro History Bulletin*, V (June, 1942), 212–15.

Meier, August. "The Negro and the Democratic Party, 1875–1915." *Phylon*, XVII (1956), 173–91.

―――. *Negro Thought in America, 1880–1915*. Ann Arbor: University of Michigan Press, 1963.

―――, and Rudwick, Elliott. *From Plantation to Ghetto*. Rev. ed. New York: Hill and Wang, 1970.

Merrill, Horace Samuel. *Bourbon Democracy of the Middle West: 1865–1896*. Baton Rouge: Louisiana State University Press, 1953.

―――. *Bourbon Leader: Grover Cleveland and the Democratic Party*. Boston: Little, Brown, 1957.

―――. *William Freeman Vilas: Doctrinaire Democrat*. Madison: State Historical Society of Wisconsin, 1954.

Merton, Robert K. *Social Theory and Social Structure*. New York: Free Press, 1957.

Miller, Kelly. *The Political Plight of the Negro*. Washington: Murray Brothers, 1913.

Minor, Henry. *The Story of the Democratic Party*. New York: Macmillan, 1928.

Mitchell, Stewart. *Horatio Seymour of New York*. Cambridge: Harvard University Press, 1938.

Moore, Clifford H. "Ohio in National Politics, 1865–1896." *Ohio Archeological and Historical Quarterly*, XXXVII (April–June, 1928), 220–427.

Munroe, John A. "The Negro in Delaware." *South Atlantic Quarterly*, LVI (Autumn, 1957), 428–44.

National Cyclopaedia of American Biography. New York: James T. White, 1906—.

Nevins, Allan. *Grover Cleveland, a Study in Courage.* New York: Dodd, Mead, 1932.

Nolen, Claude H. *The Negro's Image in the South.* Lexington: University of Kentucky Press, 1967.

Nunn, W. C. *Texas under the Carpetbaggers.* Austin: University of Texas Press, 1962.

Olcott, Charles S. *The Life of William McKinley.* 2 vols. Boston: Houghton Mifflin, 1916.

Osthaus, Carl R. *Freedmen, Philanthropy, and Fraud: A History of the Freedman's Savings Bank.* Urbana: University of Illinois Press, 1976.

Ottley, Roi. *"New World A-Coming": Inside Black America.* Boston: Houghton Mifflin, 1943.

Palmer, George Thomas. *A Conscientious Turncoat: The Story of John M. Palmer, 1817–1900.* New Haven: Yale University Press, 1941.

Parrish, William E. *Missouri under Radical Rule, 1865–1870.* Columbia: University of Missouri Press, 1965.

Patrick, Rembert W. *The Reconstruction of the Nation.* New York: Oxford University Press, 1967.

Peck, Harry Thurston. *Twenty Years of the Republic, 1885–1905.* New York: Dodd, Mead, 1906.

Perzel, Edward S. "Alexander Long, Salmon P. Chase, and the Election of 1868." *Bulletin of the Cincinnati Historical Society,* XXIII (January, 1965), 3–18.

Pessen, Edward. *Jacksonian America: Society, Personality, and Politics.* Homewood, Ill.: Dorsey Press, 1969.

Phelan, Sister Mary Cortona. *Manton Marble of the New York "World."* Washington: Catholic University of America Press, 1957.

Powell, Thomas E., ed. *The Democratic Party of Ohio.* 2 vols. N.p.: Ohio Publishing Company, 1913.

Puttkammer, Charles W., and Worthy, Ruth. "William Monroe Trotter, 1872–1934." *Journal of Negro History,* XLIII (October, 1958), 298–316.

Quarles, Benjamin. *Frederick Douglass.* Washington: Associated Publishers, 1948.

Quillin, Frank U. *The Color Line in Ohio.* Ann Arbor: George Wahr, 1913.

Rammelkamp, Julian S. *Pulitzer's "Post-Dispatch," 1878–1883.* Princeton: Princeton University Press, 1967.

Randall, Emilius O., and Ryan, Daniel J. *History of Ohio: The Rise and Progress of an American State.* 4 vols. New York: Century History Company, 1912.

Randall, James G., and Donald, David. *The Civil War and Reconstruction.* 2nd ed., rev. Boston: D. C. Heath, 1969.

Raper, Arthur F. *The Tragedy of Lynching.* Chapel Hill: University of North Carolina Press, 1933.

Rice, Lawrence D. *The Negro in Texas, 1874–1900.* Baton Rouge: Louisiana State University Press, 1971.

Richardson, Joe M. *The Negro in the Reconstruction of Florida, 1865–1877.* Florida State University Studies, no. 46. Tallahassee: Florida State University, 1965.

Riddleberger, Patrick W. "The Break in the Radical Ranks: Liberals vs. Stalwarts in the Election of 1872." *Journal of Negro History,* XLIV (April, 1959), 136–57.

————. *George Washington Julian: Radical Republican.* Indianapolis: Indiana Historical Bureau, 1966.

————. "The Radicals' Abandonment of the Negro during Reconstruction." *Journal of Negro History,* XLV (April, 1960), 88–102.

Rogers, William Warren. *One Gallused Rebellion: Agrarianism in Alabama, 1865–1896.* Baton Rouge: Louisiana State University Press, 1970.

Ross, Earle D. *The Liberal Republican Movement.* New York: Henry Holt, 1919.

Rothman, David J. *Politics and Power: The United States Senate, 1869–1901.* Cambridge: Harvard University Press, 1966.

Sackett, William Edgar. *Modern Battles of Trenton.* Trenton: John L. Murphy, 1895.

Scheiner, Seth M. *Negro Mecca: A History of the Negro in New York City, 1865–1900.* New York: New York University Press, 1965.

Schlesinger, Arthur M., and Israel, Fred L., eds. *History of American Presidential Elections, 1789–1968.* New York: Chelsea House, 1971.

Seitz, Don. *Joseph Pulitzer: His Life and Letters.* New York: Simon and Schuster, 1924.

Sheppard, William A. *Red Shirts Remembered.* Atlanta: Ruralist Press, 1940.

Shotwell, James B. *A History of the Schools of Cincinnati.* Cincinnati: School Life Company, 1902.

Sinkler, George. *The Racial Attitudes of American Presidents from Lincoln to Theodore Roosevelt.* Garden City: Doubleday, 1972.

Smith, Donnal V. "Salmon P. Chase and the Nomination of 1868." *Essays in Honor of William E. Dodd.* Ed. Avery O. Craven. Chicago: University of Chicago Press, 1935.

Smith, Samuel Denny. *The Negro in Congress, 1870–1901.* Port Washington, N.Y.: Kennikat Press, 1940.

Smith, William E. *The Francis Preston Blair Family in Politics.* 2 vols. New York: Macmillan, 1933.

Sproat, John G. *"The Best Men": Liberal Reformers in the Gilded Age.* New York: Oxford University Press, 1968.

Stephenson, Gilbert T. *Race Distinctions in American Law.* New York: D. Appleton, 1910.

Stoll, John B. *History of the Indiana Democracy, 1816–1916.* Indianapolis: Indiana Democratic Publishing Company, 1917.

Stone, Candace. *Dana and the Sun.* New York: Dodd, Mead, 1938.

Swinney, Everette. "Enforcing the Fifteenth Amendment, 1870–1877." *Journal of Southern History,* XXVIII (May, 1962), 202–18.

Tansill, Charles Callan. *The Congressional Career of Thomas F. Bayard, 1869–1885.* Washington: Georgetown University Press, 1946.

Thomas, Harrison C. *The Return of the Democratic Party to Power in 1884.* New York: By the author, 1919.

Thornbrough, Emma Lou. "The National Afro-American League, 1887–1908." *Journal of Southern History,* XXVII (November, 1961), 494–512.

———. *The Negro in Indiana before 1900.* Indianapolis: Indiana Historical Bureau, 1957.

———. *Since Emancipation: A Short History of Indiana Negroes, 1863–1963.* Indianapolis: Indiana Division, American Negro Emancipation Centennial Authority, 1963.

———. *T. Thomas Fortune: Militant Journalist.* Chicago: University of Chicago Press, 1972.

Tindall, George Brown. *South Carolina Negroes, 1877–1890.* Columbia: University of South Carolina Press, 1952.

Toppin, Edgar A. "Negro Emancipation in Historic Retrospect, Ohio: The Negro Suffrage Issue in Postbellum Ohio Politics." *Journal of Human Relations,* XI (Autumn, 1962), 232–46.

Trelease, Allen W. *White Terror: The Ku Klux Klan Conspiracy and Southern Reconstruction.* New York: Harper and Row, 1971.

Trissal, Francis M. *Public Men of Indiana: A Political History from 1860 to 1890.* 2 vols. Hammond: W. B. Conkey, 1922.

Unger, Irwin. *The Greenback Era: A Social and Political History of American Finance, 1865–1879.* Princeton: Princeton University Press, 1964.

Van Deusen, Glyndon G. *Horace Greeley: Nineteenth Century Crusader.* Philadelphia: University of Pennsylvania Press, 1953.

————. *William Henry Seward.* New York: Oxford University Press, 1967.

Van Deusen, John G. "Did the Republicans 'Colonize' Indiana in 1879?" *Indiana Magazine of History,* XXX (December, 1934), 335–46.

————. "The Exodus of 1879." *Journal of Negro History,* XXI (April, 1936), 111–29.

Voegeli, V. Jacque. *Free but Not Equal: The Midwest and the Negro during the Civil War.* Chicago: University of Chicago Press, 1967.

Wall, Joseph F. *Henry Watterson, Reconstructed Rebel.* New York: Oxford University Press, 1956.

Walls, William J. *Joseph Charles Price: Educator and Race Leader.* Boston: Christopher Publishing House, 1943.

Walters, Everett. *Joseph Benson Foraker: An Uncompromising Republican.* Columbus: Ohio State Archeological and Historical Society, 1948.

Washington, S. A. M. *George Thomas Downing: Sketch of His Life and Times.* Newport: Milne Printery, 1910.

Weaver, Valeria. "The Failure of Civil Rights, 1875–1883, and Its Repercussions." *Journal of Negro History,* LIV (October, 1969), 368–82.

Welch, Richard E., Jr. "The Federal Elections Bill of 1890: Postscripts and Prelude." *Journal of American History,* LII (December, 1965), 511–26.

Wellman, Manly Wade. *Giant in Gray: A Biography of Wade Hampton of South Carolina.* New York: Charles Scribner's Sons, 1949.

Wharton, Vernon Lane. *The Negro in Mississippi, 1865–1890.* James Sprunt Studies in History and Political Science, vol. XXVIII. Chapel Hill: University of North Carolina Press, 1947.

White, Horace. *A Life of Lyman Trumbull.* Boston: Houghton Mifflin, 1913.

Williamson, Joel. *After Slavery: The Negro in South Carolina during*

Reconstruction, 1861–1877. Chapel Hill: University of North Carolina Press, 1965.

Wood, Forrest G. *Black Scare: The Racist Response to Emancipation and Reconstruction.* Berkeley and Los Angeles: University of California Press, 1968.

Woodson, Carter G. *A Century of Negro Migration.* Washington: Association for the Study of Negro Life and History, 1918.

Woodward, C. Vann. *Origins of the New South, 1877–1913.* Vol. IX of *A History of the South.* Ed. Wendell Holmes Stephenson and E. Merton Coulter. Baton Rouge: Louisiana State University Press, 1951.

————. *Reunion and Reaction: The Compromise of 1877 and the End of Reconstruction.* Boston: Little, Brown, 1966.

————. *The Strange Career of Jim Crow.* Second rev. ed. New York: Oxford University Press, 1966.

Wright, Marion M. Thompson. *The Education of Negroes in New Jersey.* Teachers College, Columbia University Contributions to Education, no. 815. New York: Teachers College, Columbia University, 1941.

————. "Negro Suffrage in New Jersey, 1776–1875." *Journal of Negro History,* XXXIII (April, 1948), 168–224.

Wynes, Charles E. *Race Relations in Virginia, 1870–1902.* Charlottesville: University of Virginia Press, 1961.

Index